Ariel's
Harmony
of the
Gospels

Other Books by Dr. Arnold G. Fruchtenbaum

ARIEL'S
HARMONY
OF THE
GOSPELS

Based on *A Harmony of the Gospels*
by A. T. Robertson

ARNOLD G. FRUCHTENBAUM, TH.M., PH.D.

Ariel's Harmony of the Gospels (Arnold G. Fruchtenbaum, Th.M., Ph.D.)
© 2016 by Ariel Ministries
2nd Edition

ISBN 978-1-935174-62-2

Library of Congress Control Number:
2016936623

REL101000 RELIGION / Messianic Judaism / Yeshua / Jesus / Gospels / Harmony

Compiled by Arnold G. Fruchtenbaum and Jan Marek Kopytek
Edited and formatted by Christiane Jurik, M.A.
Proofread by Helen Mackie and Laurie Combs
Printed in the United States of America
Cover illustration by Jesse and Josh Gonzales (http://www.vipgraphics.net)

Published by Ariel Ministries
P.O. Box 792507
San Antonio, TX 78279-2507
www.ariel.org

Author's Dedication

This body of work is dedicated in memory of

J. Dwight Pentecost,

Professor of Biblical Studies
at Dallas Theological Seminary,
who first exposed me to teaching
the Gospels with the use of a harmony.

CHIEF DIVISIONS
OF THE HARMONY

TABLE OF CONTENTS
—DETAILED OUTLINE —

II. The Authentication of the King
— §§ 28-57 —

III. The Controversy over the King
— §§ 58–73 —

IV. The Training of the Twelve by the King
— §§ 74–98 —

V. The Opposition to the King
— §§ 99–112 —

VI. The Preparation of the Disciples by the King
— §§ 113–131 —

VII. The Official Presentation of the King
— §§ 132–144 —

VIII. The Preparation for the Death of the King
— §§ 145–164 —

IX. The Trial of the King
— §§ 165–175 —

X. The Death of the King
— §§ 176–181 —

XI. The Resurrection and Ascension of the King
— §§ 182–197 —

Appendices

Foreword

By Dr. Arnold G. Fruchtenbaum

Very little of *Ariel's Harmony of the Gospels* originated with me; it is largely based on the harmony of A. T. Robertson,[1] which in turn was based on a previous harmony by John A. Broadus. But there are some differences:

First, where more than one Gospel is listed, the verses will be placed in parallel columns, as in A. T. Robertson's harmony. The one difference is that whereas the first column in his harmony was Mark, reflecting Robertson's view of a Markan priority, this work will follow the present New Testament order of the Gospels: Matthew, Mark, Luke, and John.

Second, Robertson largely followed a geographical approach, whereas I have chosen a thematic approach. The advantage of a thematic approach is that correlations can be seen between a teaching and an event, and vice versa. Therefore, this approach provides a better overall picture as to how things in the life of the Messiah were related to each other. The significance of details which may have seemed to be casually mentioned becomes clear.

---

[1] A. T. Robertson, *A Harmony of the Gospels for Students of the Life of Christ* (New York: Harper & Row, Publishers, 1920).

Third, I follow Luke's order of events, as did Robertson, but in those places where Robertson chose to deviate from that Gospel, this harmony will continue to follow Luke's order.

Fourth, the division titles largely, but not exclusively, follow the outline of J. Dwight Pentecost that was handed out to his students at Dallas Theological Seminary.[2]

The translation used in this work is the American Standard Version of 1901. However, the archaic language (e.g., *thee, thou, hast, wast,* etc.) has been modernized. One exception is the pronoun *you*. In modern English, *you* is used as both a singular and plural second person pronoun. Therefore, to more accurately translate the original Greek text, the archaic second person plural pronoun *ye* has been retained in the Scripture quotations. Furthermore, the reader will find the names of persons and places transliterated in accordance with Hebrew pronunciation. An index with the most important names can be found on the next page.

---

[2] Pentecost eventually incorporated the outline into his book, *The Words and Works of Jesus Christ* (Grand Rapids, MI: Zondervan Publishing House, 1981).

Index of Names

This harmony of the Gospels uses the Hebrew names of the people and places mentioned in the accounts, albeit in a transliterated form. This index contains the names of the most important persons and leaves out those that are only mentioned in Matthew's and Luke's genealogies.

Aharon = Aaron

Andrei = Andrew

Avraham = Abraham

Bar Abba = Barabbas

Bar Talmai = Bartholomew

Bartimai = Bartimaeus

Beit Anyah = Bethany

Beit Chesda = Bethesda

Beit Lechem = Bethlehem

Beit Tzaida = Bethsaida

Berechyah = Barachiah

Bnei Regesh = Boanerges

Chakeil D'ma = Akeldama

Chalphi = Alphaeus

Chanan = Annas

Kirenyah = Cyrene

Dalmanuta = Dalmanutha

Didymos = Didymus

Einon = Aenon

Elazar = Lazarus

Elisheva = Elizabeth

Eliyahu = Elijah

Gavriel = Gabriel

Galil = Galilee

Gat Shemen = Gethsemane

Ginosar = Gennesaret

Golgota = Calvary

Hevel = Abel

Kayapha = Caiaphas

Keipha = Cephas

Kfar Nachum = Capernaum

Kliyopas = Cleopas

Magdalit = Magdalene

Marta = Martha

Mattai = Matthew

Miriam = Mary

Mosheh = Moses

Nakdimon = Nicodemus

Natzeret = Nazareth

Netanel = Nathanael

Noach = Noah

Ramatayim = Arimathaea

Shaleim = Salim

Shiloach = Siloam

Shimon = Simon

Shlomoh = Solomon

Shomron = Samaria

Shoshanah = Susanna

Taddai = Thaddaeus

Talyeta = Talitha

Timai = Timaeus

Toma = Thomas

Tverya = Tiberias

Tzarfat = Zarephath

Tzidon = Sidon

Tzor = Tyre

Yaakov = Jacob, James

Yair = Jairus

Yarden = Jordan

Yehudah = Judea, Judah, Judas

Yehudah Ish Kriyot = Judas Iscariot

Yerushalayim = Jerusalem

Yeshayahu = Isaiah

Yeshua = Jesus

Yirmeyahu = Jeremiah

Yishai = Jesse

Yisrael = Israel

Yitzchak = Isaac

Yochanah = Joanna

Yochanan = John

Yonah = Jonah

Yosei = Joses

Yoseph = Joseph

Zakkai = Zacchaeus

Zavdi = Zebedee

Zecharyah = Zechariah

Zvulun = Zebulun

Introductory Material
— §§ 1–2 —

[§ 1]—A. Luke's Prologue:
The Sources of Knowledge

Luke 1:1-4

[1] Forasmuch as many have taken in hand to draw up a narrative concerning those matters which have been fulfilled among us, [2] even as they delivered them unto us, who from the beginning were eyewitnesses and ministers of the word, [3] it seemed good to me also, having traced the course of all things accurately from the first, to write unto you in order, most excellent Theophilus; [4] that you might know the certainty concerning the things wherein you were instructed.

[§ 2]—B. The Prologue in the Gospel of John: The Preexistence of the Messiah

John 1:1-18

[1] In the beginning was the Word, and the Word was with God, and the Word was God. [2] The same was in the beginning with God. [3] All things were made through him; and without him was not anything made that has been made. [4] In him was life; and the life was the light of men. [5] And the light shines in the darkness; and the darkness apprehended it not. [6] There came a man, sent from God, whose name was Yochanan. [7] The same came for witness, that he might bear witness of the light, that all might believe through him. [8] He was not the light, but <came> that he might bear witness of the light. [9] There was the true light, <even the light> which lights every man, coming into the world. [10] He was in the world, and the world was made through him, and the world knew him not. [11] He came unto his own, and they that were his own received him not. [12] But as many as received him, to them gave he the right to become children of God, <even> to them that believe on his name: [13] who were born, not of blood, nor of the will of the flesh, nor of the will of man, but of God. [14] And the Word became flesh, and dwelled[1] among us (and we beheld his glory, glory as of the only begotten from the Father), full of grace and truth. [15] Yochanan bore witness of him, and cried, saying, This was he of whom I said, He that comes after me is become before me: for he was before me. [16] For of his fullness we all received, and grace for grace. [17] For the law was given through Mosheh; grace and truth came through Yeshua the Messiah. [18] No man has seen God at any time; the only begotten Son, who is in the bosom of the Father, he has declared <him>.

---

[1] Greek: *tabernacled*.

I. THE INTRODUCTION
OF THE KING
— §§ 3–27 —

[§§ 3–19]—A. The Arrival of the King

[§ 3]—1. The Genealogy of the King

Matthew 1:1-17	Luke 3:23d-38
[1] The book of the generation of Yeshua the Messiah, the son of David, the son of Avraham. [2] Avraham begat Yitzchak; and Yitzchak begat Yaakov; and Yaakov begat	[23d] being the son (as was supposed) of Yoseph, the <son> of Eili, [24] the <son> of Mattat, the <son> of Levi, the <son> of Malchi, the <son> of Yannai, the <son> of Yoseph, [25] the

Yehudah and his brethren; [3] and Yehudah begat Peretz and Zerach of Tamar; and Peretz begat Chetzron; and Chetzron begat Ram; [4] and Ram begat Amminadav; and Amminadav begat Nachshon; and Nachshon begat Salmon; [5] and Salmon begat Boaz of Rachav; and Boaz begat Oved of Ruth; and Oved begat Yishai; [6] and Yishai begat David the king. And David begat Shlomoh of her <that had been the wife> of Uriyah; [7] and Shlomoh begat Rahavam; and Rahavam begat Aviyah; and Aviyah begat Asa; [8] and Asa begat Yehoshaphat; and Yehoshaphat begat Yoram; and Yoram begat Uziyahu; [9] and Uziyahu begat Yotam; and Yotam begat Achaz; and Achaz begat Chizkiyahu; [10] and Chizkiyahu begat Menasheh; and Menasheh begat Amon; and Amon begat Yoshiyahu; [11] and Yoshiyahu begat Yechanyahu and his brethren, at the time of the carrying away to Babylon. [12] And after the carrying away to Babylon, Yechanyahu begat Shealtiel; and Shealtiel begat Zerubbavel; [13] and Zerubbavel begat Avihud; and Avihud begat Elyakim; and Elyakim begat Azur; [14] and Azur begat Zadok; and Zadok begat Achim; and Achim begat Eliud; [15] and Eliud begat Eleazar; and Eleazar begat Matthan; and Matthan begat Yaakov; [16] and Yaakov begat Yoseph the husband of Miriam, of whom

<son> of Mattithyahu, the <son> of Amotz, the <son> of Nachum, the <son> of Chesli, the <son> of Naggai, [26] the <son> of Machat, the <son> of Mattithyahu, the <son> of Shmi, the <son> of Yoseph, the <son> of Yodah, [27] the <son> of Yochanan, the <son> of Reisha, the <son> of Zerubbavel, the <son> of Shealtiel, the <son> of Neiri, [28] the <son> of Malchi, the <son> of Addi, the <son> of Kosam, the <son> of Elmadan, the <son> of Eir, [29] the <son> of Yeshua, the <son> of Eliezer, the <son> of Yorim, the <son> of Mattiat, the <son> of Levi, [30] the <son> of Shmion, the <son> of Yehudah, the <son> of Yoseph, the <son> of Yonam, the <son> of Eliakim, [31] the <son> of Malah, the <son> of Manna, the <son> of Mattatah, the <son> of Natan, the <son> of David, [32] the <son> of Yishai, the <son> of Oved, the <son> of Boaz, the <son> of Salmon, the <son> of Nachshon, [33] the <son> of Amminadav, the <son> of Arni, the <son> of Chetzron, the <son> of Peretz, the <son> of Yehudah, [34] the <son> of Yaakov, the <son> of Yitzchak, the <son> of Avraham, the <son> of Terach, the <son> of Nachor, [35] the <son> of Serug, the <son> of Reu, the <son> of Peleg, the <son> of Eiver, the <son> of Shelach [36] the <son> of Cainan, the <son> of Arpachshad, the <son> of Shem, the

was born Yeshua, who is called Messiah. [17] So all the generations from Avraham unto David are fourteen generations; and from David unto the carrying away to Babylon fourteen generations; and from the carrying away to Babylon unto the Messiah fourteen generations. [1]

<son> of Noach, the <son> of Lemech, [37] the <son> of Metushelach, the <son> of Chanoch, the <son> of Yered, the <son> of Mahalaleel, the <son> of Kainan, [38] the <son> of Enosh, the <son> of Shet, the <son> of Adam, the <son> of God. [2]

[§§ 4–11]—2. The Advent of the King

[§ 4]—a. The Annunciation of Yochanan's Birth to Zecharyah

Luke 1:5-25

[5] There was in the days of Herod, king of Yehudah, a certain priest named Zecharyah, of the course of Aviyah: and he had a wife of the daughters of Aharon, and her name was Elisheva. [6] And they were both righteous before God, walking in all the commandments and ordinances of the Lord blameless. [7] And they had no child, because that Elisheva was barren, and they both were <now> well stricken in years. [8] Now it came to pass, while he executed the priest's office before God in the order of his course, [9] according to the custom of the priest's office, his lot was to enter into the temple of the Lord and burn incense. [10] And the whole multitude of the people were praying without at the hour of incense. [11] And there appeared unto him an angel of the Lord standing on the right side of the altar of incense. [12] And Zecharyah was troubled when he saw <him>, and fear fell upon him. [13] But the angel said unto him, Fear not, Zecharyah: because your supplication is heard, and your wife Elisheva shall bear you a son, and you shall call his name Yochanan. [14] And you shall have joy and gladness; and many shall rejoice at his birth. [15] For he shall be great in the sight of the Lord, and he shall drink no wine nor strong drink; and he shall be filled with

---

[1] Cf. I Chron. 1:34; 2:1-15; 3:1-19.

[2] Cf. I Chron. 1:1-4, 24-28; 2:1-15; 3:17; Ruth 4:18-22.

the Holy Spirit, even from his mother's womb. [16] And many of the children of Yisrael shall be turned unto the Lord their God. [17] And he shall go before his face in the spirit and power of Eliyahu, to turn the hearts of the fathers to the children, and the disobedient <to walk> in the wisdom of the just; to make ready for the Lord a people prepared <for him>. [18] And Zecharyah said unto the angel, Whereby shall I know this? for I am an old man, and my wife well stricken in years. [19] And the angel answering said unto him, I am Gavriel, that stands in the presence of God; and I was sent to speak unto you, and to bring you these good tidings. [20] And behold, you shall be silent and not able to speak, until the day that these things shall come to pass, because you believed not my words, which shall be fulfilled in their season. [21] And the people were waiting for Zecharyah, and they marveled while he tarried in the temple. [22] And when he came out, he could not speak unto them: and they perceived that he had seen a vision in the temple: and he continued making signs unto them, and remained dumb. [23] And it came to pass, when the days of his ministration were fulfilled, he departed unto his house.

[24] And after these days Elisheva his wife conceived; and she hid herself five months, saying, [25] Thus has the Lord done unto me in the days wherein he looked upon <me>, to take away my reproach among men.

[§ 5]—b. The Annunciation of Yeshua's Birth to Miriam

Luke 1:26-38

[26] Now in the sixth month the angel Gavriel was sent from God unto a city of Galil, named Natzeret, [27] to a virgin betrothed to a man whose name was Yoseph, of the house of David; and the virgin's name was Miriam. [28] And he came in unto her, and said, Hail, you that are highly favored, the Lord <is> with you. [29] But she was greatly troubled at the saying, and cast in her mind what manner of salutation this might be. [30] And the angel said unto her, Fear not, Miriam: for you have found favor with God. [31] And behold, you shall conceive in your womb, and bring forth a son, and shall call his name YESHUA. [32] He shall be great, and shall be called the Son of the Most High: and the Lord God shall give unto him the throne of his father David: [33] and he shall reign over the house of Yaakov forever; and of his kingdom there

shall be no end. [34] And Miriam said unto the angel, How shall this be, seeing I know not a man? [35] And the angel answered and said unto her, The Holy Spirit shall come upon you, and the power of the Most High shall overshadow you: wherefore also the holy thing which is begotten shall be called the Son of God. [36] And behold, Elisheva your kinswoman, she also has conceived a son in her old age; and this is the sixth month with her that was called barren. [37] For no word from God shall be void of power. [38] And Miriam said, Behold, the handmaid of the Lord; be it unto me according to your word. And the angel departed from her.

[§ 6]—c. The Visit of Miriam to Elisheva

Luke 1:39-45

[39] And Miriam arose in these days and went into the hill country with haste, into a city of Judah; [40] and entered into the house of Zecharyah and saluted Elisheva. [41] And it came to pass, when Elisheva heard the salutation of Miriam, the babe leaped in her womb; and Elisheva was filled with the Holy Spirit; [42] and she lifted up her voice with a loud cry, and said, Blessed <are> you among women, and blessed <is> the fruit of your womb. [43] And whence is this to me, that the mother of my Lord should come unto me? [44] For behold, when the voice of your salutation came into mine ears, the babe leaped in my womb for joy. [45] And blessed <is> she that believed; for there shall be a fulfillment of the things which have been spoken to her from the Lord.

[§ 7]—d. The Song of Miriam

Luke 1:46-56

[46] And Miriam said,
My soul does magnify the Lord,
[47] And my spirit has rejoiced in God my Savior.
[48] For he has looked upon the low estate of his handmaid: For behold, from henceforth all generations shall call me blessed.
[49] For he that is mighty has done to me great things; And holy is his name.

50 And his mercy is unto generations and generations on them that fear him.

51 He has showed strength with his arm; He has scattered the proud in the imagination of their heart.

52 He has put down princes from <their> thrones, And has exalted them of low degree.

53 The hungry he has filled with good things; And the rich he has sent empty away.

54 He has given help to Yisrael his servant, That he might remember mercy

55 (As he spoke unto our fathers) Toward Avraham and his seed forever.

56 And Miriam abode with her about three months, and returned unto her house.

[§ 8]—e. The Birth of Yochanan

Luke 1:57-80

57 Now Elisheva's time was fulfilled that she should be delivered; and she brought forth a son. 58 And her neighbors and her kinsfolk heard that the Lord had magnified his mercy towards her; and they rejoiced with her. 59 And it came to pass on the eighth day that they came to circumcise the child; and they would have called him Zecharyah, after the name of the father. 60 And his mother answered and said, Not so; but he shall be called Yochanan. 61 And they said unto her, There is none of your kindred that is called by this name. 62 And they made signs to his father, what he would have him called. 63 And he asked for a writing tablet, and wrote, saying, His name is Yochanan. And they marveled all. 64 And his mouth was opened immediately, and his tongue <loosed>, and he spoke, blessing God. 65 And fear came on all that dwelled round about them: and all these sayings were noised abroad throughout all the hill country of Yehudah. 66 And all that heard them laid them up in their heart, saying, What then shall this child be? For the hand of the Lord was with him. 67 And his father Zecharyah was filled with the Holy Spirit, and prophesied, saying,

68 Blessed <be> the Lord, the God of Yisrael;
For he has visited and wrought redemption for his people,

⁶⁹ And has raised up a horn of salvation for us
In the house of his servant David

⁷⁰ (As he spoke by the mouth of his holy prophets that have been from of old),

⁷¹ Salvation from our enemies, and from the hand of all that hate us;

⁷² To show mercy towards our fathers,
And to remember his holy covenant;

⁷³ The oath which he spoke unto Avraham our father,

⁷⁴ To grant unto us that we being delivered out of the hand of our enemies Should serve him without fear,

⁷⁵ In holiness and righteousness before him all our days.

⁷⁶ Yea and you, child, shall be called the prophet of the Most High:
For you shall go before the face of the Lord to make ready his ways;

⁷⁷ To give knowledge of salvation unto his people
In the remission of their sins,

⁷⁸ Because of the tender mercy of our God,
Whereby the dayspring from on high shall visit us,

⁷⁹ To shine upon them that sit in darkness and the shadow of death;
To guide our feet into the way of peace.

⁸⁰ And the child grew, and waxed strong in spirit, and was in the deserts till the day of his showing unto Yisrael.

[§ 9]—f. The Annunciation of Yeshua's Birth to Yoseph

Matthew 1:18-25

¹⁸ Now the birth of Yeshua the Messiah was on this wise: When his mother Miriam had been betrothed to Yoseph, before they came together she was found with child of the Holy Spirit. ¹⁹ And Yoseph her husband, being a righteous man, and not willing to make her a public example, was minded to put her away privately. ²⁰ But when he thought on these things, behold, an angel of the Lord appeared unto him in a dream, saying, Yoseph, you son of David, fear not to take unto you Miriam your wife: for that which is conceived in her is of the Holy Spirit. ²¹ And she shall bring forth a son; and you shall call his name YESHUA; for it is he that shall save his people from their sins. ²² Now all this is come to pass that it might be fulfilled which was spoken by the Lord through the prophet, saying,

[23] Behold, the virgin shall be with child, and shall bring forth a son,
And they shall call his name Immanuel;

which is, being interpreted, God with us. [24] And Yoseph arose from his sleep, and did as the angel of the Lord commanded him, and took unto him his wife; [25] and knew her not till she had brought forth a son: and he called his name YESHUA.

[§ 10]—g. The Birth of the King

Luke 2:1-7

[1] Now it came to pass in those days, there went out a decree from Caesar Augustus, that all the world should be enrolled. [2] This was the first enrolment made when Quirinius was governor of Syria. [3] And all went to enroll themselves, everyone to his own city. [4] And Yoseph also went up from Galil, out of the city of Natzeret, into Yehudah, to the city of David, which is called Beit Lechem, because he was of the house and family of David; [5] to enroll himself with Miriam, who was betrothed to him, being great with child. [6] And it came to pass, while they were there, the days were fulfilled that she should be delivered. [7] And she brought forth her firstborn son; and she wrapped him in swaddling clothes, and laid him in a manger, because there was no room for them in the inn.

[§ 11]—h. The Announcement to the Shepherds

Luke 2:8-20

[8] And there were shepherds in the same country abiding in the field, and keeping watch by night over their flock. [9] And an angel of the Lord stood by them, and the glory of the Lord shone round about them: and they were sore afraid. [10] And the angel said unto them, Be not afraid; for behold, I bring you good tidings of great joy which shall be to all the people: [11] for there is born to you this day in the city of David a Savior, who is Messiah the Lord. [12] And this <is> the sign unto you: Ye shall find a babe wrapped in swaddling clothes, and lying in a manger. [13] And suddenly there was with the angel a multitude of the heavenly host praising God, and saying,

¹⁴ Glory to God in the highest,
And on earth peace among men
in whom he is well pleased.

¹⁵ And it came to pass, when the angels went away from them into heaven, the shepherds said one to another, Let us now go even unto Beit Lechem, and see this thing that is come to pass, which the Lord has made known unto us. ¹⁶ And they came with haste, and found both Miriam and Yoseph, and the babe lying in the manger. ¹⁷ And when they saw it, they made known concerning the saying which was spoken to them about this child. ¹⁸ And all that heard it wondered at the things which were spoken unto them by the shepherds. ¹⁹ But Miriam kept all these sayings, pondering them in her heart. ²⁰ And the shepherds returned, glorifying and praising God for all the things that they had heard and seen, even as it was spoken unto them.

[§§ 12–19]—3. His Infancy and Childhood

[§ 12]—a. The Circumcision

Luke 2:21

²¹ And when eight days were fulfilled for circumcising him, his name was called YESHUA, which was so called by the angel before he was conceived in the womb.

[§ 13]—b. The Presentation

Luke 2:22-38

²² And when the days of their purification according to the law of Mosheh were fulfilled, they brought him up to Yerushalayim, to present him to the Lord ²³ (as it is written in the law of the Lord, Every male that opens the womb shall be called holy to the Lord), ²⁴ and to offer a sacrifice according to that which is said in the law of the Lord, A pair of turtledoves, or two young pigeons. ²⁵ And behold, there was a man in Yerushalayim whose name was Simeon; and this man was righteous and devout, looking for the consolation of Yisrael: and the Holy Spirit was upon him. ²⁶ And it had been

revealed unto him by the Holy Spirit, that he should not see death, before he had seen the Lord's Messiah. [27] And he came in the Spirit into the temple: and when the parents brought in the child Yeshua, that they might do concerning him after the custom of the law, [28] then he received him into his arms, and blessed God, and said,

> [29] Now let you your servant depart, Lord, According to your word, in peace;
>
> [30] For mine eyes have seen your salvation,
>
> [31] Which you have prepared before the face of all peoples;
>
> [32] A light for revelation to the Gentiles, And the glory of your people Yisrael.

[33] And his father and his mother were marveling at the things which were spoken concerning him; [34] and Simeon blessed them, and said unto Miriam his mother, Behold, this <child> is set for the falling and the rising of many in Yisrael; and for a sign which is spoken against; [35] yea and a sword shall pierce through your own soul; that thoughts out of many hearts may be revealed.

[36] And there was one Hannah, a prophetess, the daughter of Penuel, of the tribe of Asher (she was of a great age, having lived with a husband seven years from her virginity, [37] and she had been a widow even unto eighty and four years), who departed not from the temple, worshipping with fastings and supplications night and day. [38] And coming up at that very hour she gave thanks unto God, and spoke of him to all them that were looking for the redemption of Yerushalayim.

[§§ 14–16]—c. His Infancy

[§ 14] —(1) In Beit Lechem

Matthew 2:1-12

[1] Now when Yeshua was born in Beit Lechem of Yehudah in the days of Herod the king, behold, Wise-men[3] from the east came to Yerushalayim, saying, [2] Where is he that is born King of the Jews? for we saw his star in the east, and are come to worship him. [3] And when Herod the king heard it, he was troubled, and all Yerushalayim with him. [4] And gathering together all the chief priests and scribes of the people, he inquired of them where the Messiah should be born. [5] And they said unto him, In Beit Lechem of Yehudah: for thus it is written through the prophet,

> [6] And you Beit Lechem, land of Yehudah, are in no wise least among the princes of Yehudah: for out of you shall come forth a governor, who shall be shepherd of my people Yisrael.

[7] Then Herod privately called the Wise-men, and learned of them exactly what time the star appeared. [8] And he sent them to Beit Lechem, and said, Go and search out exactly concerning the young child; and when ye have found <him>, bring me word, that I also may come and worship him. [9] And they, having heard the king, went their way; and lo, the star, which they saw in the east, went before them, till it came and stood over where the young child was. [10] And when they saw the star, they rejoiced with exceeding great joy. [11] And they came into the house and saw the young child with Miriam his mother; and they fell down and worshipped him; and opening their treasures they offered unto him gifts, gold and frankincense and myrrh. [12] And being warned <of God> in a dream that they should not return to Herod, they departed into their own country another way.

---

[3] Or, *Magi.*

[§ 15] —(2) In Egypt

Matthew 2:13-18

[13] Now when they were departed, behold, an angel of the Lord appeared to Yoseph in a dream, saying, Arise and take the young child and his mother, and flee into Egypt[4], and be you there until I tell you: for Herod will seek the young child to destroy him. [14] And he arose and took the young child and his mother by night, and departed into Egypt; [15] and was there until the death of Herod: that it might be fulfilled which was spoken by the Lord through the prophet, saying, Out of Egypt did I call my son. [16] Then Herod, when he saw that he was mocked of the Wise-men, was exceedingly angry, and sent forth, and slew all the male children that were in Beit Lechem, and in all the borders thereof, from two years old and under, according to the time which he had exactly learned of the Wise-men. [17] Then was fulfilled that which was spoken through Yermiyahu the prophet, saying,

[18] A voice was heard in Ramah,
  weeping and great mourning,
  Rachel weeping for her children;
  And she would not be comforted,
  because they are not.

[§ 16] —(3) In Natzeret

Matthew 2:19-23	Luke 2:39
[19] But when Herod was dead, behold, an angel of the Lord appeared in a dream to Yoseph in Egypt, saying, [20] Arise and take the young child and his mother, and go into the land of Yisrael: for they are dead that	[39] And when they had accomplished all things that were according to the law of the Lord, they returned into Galil, to their own city Natzeret.

---

[4] Hebrew: *Mitzrayim.*

sought the young child's life. [21] And he arose and took the young child and his mother, and came into the land of Yisrael. [22] But when he heard that Archelaus was reigning over Yehudah in the room of his father Herod, he was afraid to go thither; and being warned <of God> in a dream, he withdrew into the parts of Galil, [23] and came and dwelled in a city called Natzeret; that it might be fulfilled which was spoken through the prophets, that he should be called a Nazarene.

[§§ 17–19]—d. His Boyhood

[§ 17]—(1) His Growth

Luke 2:40

[40] And the child grew, and waxed strong, filled with wisdom: and the grace of God was upon him.

[§ 18]—(2) The Visit to Yerushalayim

Luke 2:41-50

[41] And his parents went every year to Yerushalayim at the feast of the Passover. [42] And when he was twelve years old, they went up after the custom of the feast; [43] and when they had fulfilled the days, as they were returning, the boy Yeshua tarried behind in Yerushalayim; and his parents knew it not; [44] but supposing him to be in the company, they went a day's journey; and they sought for him among their kinsfolk and acquaintance: [45] and when they found him not, they returned to Yerushalayim, seeking for him. [46] And

it came to pass, after three days they found him in the temple, sitting in the midst of the teachers, both hearing them, and asking them questions: [47] and all that heard him were amazed at his understanding and his answers. [48] And when they saw him, they were astonished; and his mother said unto him, Son, why have you thus dealt with us? Behold, your father and I sought you sorrowing. [49] And he said unto them, How is it that ye sought me? Knew ye not that I must be in my Father's house[5]? [50] And they understood not the saying which he spoke unto them.

[§ 19]—(3) His Development

Luke 2:51-52

[51] And he went down with them, and came to Natzeret; and he was subject unto them: and his mother kept all <these> sayings in her heart. [52] And Yeshua advanced in wisdom and stature, and in favor with God and men.

[§§ 20–23]—
B. The Forerunner and Herald of the King

[§ 20]—1. The Message to Yochanan

Mark 1:1	Luke 3:1-2
[1] The beginning of the gospel of Yeshua Messiah[6], the Son of God.	[1] Now in the fifteenth year of the reign of Tiberius Caesar, Pontius Pilate being governor of Yehudah, and Herod being tetrarch of Galil, and his brother Philip tetrarch of the

---

[5] Or, *about my Father's business.*

[6] Hebrew: *Mashiach.*

region of Ituraea and Trachonitis, and Lysanias tetrarch of Abilene, [2] in the high priesthood of Chanan and Kayapha, the word of God came unto Yochanan the son of Zecharyah in the wilderness.

[§ 21]—2. The Message by Yochanan

Matthew 3:1-6	Mark 1:2-6	Luke 3:3-6
[1] And in those days came Yochanan the Baptizer, preaching in the wilderness of Yehudah, saying, [2] Repent ye; for the kingdom of heaven is at hand. [3] For this is he that was spoken of through Yeshayahu the prophet, saying,	[2] Even as it is written in Yeshayahu the prophet,	[3] And he came into all the region round about the Yarden, preaching the baptism of repentance unto remission of sins; [4] as it is written in the book of the words of Yeshayahu the prophet,
	Behold, I send my messenger before your face, Who shall prepare your way.	
The voice of one crying in the wilderness, Make ye ready the way of the Lord, make his paths straight.	[3] The voice of one crying in the wilderness, Make ye ready the way of the Lord, Make his paths straight;	The voice of one crying in the wilderness, make ye ready the way of the Lord, Make his paths straight. [5] Every valley shall be filled, And every mountain and hill shall be brought low; And the

17

crooked shall become straight, And the rough ways smooth; [6] And all flesh shall see the salvation of God.

[4] Now Yochanan himself had his raiment of camel's hair, and a leathern girdle about his loins; and his food was locusts and wild honey.

[5] Then went out unto him Yerushalayim, and all Yehudah, and all the region round about the Yarden; [6] and they were baptized of him in the river Yarden, confessing their sins.

[4] Yochanan came, who baptized in the wilderness and preached the baptism of repentance unto remission of sins. [6] And Yochanan was clothed with camel's hair, and <had> a leathern girdle about his loins, and did eat locusts and wild honey. [5] And there went out unto him all the country of Yehudah, and all they of Yerushalayim; And they were baptized of him in the river Yarden, confessing their sins.

[§ 22]—3. The Explanation by Yochanan

Matthew 3:7-10

[7] But when he saw many of the Pharisees and Sadducees coming to his baptism, he said unto them, Ye offspring of vipers, who warned you to flee from the wrath to come?

Luke 3:7-14

[7] He said therefore to the multitudes that went out to be baptized of him, Ye offspring of vipers, who warned you to flee from the wrath to come? [8] Bring forth therefore fruits worthy

⁸ Bring forth therefore fruit worthy of repentance: ⁹ and think not to say within yourselves, We have Avraham to our father: for I say unto you, that God is able of these stones to raise up children unto Avraham. ¹⁰ And even now the axe lies at the root of the trees: every tree therefore that brings not forth good fruit is hewn down, and cast into the fire.

of repentance, and begin not to say within yourselves, We have Avraham to our father: for I say unto you, that God is able of these stones to raise up children unto Avraham. ⁹ And even now the axe also lies at the root of the trees: every tree therefore that brings not forth good fruit is hewn down, and cast into the fire.

¹⁰ And the multitudes asked him, saying, What then must we do? ¹¹ And he answered and said unto them, He that has two coats, let him impart to him that has none; and he that has food, let him do likewise. ¹² And there came also publicans to be baptized, and they said unto him, Teacher, what must we do? ¹³ And he said unto them, Extort no more than that which is appointed you. ¹⁴ And soldiers also asked him, saying, And we, what must we do? And he said unto them, Extort from no man by violence, neither accuse <anyone> wrongfully; and be content with your wages.

[§ 23]—4. The Promise by Yochanan

Matthew 3:11-12	Mark 1:7-8	Luke 3:15-18
		[15] And as the people were in expectation, and all men reasoned in their hearts concerning Yochanan, whether haply he were the Messiah;
	[7] And he preached, saying,	[16] Yochanan answered, saying unto them all,
[11] I indeed baptize you in water unto repentance: but he that comes after me is mightier than I, whose shoes I am not worthy to bear: he shall baptize you in the Holy Spirit and <in> fire: [12] whose fan is in his hand, and he will thoroughly cleanse his threshingfloor; and he will gather his wheat into the garner, but the chaff he will burn up with unquenchable fire.	There comes after me he that is mightier than I, the latchet of whose shoes I am not worthy to stoop down and unloose. [8] I baptized you in water; But he shall baptize you in the Holy Spirit.	I indeed baptize you with water; but there comes he that is mightier than I, the latchet of whose shoes I am not worthy to unloose: he shall baptize you in the Holy Spirit and <in> fire: [17] whose fan is in his hand, thoroughly to cleanse his threshingfloor, and to gather the wheat into his garner; but the chaff he will burn up with unquenchable fire. [18] With many other exhortations therefore preached he good tidings unto the people;
		(Luke 3:19-20 in § 35)

[§§ 24–27]—C. The Approval of the King

[§ 24]—1. At His Baptism

Matthew 3:13-17	Mark 1:9-11	Luke 3:21-23c
[13] Then came Yeshua from Galil to the Yarden unto Yochanan, to be baptized of him. [14] But Yochanan would have hindered him, saying, I have need to be baptized of you, and you come to me? [15] But Yeshua answering said unto him, Suffer <it> now: for thus it becomes us to fulfill all righteousness. Then he suffered him.	[9] And it came to pass in those days that Yeshua came from Natzeret of Galil, and was baptized of Yochanan in the Yarden.	[21] Now it came to pass, when all the people were baptized,
[16] And Yeshua when he was baptized, went up straightway from the water: and lo, the heavens were opened unto him,	[10] And straightway coming up out of the water, he saw the heavens rent asunder,	that, Yeshua also having been baptized, and praying, the heaven was opened,
and he saw the Spirit of God descending as a dove, and coming upon him;	and the Spirit as a dove descending upon him:	[22] and the Holy Spirit descended in a bodily form, as a dove, upon him,
[17] and lo, a voice out of the heavens, saying, This is my beloved Son, in whom I am well pleased.	[11] And a voice came out of the heavens, You are my beloved Son, in you I am well pleased.	and a voice came out of heaven, You are my beloved Son; in you I am well pleased.

23 And Yeshua himself, when he began <to teach>, was about thirty years of age,

(Luke 23d-38 in § 3)

[§ 25]—2. Through the Temptation

Matthew 4:1-11

1 Then was Yeshua led up of the Spirit into the wilderness to be tempted of the devil. 2 And when he had fasted forty days and forty nights, he afterward hungered.

3 And the tempter came and said unto him, If you are the Son of God, command that these stones become bread. 4 But he answered and said, It is written,

Man shall not live by bread alone, but by every word that proceeds out of the mouth of God.

Mark 1:12-13

12 And straightway the Spirit drives him forth into the wilderness. 13 And he was in the wilderness forty days tempted of Satan; And he was with the wild beasts; And the angels ministered unto him.

Luke 4:1-13

1 And Yeshua, full of the Holy Spirit, returned from the Yarden, and was led in the Spirit in the wilderness 2 during forty days, being tempted of the devil. And he did eat nothing in those days: and when they were completed, he hungered. 3 And the devil said unto him, if you are the Son of God, command this stone that it become bread.

4 And Yeshua answered unto him, It is written,

Man shall not live by bread alone.

Mt. cont.: [5] Then the devil takes him into the holy city; and he set him on the pinnacle of the temple, [6] and said unto him, If you are the Son of God, cast yourself down: for it is written,

> He shall give his angels charge concerning you: and, On their hands they shall bear you up, lest haply you dash your foot against a stone.

[7] Yeshua said unto him, Again it is written,

> You shall not make trial of the Lord your God.

[8] Again, the devil takes him unto an exceeding high mountain, and shows him all the kingdoms of the world, and the glory of them; [9] and he said unto him, All these things will I give you, if you will fall down and worship me. [10] Then said Yeshua unto him, Get you hence, Satan: for it is written,

> You shall worship the Lord your God, and him only shall you serve.

[11] Then the devil left him; and behold, angels came and ministered unto him.

Lk. Cont.: [5] And he led him up, and showed him all the kingdoms of the world in a moment of time.

[6] And the devil said unto him, To you will I give all this authority, and the glory of them: for it has been delivered unto me; and to whomsoever I will I give it. [7] If you therefore will worship before me, it shall all be yours.

[8] And Yeshua answered and said unto him, It is written,

> You shall worship the Lord your God, and him only shall you serve.

[9] And he led him to Yerushalayim, and set him on the pinnacle of the temple, and said unto him, If you are the Son of God, cast yourself down from hence: [10] for it is written,

> He shall give his angels charge concerning you, to guard you:

[11] and, On their hands they shall bear you up, Lest haply you dash your foot against a stone.

[12] And Yeshua answering said unto him, It is said,

> You shall not make trial of the Lord your God.

[13] And when the devil had completed every temptation, he departed from him for a season.

[§§ 26–27]—3. By His Herald

[§ 26]—a. Yochanan's Testimony before Leaders

John 1:19-28

[19] And this is the witness of Yochanan, when the Jews sent unto him from Yerushalayim priests and Levites to ask him, Who are you? [20] And he confessed, and denied not; and he confessed, I am not the Messiah. [21] And they asked him, What then? Are you Eliyahu? And he said, I am not. Are you the prophet? And he answered, No. [22] They said therefore unto him, Who are you? That we may give an answer to them that sent us. What do you say of yourself? [23] He said, I am the voice of one crying in the wilderness, Make straight the way of the Lord, as said Yeshayahu the prophet. [24] And they had been sent from the Pharisees. [25] And they asked him, and said unto him, Why then do you baptize, if you are not the Messiah, neither Eliyahu, neither the prophet? [26] Yochanan answered them, saying, I baptize in water: in the midst of you stands one whom ye know not, [27] <even> he that comes after me, the latchet of whose shoe I am not worthy to unloose. [28] These things were done in Beit Anyah beyond the Yarden, where Yochanan was baptizing.

[§ 27]—b. Yochanan's Testimony to Yeshua

John 1:29-34

[29] On the morrow he sees Yeshua coming unto him, and said, Behold, the Lamb of God, that takes away the sin of the world! [30] This is he of whom I said, After me comes a man who is become before me: for he was before me. [31] And I knew him not; but that he should be made manifest to Yisrael, for this cause came I baptizing in water. [32] And Yochanan bore witness, saying, I have beheld the Spirit descending as a dove out of heaven; and it abode upon him. [33] And I knew him not: but he that sent me to baptize in water, he said unto me, Upon whomsoever you shall see the Spirit descending, and abiding upon him, the same is he that baptizes in the Holy Spirit. [34] And I have seen, and have borne witness that this is the Son of God.

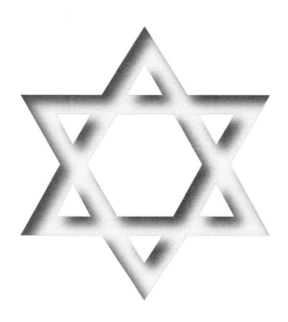

II. The Authentication of the King
— §§ 28–57 —

[§§ 28–37]—A. Acceptance of His Person

[§ 28]—1. The Belief by the First Disciples

John 1:35-51

[35] Again on the morrow Yochanan was standing, and two of his disciples; [36] and he looked upon Yeshua as he walked, and said, Behold, the Lamb of God! [37] And the two disciples heard him speak, and they followed Yeshua. [38] And Yeshua turned, and beheld them following, and said unto them, What seek ye? And they said unto him, Rabbi (which is to say, being inter-

preted, Teacher), where do you live? [39] He said unto them, Come, and ye shall see. They came therefore and saw where he abode; and they abode with him that day: it was about the tenth hour. [40] One of the two that heard Yochanan <speak>, and followed him, was Andrei, Shimon Peter's brother. [41] He found first his own brother Shimon, and said unto him, We have found the Messiah (which is, being interpreted, Christ). [42] He brought him unto Yeshua. Yeshua looked upon him, and said, You are Shimon the son of Yochanan: you shall be called Keipha – which is by interpretation, Peter. [43] On the morrow he was minded to go forth into Galil, and he found Philip: and Yeshua said unto him, Follow me. [44] Now Philip[1] was from Beit Tzaida, of the city of Andrei and Peter. [45] Philip found Netanel, and said unto him, We have found him, of whom Mosheh in the law, and the prophets, wrote, Yeshua of Natzeret, the son of Yoseph. [46] And Netanel said unto him, Can any good thing come out of Natzeret? Philip said unto him, Come and see. [47] Yeshua saw Netanel coming to him, and said of him, Behold, an Israelite indeed, in whom is no guile! [48] Netanel said unto him, From where do you know me? Yeshua answered and said unto him, Before Philip called you, when you were under the fig tree, I saw you. [49] Netanel answered him, Rabbi, you are the Son of God; you are King of Yisrael. [50] Yeshua answered and said unto him, Because I said unto you, I saw you underneath the fig tree, you believe? You shall see greater things than these. [51] And he said unto him, Verily, verily, I say unto you, Ye shall see the heaven opened, and the angels of God ascending and descending upon the Son of man.

[§ 29]—2. The Belief Through the First Miracle

John 2:1-11

[1] And the third day there was a marriage in Kana of Galil; and the mother of Yeshua was there: [2] and Yeshua also was bidden, and his disciples, to the marriage. [3] And when the wine failed, the mother of Yeshua said unto him, They have no wine. [4] And Yeshua said unto her, Woman, what have I to do with you? Mine hour is not yet come. [5] His mother said unto the servants,

---

[1] Greek: *Philipos.*

Whatsoever he says unto you, do it. [6] Now there were six water pots of stone set there after the Jews' manner of purifying, containing two or three firkins apiece. [7] Yeshua said unto them, Fill the water pots with water. And they filled them up to the brim. [8] And he said unto them, Draw out now, and bear unto the ruler of the feast. And they bore it. [9] And when the ruler of the feast tasted the water now become wine, and knew not from where it was (but the servants that had drawn the water knew), the ruler of the feast called the bridegroom, [10] and said unto him, Every man sets on first the good wine; and when <men> have drunk freely, <then> that which is worse: you have kept the good wine until now. [11] This beginning of his signs did Yeshua in Kana of Galil, and manifested his glory; and his disciples believed on him.

[§ 30]—3. The Sojourn in Kfar Nachum

John 2:12

[12] After this he went down to Kfar Nachum, he, and his mother, and <his> brethren, and his disciples; and there they abode not many days.

[§ 31]—4. The First Possession of the Temple

John 2:13-22

[13] And the Passover of the Jews was at hand, and Yeshua went up to Yerushalayim. [14] And he found in the temple those that sold oxen and sheep and doves, and the changers of money sitting: [15] and he made a scourge of cords, and cast all out of the temple, both the sheep and the oxen; and he poured out the changers' money, and overthrew their tables; [16] and to them that sold the doves he said, Take these things hence; make not my Father's house a house of merchandise. [17] His disciples remembered that it was written, Zeal for your house shall eat me up. [18] The Jews therefore answered and said unto him, What sign do you show unto us, seeing that you do these things? [19] Yeshua answered and said unto them, Destroy this temple, and in three days I will raise it up. [20] The Jews therefore said, Forty and six years was this temple in building, and you will raise it up in three days? [21] But he spoke of the temple of his body. [22] When therefore he was

raised from the dead, his disciples remembered that he spoke this; and they believed the scripture, and the word which Yeshua had said.

[§§ 32–33]—5. Acceptance in Yehuda

[§ 32]—a. Faith in His Signs

John 2:23-25

23 Now when he was in Yerushalayim at the Passover, during the feast, many believed on his name, beholding his signs which he did. 24 But Yeshua did not trust himself unto them, for that he knew all men, 25 and because he needed not that anyone should bear witness concerning man; for he himself knew what was in man.

[§ 33]—b. The Explanation to Nakdimon

John 3:1-21

1 Now there was a man of the Pharisees, named Nakdimon, a ruler of the Jews: 2 the same came unto him by night, and said to him, Rabbi, we know that you are a teacher come from God; for no one can do these signs that you do, except God be with him. 3 Yeshua answered and said unto him, Verily, verily, I say unto you, Except one be born anew, he cannot see the kingdom of God. 4 Nakdimon said unto him, How can a man be born when he is old? Can he enter a second time into his mother's womb, and be born? 5 Yeshua answered, Verily, verily, I say unto you, Except one be born of water and the Spirit, he cannot enter into the kingdom of God! 6 That which is born of the flesh is flesh; and that which is born of the Spirit is spirit. 7 Marvel not that I said unto you, Ye must be born anew. 8 The wind blows where it will, and you hear the voice thereof, but know not from where it comes, and whither it goes: so is everyone that is born of the Spirit. 9 Nakdimon answered and said unto him, How can these things be? 10 Yeshua answered and said unto him, Are you the teacher of Yisrael, and understand not these things? 11 Verily, verily, I say unto you, We speak that which we know, and bear witness of that which we have seen; and ye re-

ceive not our witness. [12] If I told you earthly things and ye believe not, how shall ye believe if I tell you heavenly things? [13] And no one has ascended into heaven, but he that descended out of heaven, <even> the Son of man, who is in heaven. [14] And as Mosheh lifted up the serpent in the wilderness, even so must the Son of man be lifted up; [15] that whosoever believes may in him have eternal life. [16] For God so loved the world, that he gave his only begotten Son, that whosoever believes on him should not perish, but have eternal life. [17] For God sent not the Son into the world to judge the world; but that the world should be saved through him. [18] He that believes on him is not judged: he that believes not has been judged already, because he has not believed on the name of the only begotten Son of God. [19] And this is the judgment, that the light is come into the world, and men loved the darkness rather than the light; for their works were evil. [20] For everyone that does evil hates the light, and comes not to the light, lest his works should be reproved. [21] But he that does the truth comes to the light, that his works may be made manifest, that they have been wrought in God.

[§ 34]—6. Yochanan's Witness

John 3:22-36

[22] After these things came Yeshua and his disciples into the land of Yehudah; and there he tarried with them, and baptized. [23] And Yochanan also was baptizing in Einon near to Shaleim, because there was much water there: and they came, and were baptized. [24] For Yochanan was not yet cast into prison. [25] There arose therefore a questioning on the part of Yochanan's disciples with a Jew about purifying. [26] And they came unto Yochanan, and said to him, Rabbi, he that was with you beyond the Yarden, to whom you have borne witness, behold, the same baptizes, and all men come to him. [27] Yochanan answered and said, A man can receive nothing, except it have been given him from heaven. [28] Ye yourselves bear me witness, that I said, I am not the Messiah, but, that I am sent before him. [29] He that has the bride is the bridegroom: but the friend of the bridegroom, that stands and hears him, rejoices greatly because of the bridegroom's voice: this my joy therefore is made full. [30] He must increase, but I must decrease. [31] He that comes from above is above all: he that is of the earth is of the earth, and of the earth he speaks: he that comes from heaven is above all. [32] What he has

seen and heard, of that he bears witness; and no man receives his witness. [33] He that has received his witness has set his seal to <this>, that God is true. [34] For he whom God has sent speaks the words of God: for he gives not the Spirit by measure. [35] The Father loves the Son, and has given all things into his hand. [36] He that believes on the Son has eternal life; but he that obeys not the Son shall not see life, but the wrath of God abides on him.

[§ 35]—7. Yochanan's Imprisonment

John 4:1-4

[1] When therefore the Lord knew that the Pharisees had heard that Yeshua was making and baptizing more disciples than Yochanan [2] (although Yeshua himself baptized not, but his disciples), [3] he left Yehudah, and departed again into Galil. [4] And he must needs pass through Shomron.

Luke 3:19-20

[19] but Herod the tetrarch, being reproved by him for Herodias his brother's wife, and for all the evil things which Herod had done, [20] added this also to them all, that he shut up Yochanan in prison.

Matthew 4:12	Mark 1:14a	Luke 4:14a
[12] Now when he heard that Yochanan was delivered up, he withdrew into Galil;	[14] Now after Yochanan was delivered up, Yeshua came into Galil,	[14] And Yeshua returned in the power of the Spirit into Galil:

[§ 36]—8. The Acceptance in Shomron

John 4:5-42

[5] So he came to a city of Shomron, called Sychar[2], near to the parcel of ground that Yaakov gave to his son Yoseph: [6] and Yaakov's well was there. Yeshua therefore, being wearied with his journey, sat thus by the well. It was about the sixth hour. [7] There came a woman of Shomron to draw water: Yeshua said unto her, Give me to drink. [8] For his disciples were gone away into the city to buy food. [9] The Samaritan woman therefore said unto him, How is it that you, being a Jew, asks drink of me, who am a Samaritan woman? (For Jews have no dealings with Samaritans.) [10] Yeshua answered and said unto her, If you knew the gift of God, and who it is that says to you, Give me to drink; you would have asked of him, and he would have given you living water. [11] The woman said unto him, Sir, you have nothing to draw with, and the well is deep: from where then have you that living water? [12] Are you greater than our father Yaakov, who gave us the well, and drank thereof himself, and his sons, and his cattle? [13] Yeshua answered and said unto her, Everyone that drinks of this water shall thirst again: [14] but whosoever drinks of the water that I shall give him shall never thirst; but the water that I shall give him shall become in him a well of water springing up unto eternal life. [15] The woman said unto him, Sir, give me this water, that I thirst not, neither come all the way hither to draw. [16] Yeshua said unto her, Go, call your husband, and come hither. [17] The woman answered and said unto him, I have no husband. Yeshua said unto her, You said well, I have no husband: [18] for you have had five husbands; and he whom you now have is not your husband: this have you said truly. [19] The woman said unto him, Sir, I perceive that you are a prophet. [20] Our fathers worshipped in this mountain[3]; and ye say, that in Yerushalayim is the place where men ought to worship. [21] Yeshua said unto her, Woman, believe me, the hour comes, when neither in this mountain, nor in Yerushalayim, shall ye worship the Father. [22] Ye worship that which ye know not: we worship that which we know; for salvation is from the Jews. [23] But the hour comes, and now is,

---

[2] By the city of Shechem (in Arabic: *Nablus*).

[3] Mount Gerizim, in the immediate vicinity of Shechem.

when the true worshippers shall worship the Father in spirit and truth: for such does the Father seek to be his worshippers. [24] God is a Spirit: and they that worship him must worship in spirit and truth. [25] The woman said unto him, I know that Messiah comes (he that is called Christ): when he is come, he will declare unto us all things. [26] Yeshua said unto her, I that speak unto you am <he>.

[27] And upon this came his disciples; and they marveled that he was speaking with a woman; yet no man said, What are you seeking? or, Why are you speaking with her? [28] So the woman left her waterpot, and went away into the city, and said to the people, [29] Come, see a man, who told me all things that <ever> I did: can this be the Messiah? [30] They went out of the city, and were coming to him. [31] In the mean while the disciples prayed him, saying, Rabbi, eat. [32] But he said unto them, I have meat to eat that ye know not. [33] The disciples therefore said one to another, Has any man brought him <anything> to eat? [34] Yeshua said unto them, My meat is to do the will of him that sent me, and to accomplish his work. [35] Say not ye, There are yet four months, and <then> comes the harvest? Behold, I say unto you, Lift up your eyes, and look on the fields, that they are white already unto harvest. [36] He that reaps receives wages, and gathers fruit unto life eternal; that he that sows and he that reaps may rejoice together. [37] For herein is the saying true, One sows, and another reaps. [38] I sent you to reap that whereon ye have not labored: others have labored, and ye are entered into their labor. [39] And from that city many of the Samaritans believed on him because of the word of the woman, who testified, He told me all things that <ever> I did. [40] So when the Samaritans came unto him, they besought him to abide with them: and he abode there two days. [41] And many more believed because of his word; [42] and they said to the woman, Now we believe, not because of your speaking: for we have heard for ourselves, and know that this is indeed the Savior of the world.

[§ 37]—9. The Acceptance in Galil

John 4:43-45

[43] And after the two days he went forth from thence into Galil. [44] For Yeshua himself testified, that a prophet has no honor in his own country. [45] So

when he came into Galil, the Galileans received him, having seen all the things that he did in Yerushalayim at the feast: for they also went unto the feast.

[§§ 38–57]—B. The Authority of the King

[§ 38]—1. Messiah's Authority to Preach

Matthew 4:17	Mark 1:14b-15	Luke 4:14b-15
[17] From that time began Yeshua to preach, and to say, Repent ye; for the kingdom of heaven is at hand.	[14] preaching the gospel of God, [15] and saying, The time is fulfilled, and the kingdom of God is at hand: repent ye, and believe in the gospel.	[14] and a fame went out concerning him through all the region round about. [15] And he taught in their synagogues, being glorified of all.

[§ 39]—2. The Messiah's Authority to Heal

John 4:46-54

[46] He came therefore again unto Kana of Galil, where he made the water wine. And there was a certain nobleman, whose son was sick at Kfar Nachum. [47] When he heard that Yeshua was come out of Yehudah into Galil, he went unto him, and besought <him> that he would come down, and heal his son; for he was at the point of death. [48] Yeshua therefore said unto him, Except ye see signs and wonders, ye will in no wise believe. [49] The nobleman said unto him, Sir, come down ere my child die. [50] Yeshua said unto him, Go your way; your son lives. The man believed the word that Yeshua spoke unto him, and he went his way. [51] And as he was now going down, his servants met him, saying, that his son lived. [52] So he inquired of them the hour when he began to amend. They said therefore unto him, Yesterday at the seventh hour the fever left him. [53] So the father knew that <it was> at that hour in which Yeshua said unto him, your son lives: and himself believed,

and his whole house. [54] This is again the second sign that Yeshua did, having come out of Yehudah into Galil.

[§ 40]—3. The Initial Rejection in Natzeret

Luke 4:16-31

[16] And he came to Natzeret, where he had been brought up: and he entered, as his custom was, into the synagogue on the Sabbath day, and stood up to read. [17] And there was delivered unto him the book of the prophet Yeshayahu. And he opened the book, and found the place where it was written,

[18] The Spirit of the Lord is upon me,

 Because he anointed me to preach good tidings to the poor:

 He has sent me to proclaim release to the captives,

 And recovering of sight to the blind,

 To set at liberty them that are bruised,

[19] To proclaim the acceptable year of the Lord.

[20] And he closed the book, and gave it back to the attendant, and sat down: and the eyes of all in the synagogue were fastened on him. [21] And he began to say unto them, Today has this scripture been fulfilled in your ears. [22] And all bore him witness, and wondered at the words of grace which proceeded out of his mouth: and they said, Is not this Yoseph's son? [23] And he said unto them, Doubtless ye will say unto me this parable, Physician, heal yourself: whatsoever we have heard done at Kfar Nachum, do also here in your own country. [24] And he said, Verily I say unto you, No prophet is acceptable in his own country. [25] But of a truth I say unto you, There were many widows in Yisrael in the days of Eliyahu, when the heaven was shut up three years and six months, when there came a great famine over all the land; [26] and unto none of them was Eliyahu sent, but only to Tzarfat, in the land of Tzidon, unto a woman that was a widow. [27] And there were many lepers in Yisrael in the time of Elisha the prophet; and none of them was cleansed, but only Naaman the Syrian[4]. [28] And they were all filled with wrath in the synagogue,

---

[4] Hebrew: *Aramean.*

as they heard these things; [29] and they rose up, and cast him forth out of the city, and led him unto the brow of the hill whereon their city was built, that they might throw him down headlong. [30] But he passing through the midst of them went his way. [31] And he came down to Kfar Nachum, a city of Galil.

[§ 41]—4. The Headquarters in Kfar Nachum

Matthew 4:13-16

[13] and leaving Natzeret, he came and dwelled in Kfar Nachum, which is by the sea, in the borders of Zvulun and Naphtali: [14] that it might be fulfilled which was spoken through Yeshayahu the prophet, saying,

[15] The land of Zvulun and the land of Naphtali,

 toward the sea, beyond the Yarden,

 Galil of the Gentiles,

[16] the people that sat in darkness

 saw a great light,

 and to them that sat in the region and shadow of death,

 to them did light spring up.

[§ 42]—5. Messiah's Authority over Demons

Mark 1:21-28

[21] And they go into Kfar Nachum; and straightway on the Sabbath day he entered into the synagogue and taught. [22] And they were astonished at his teaching: For he taught them as having authority, and not as the scribes. [23] And straightway there was in their synagogue a man with an unclean spirit; and he cried out, [24] saying, What have we to do with you, Yeshua you Nazarene? Are you come to destroy us? I know you who

Luke 4:31b-37

[31] And he was teaching them on the Sabbath day: [32] and they were astonished at his teaching; for his word was with authority.

[33] And in the synagogue there was a man, that had a spirit of an unclean demon; and he cried out with a loud voice, [34] Ah! What have we to do with you, Yeshua you Nazarene? Are you come to destroy us? I know you

you are, the Holy One of God. [25] And Yeshua rebuked him, saying, Hold your peace, and come out of him. [26] And the unclean spirit, tearing him and crying with a loud voice, came out of him.

[27] And they were all amazed, insomuch that they questioned among themselves, saying, What is this? A new teaching! With authority he commands even the unclean spirits, and they obey him.

[28] And the report of him went out straightway everywhere into all the region of Galil round about.

who you are, the Holy One of God. [35] And Yeshua rebuked him, saying, Hold your peace, and come out of him. And when the demon had thrown him down in the midst, he came out of him, having done him no hurt. [36] And amazement came upon all, and they spoke together, one with another, saying, What is this word? For with authority and power he commands the unclean spirits, and they come out.

[37] And there went forth a rumor concerning him into every place of the region round about.

[§ 43]—6. Messiah's Authority over Disease

Matthew 8:14-17	Mark 1:29-34	Luke 4:38-41
	[29] And straightway, when they were come out of the synagogue, they came into the house of Shimon and Andrei, with Yaakov and Yochanan.	[38] And he rose up from the synagogue, and entered into the house of Shimon.
[14] And when Yeshua was come into Peter's house, he saw his wife's mother lying sick of a fever.	[30] Now Shimon's wife's mother lay sick of a fever; and straightway they tell him of her:	And Shimon's wife's mother was holden with a great fever; and they besought him for her.
[15] And he touched her hand,	[31] and he came and took her by the hand, and raised her up;	[39] And he stood over her, and rebuked the fever;
and the fever left her,	and the fever left her,	and it left her: and

and she arose, and ministered unto him.

[16] And when even was come, they brought unto him many possessed with demons: and he cast out the spirits with a word, and healed all that were sick: [17] that it might be fulfilled which was spoken through Yeshayahu the prophet, saying: Himself took our infirmities, and bore our diseases.

and she ministered unto them.

[32] And at even, when the sun did set, they brought unto him all that were sick, and them that were possessed with demons. [33] And all the city was gathered together at the door. [34] And he healed many that were sick with divers diseases, and cast out many demons; and he suffered not the demons to speak, because they knew him.

immediately she rose up and ministered unto them.

[40] And when the sun was setting, all they that had any sick with divers diseases brought them unto him; and he laid his hands on every one of them, and healed them. [41] And demons also came out from many, crying out, and saying, You are the Son of God. And rebuking them, he suffered them not to speak, because they knew that he was the Messiah.

[§ 44]—7. Messiah's Authority to Preach

Matthew 4:23-25	Mark 1:35-39	Luke 4:42-44
	[35] And in the morning, a great while before day, he rose up and went out, and departed into a desert place, and there prayed. [36] And Shimon and they that were with him followed after him; [37] and they found him, and say unto him,	[42] And when it was day, he came out and went into a desert place: and the multitudes sought after him, and came unto him, and would have stayed him, that he should not go from them. [43] But he said unto them, I must preach the good tid-

	All are seeking you. [38] And he said unto them, Let us go elsewhere into the next towns, that I may preach there also; for to this end came I forth.	ings of the kingdom of God to the other cities also: for therefore was I sent.
[23] And Yeshua went about in all Galil, teaching in their synagogues, and preaching the gospel of the kingdom, and healing all manner of disease and all manner of sickness among the people.	[39] And he went into their synagogues throughout all Galil, preaching and casting out demons.	[44] And he was preaching in the synagogues of Galil.

Mt. cont.: [24] And the report of him went forth into all Syria: and they brought unto him all that were sick, holden with divers diseases and torments, possessed with demons, and epileptic, and palsied; and he healed them. [25] And there followed him great multitudes from Galil and Decapolis and Yerushalayim and Yehudah and <from> beyond the Yarden.

[§ 45]—8. Messiah's Authority over Nature

Matthew 4:18-22	Mark 1:16-20	Luke 5:1-11
[18] And walking by the sea of Galil, he saw two brethren, Shimon who is called Peter, and Andrei his brother, casting a net into the sea; for they were	[16] And passing along by the sea of Galil, he saw Shimon and Andrei the brother of Shimon casting a net in the sea; for they were fishers.	[1] Now it came to pass, while the multitude pressed upon him and heard the word of God, that he was standing by the lake of Ginosar; [2] and he saw two boats

fishers. [19] And he said unto them, Come ye after me, and I will make you fishers of men. [20] And they straightway left the nets, and followed him. [21] And going on from thence he saw two other brethren, Yaakov the <son> of Zavdi, and Yochanan his brother, in the boat with Zavdi their father, mending their nets; and he called them. [22] And they straightway left the boat and their father, and followed him.

[17] And Yeshua said unto them, Come ye after me, and I will make you to become fishers of men. [18] And straightway they left the nets, and followed him. [19] And going on a little further, he saw Yaakov the <son> of Zavdi, and Yochanan his brother, who also were in the boat mending the nets. [20] And straightway he called them: and they left their father Zavdi in the boat with the hired servants, and went after him.

standing by the lake: but the fishermen had gone out of them, and were washing their nets. [3] And he entered into one of the boats, which was Shimon's, and asked him to put out a little from the land. And he sat down and taught the multitudes out of the boat.

Lk. cont.: [4] And when he had left speaking, he said unto Shimon, Put out into the deep, and let down your nets for a draught. [5] And Shimon answered and said, Master, we toiled all night, and took nothing: but at your word I will let down the nets. [6] And when they had done this, they inclosed a great multitude of fishes; and their nets were breaking; [7] and they beckoned unto their partners in the other boat, that they should come and help them. And they came, and filled both the boats, so that they began to sink. [8] But Shimon Peter, when he saw it, fell down at Yeshua's knees, saying, Depart from me; for I am a sinful man, O Lord. [9] For he was amazed, and all that were with him, at the draught of the fishes which they had taken; [10] and so were also Yaakov and Yochanan, sons of Zavdi, who were partners with Shimon. And Yeshua said unto Shimon, Fear not; from henceforth you shall catch men. [11] And when they had brought their boats to land, they left all, and followed him.

[§ 46]—9. Messiah's Authority over Defilement: The Healing of the Jewish Leper

Matthew 8:2-4	Mark 1:40-45	Luke 5:12-16
[2] And behold, there came to him a leper and worshipped him, saying, Lord,	[40] And there comes to him a leper, beseeching him, and kneeling down to him, and saying unto him,	[12] And it came to pass, while he was in one of the cities, behold, a man full of leprosy: and when he saw Yeshua, he fell on his face, and besought him, saying,
if you will, you can make me clean. [3] And he stretched forth his hand, and touched him, saying, I will; you be made clean.	If you will, you can make me clean. [41] And being moved with compassion, he stretched forth his hand, and touched him, and said unto him, I will; you be made clean.	Lord, if you will, you can make me clean. [13] And he stretched forth his hand, and touched him, saying, I will; you be made clean.
And straightway his leprosy was cleansed.	[42] And straightway the leprosy departed from him, and he was made clean. [43] And he strictly charged him, and straightway sent him out, [44] and said unto him, See you say nothing to any man: but go show yourself to the priest, and offer for your cleansing the things which Mosheh commanded, for a testimony unto them.	And straightway the leprosy departed from him.
[4] And Yeshua said unto him, See you tell no man; but go, show yourself to the priest, and offer the gift that Mosheh commanded, for a testimony unto them.		[14] And he charged him to tell no man: but go your way, and show yourself to the priest, and offer for your cleansing, according as Mosheh commanded, for a testimony unto them.

<table>
<tr>
<td>

⁴⁵ But he went out, and began to publish it much, and to spread abroad the matter, insomuch that Yeshua could no more openly enter into a city, but was without in desert places: and they came to him from every quarter.

</td>
<td>

¹⁵ But so much the more went abroad the report concerning him: and great multitudes came together to hear, and to be healed of their infirmities.

¹⁶ But he withdrew himself in the deserts, and prayed.

</td>
</tr>
</table>

[§ 47]—10. Messiah's Authority to Forgive Sin

Matthew 9:1-8	Mark 2:1-12	Luke 5:17-26
¹ And he entered into a boat, and crossed over, and came into his own city.	¹ And when he entered again into Kfar Nachum after some days, it was noised that he was in the house. ² And many were gathered together, so that there was no longer room <for them>, no, not even about the door: and he spoke the word unto them.	¹⁷ And it came to pass on one of those days, that he was teaching; and there were Pharisees and doctors of the law sitting by, who were come out of every village of Galil and Yehudah and Yerushalayim: and the power of the Lord was with him to heal.
² And behold, they brought to him a man sick of the palsy, lying on a bed:	³ And they come, bringing unto him a man sick of the palsy, borne of four.	¹⁸ And behold, men bring on a bed a man that was palsied: and they sought to bring him in, and to lay him before him.

and Yeshua seeing their faith said unto the sick of the palsy, Son, be of good cheer; your sins are forgiven. ³ And behold, certain of the scribes said within themselves, This man blasphemes.

⁴ And Yeshua knowing their thoughts said,

Wherefore think ye evil in your hearts? ⁵ For which is easier, to say, your sins are forgiven; or to say, Arise, and walk?

---

⁴ And when they could not come near unto him for the crowd, they uncovered the roof where he was: and when they had broken it up, they let down the bed whereon the sick of the palsy lay. ⁵ And Yeshua seeing their faith said unto the sick of the palsy, Son, your sins are forgiven. ⁶ But there were certain of the scribes sitting there, and reasoning in their hearts, ⁷ Why does this man thus speak? He blasphemes: who can forgive sins but one, <even> God? ⁸ And straightway Yeshua, perceiving in his spirit that they so reasoned within themselves, said unto them, Why reason ye these things in your hearts? ⁹ Which is easier, to say to the sick of the palsy, your sins are forgiven; or to say, Arise, and take up your bed, and walk?

---

¹⁹ And not finding by what <way> they might bring him in because of the multitude, they went up to the house-top, and let him down through the tiles with his couch into the midst before Yeshua.

²⁰ And seeing their faith, he said, Man, your sins are forgiven you.

²¹ And the scribes and the Pharisees began to reason, saying, Who is this that speaks blasphemies? Who can forgive sins, but God alone?

²² But Yeshua perceiving their reasonings, answered and said unto them,

Why reason ye in your hearts? ²³ Which is easier, to say, your sins are forgiven you; or to say, Arise and walk?

6 But that ye may know that the Son of man has authority on earth to forgive sins (then he said to the sick of the palsy), Arise, and take up your bed, and go up unto your house.

7 And he arose, and departed to his house.

8 But when the multitudes saw it, they were afraid, and glorified God, who had given such authority unto men.

10 But that ye may know that the Son of man has authority on earth to forgive sins (he said to the sick of the palsy), 11 I say unto you, Arise, take up your bed, and go unto your house. 12 And he arose, and straightway took up the bed, and went forth before them all; insomuch that they were all amazed, and glorified God, saying, We never saw it on this fashion.

24 But that ye may know that the Son of man has authority on earth to forgive sins (he said unto him that was palsied), I say unto you, Arise, and take up your couch, and go unto your house. 25 And immediately he rose up before them, and took up that whereon he lay, and departed to his house, glorifying God. 26 And amazement took hold on all, and they glorified God; and they were filled with fear, saying, We have seen strange things today.

[§ 48]—11. Messiah's Authority over Men

Matthew 9:9-13	Mark 2:13-17	Luke 5:27-32
9 And as Yeshua passed by from thence, he saw a man, called Mattai, sitting at the place of toll: and he said unto him, Follow me. And he arose, and followed him.	13 And he went forth again by the sea side; and all the multitude resorted unto him, and he taught them. 14 And as he passed by, he saw Levi the <son> of Chalphi sitting at the place of toll, and he said unto him, Follow	27 And after these things he went forth, and beheld a publican, named Levi, sitting at the place of toll, and said unto him, Follow me. 28 And he forsook all, and rose up and followed him.

me. And he arose and followed him.

¹⁵ And it came to pass, that he was sitting at meat in his house, and many publicans and sinners sat down with Yeshua and his disciples: for there were many, and they followed him.

¹⁰ And it came to pass, as he sat at meat in the house, behold, many publicans and sinners came and sat down with Yeshua and his disciples.

²⁹ And Levi made him a great feast in his house: and there was a great multitude of publicans and of others that were sitting at meat with them.

¹¹ And when the Pharisees saw it, they said unto his disciples, Why eats your Teacher with the publicans and sinners?

¹⁶ And the scribes of the Pharisees, when they saw that he was eating with the sinners and publicans, said unto his disciples, <How is it> that he eats and drinks with publicans and sinners?

³⁰ And the Pharisees and their scribes murmured against his disciples, saying, Why do ye eat and drink with the publicans and sinners?

¹² But when he heard it, he said, They that are whole have no need of a physician, but they that are sick. ¹³ But go ye and learn what <this> means, I desire mercy, and not sacrifice, for I came not to call the righteous, but sinners.

¹⁷ And when Yeshua heard it, he said unto them, They that are whole have no need of a physician, but they that are sick: I came not to call the righteous, but sinners.

³¹ And Yeshua answering said unto them, They that are in health have no need of a physician; but they that are sick. ³² I am not come to call the righteous but sinners to repentance.

[§ 49]—12. Messiah's Authority over Tradition

Matthew 9:14-17	Mark 2:18-22	Luke 5:33-39
[14] Then come to him the disciples of Yochanan, saying, Why do we and the Pharisees fast often, but your disciples fast not?	[18] And Yochanan's disciples and the Pharisees were fasting: and they come and say unto him, Why do Yochanan's disciples and the disciples of the Pharisees fast, but your disciples fast not?	[33] And they said unto him, The disciples of Yochanan fast often, and make supplications; likewise also the \<disciples\> of the Pharisees; but yours eat and drink.
[15] And Yeshua said unto them, Can the sons of the bridechamber mourn, as long as the bridegroom is with them?	[19] And Yeshua said unto them, Can the sons of the bridechamber fast, while the bridegroom is with them? As long as they have the bridegroom with them, they cannot fast. [20] But the days will come, when the bridegroom shall be taken away from them, and then will they fast in that day.	[34] And Yeshua said unto them, Can ye make the sons of the bridechamber fast, while the bridegroom is with them?
But the days will come, when the bridegroom shall be taken away from them, and then will they fast.		[35] But the days will come; and when the bridegroom shall be taken away from them, then will they fast in those days. [36] And he spoke also a parable unto them:
[16] And no man puts a piece of undressed cloth upon an old garment; for that which should fill it up takes from the garment, and a worse rent is made.	[21] No man sows a piece of undressed cloth on an old garment: else that which should fill it up takes from it, the new from the old, and a worse rent is made.	No man tears a piece from a new garment and puts it upon an old garment; else he will tear the new, and also the piece from the new will not agree with the old.

¹⁷ Neither do \<men\> put new wine into old wineskins: else the skins burst, and the wine is spilled, and the skins perish: but they put new wine into fresh wineskins, and both are preserved.

²² And no man puts new wine into old wineskins; else the wine will burst the skins, and the wine perishes, and the skins: but \<they put\> new wine into fresh wineskins.

³⁷ And no man puts new wine into old wineskins; else the new wine will burst the skins, and itself will be spilled, and the skins will perish. ³⁸ But new wine must be put into fresh wineskins. ³⁹ And no man having drunk old \<wine\> desires new; for he said, The old is good.

[§§ 50–52]—13. Messiah's Authority over the Sabbath

[§ 50]—a. Through the Healing of a Paralytic

John 5:1-47

¹ After these things there was a feast of the Jews; and Yeshua went up to Yerushalayim.

² Now there is in Yerushalayim by the sheep \<gate\> a pool, which is called in Hebrew Beit Chesda, having five porches. ³ In these lay a multitude of them that were sick, blind, halt, withered.⁵ ⁵ And a certain man was there, who had been thirty and eight years in his infirmity. ⁶ When Yeshua saw him lying, and knew that he had been now a long time \<in that case\>, he said unto him, Would you be made whole? ⁷ The sick man answered him, Sir, I have no man, when the water is troubled, to put me into the pool: but while I am coming, another steps down before me. ⁸ Yeshua said unto him,

---

⁵ Many ancient authorities insert wholly or in part: "waiting for the moving of the water, ⁴ for an angel of the Lord went down at certain seasons into the pool, and troubled the water: whosoever then first after the troubling of the waters stepped in was made whole, with whatsoever disease he was holden."

Arise, take up your bed, and walk. [9] And straightway the man was made whole, and took up his bed and walked.

Now it was the Sabbath on that day. [10] So the Jews said unto him that was cured, It is the Sabbath, and it is not lawful for you to take up your bed. [11] But he answered them, He that made me whole, the same said unto me, Take up your bed, and walk. [12] They asked him, Who is the man that said unto you, Take up <your bed>, and walk? [13] But he that was healed knew not who it was; for Yeshua had conveyed himself away, a multitude being in the place. [14] Afterward Yeshua finds him in the temple, and said unto him, Behold, you are made whole: sin no more, lest a worse thing befall you. [15] The man went away, and told the Jews that it was Yeshua who had made him whole. [16] And for this cause the Jews persecuted Yeshua, because he did these things on the Sabbath. [17] But Yeshua answered them, My Father works even until now, and I work. [18] For this cause therefore the Jews sought the more to kill him, because he not only broke the Sabbath, but also called God his own Father, making himself equal with God.

[19] Yeshua therefore answered and said unto them, Verily, verily, I say unto you, The Son can do nothing of himself, but what he sees the Father doing: for what things soever he does, these the Son also does in like manner. [20] For the Father loves the Son, and shows him all things that himself does: and greater works than these will he show him, that ye may marvel. [21] For as the Father raises the dead and gives them life, even so the Son also gives life to whom he will. [22] For neither does the Father judge any man, but he has given all judgment unto the Son; [23] that all may honor the Son, even as they honor the Father. He that honors not the Son honors not the Father that sent him. [24] Verily, verily, I say unto you, He that hears my word, and believes him that sent me, has eternal life, and comes not into judgment, but has passed out of death into life. [25] Verily, verily, I say unto you, The hour comes, and now is, when the dead shall hear the voice of the Son of God; and they that hear shall live. [26] For as the Father has life in himself, even so gave he to the Son also to have life in himself: [27] and he gave him authority to execute judgment, because he is a son of man. [28] Marvel not at this: for the hour comes, in which all that are in the tombs shall hear his voice, [29] and shall come forth; they that have done good, unto the resurrection of life; and they that have done evil, unto the resurrection of judgment.

[30] I can of myself do nothing: as I hear, I judge: and my judgment is righteous; because I seek not mine own will, but the will of him that sent me. [31] If I bear witness of myself, my witness is not true. [32] It is another that bears witness of me; and I know that the witness which he witnesses of me is true. [33] Ye have sent unto Yochanan, and he has borne witness unto the truth. [34] But the witness which I receive is not from man: howbeit I say these things, that ye may be saved. [35] He was the lamp that burns and shines; and ye were willing to rejoice for a season in his light. [36] But the witness which I have is greater than <that of> Yochanan; for the works which the Father has given me to accomplish, the very works that I do, bear witness of me, that the Father has sent me. [37] And the Father that sent me, he has borne witness of me. Ye have neither heard his voice at any time, nor seen his form. [38] And ye have not his word abiding in you: for whom he sent, him ye believe not. [39] Ye search the scriptures, because ye think that in them ye have eternal life; and these are they which bear witness of me; [40] and ye will not come to me, that ye may have life. [41] I receive not glory from men. [42] But I know you, that ye have not the love of God in yourselves. [43] I am come in my Father's name, and ye receive me not: if another shall come in his own name, him ye will receive. [44] How can ye believe, who receive glory one of another, and the glory that <comes> from the only God ye seek not? [45] Think not that I will accuse you to the Father: there is one that accuses you, <even> Mosheh, on whom ye have set your hope. [46] For if ye believed Mosheh, ye would believe me; for he wrote of me. [47] But if ye believe not his writings, how shall ye believe my words?

[§ 51]—b. Through the Controversy over Grain

Matthew 12:1-8	Mark 2:23-28	Luke 6:1-5
[1] At that season Yeshua went on the Sabbath day through the wheatfields; and his disciples were hungry and began to pluck ears and to eat.	[23] And it came to pass, that he was going on the Sabbath day through the wheatfields; and his disciples began, as they went, to pluck the ears.	[1] Now it came to pass on a Sabbath that he was going through the wheatfields; and his disciples plucked the ears, and did eat, rubbing them in their hands.

2 But the Pharisees, when they saw it, said unto him, Behold, your disciples do that which it is not lawful to do upon the Sabbath. 3 But he said unto them, Have ye not read what David did, when he was hungry, and they that were with him;

4 how he entered into the house of God, and ate the showbread, which it was not lawful for him to eat, neither for them that were with him, but only for the priests? 5 Or have ye not read in the law, that on the Sabbath day the priests in the temple profane the Sabbath, and are guiltless? 6 But I say unto you, that one greater than the temple is here. 7 But if ye had known what this means, I desire mercy, and not sacrifice, ye would not have condemned the guiltless.

24 And the Pharisees said unto him, Behold, why do they on the Sabbath day that which is not lawful? 25 And he said unto them, Did ye never read what David did, when he had need, and was hungry, he, and they that were with him?

26 How he entered into the house of God when Abiathar was high priest, and ate the showbread, which it is not lawful to eat save for the priests, and gave also to them that were with him?

27 And he said unto them, The Sabbath was made for man, and not man for the Sabbath:

2 But certain of the Pharisees said, Why do ye that which it is not lawful to do on the Sabbath day? 3 And Yeshua answering them said, Have ye not read even this, what David did, when he was hungry, he, and they that were with him;

4 how he entered into the house of God, and took and ate the showbread, and gave also to them that were with him; which it is not lawful to eat save for the priests alone?

5 And he said unto them,

[8] For the Son of man is lord of the Sabbath.	[28] so that the Son of man is lord even of the Sabbath.	The Son of man is lord of the Sabbath.

[§ 52]—c. Through the Healing of a Man with a Withered Hand

Matthew 12:9-14	Mark 3:1-6	Luke 6:6-11
[9] And he departed thence, and went into their synagogue: [10] and behold, a man having a withered hand.	[1] And he entered again into the synagogue; and there was a man there who had his hand withered.	[6] And it came to pass on another Sabbath that he entered into the synagogue and taught: and there was a man there, and his right hand was withered. [7] And the scribes and the Pharisees watched him, whether he would heal on the Sabbath; that they might find how to accuse him. [8] But he knew their thoughts; and he said to the man that had his hand withered, Rise up, and stand forth in the midst. And he arose and stood forth. [9] And Yeshua said unto them, I ask you, Is it lawful on the Sabbath to do good, or to do harm? To save a life, or to destroy it? [10] And he
And they asked him, saying, Is it lawful to heal on the Sabbath day? That they might accuse him.	[2] And they watched him, whether he would heal him on the Sabbath day; that they might accuse him.	
	[3] And he said unto the man that had his hand withered, Stand forth.	
[11] And he said unto them, What man shall there be of you, that shall have one sheep, and if this fall into a pit on the Sabbath day, will he not lay hold on	[4] And he said unto them, Is it lawful on the Sabbath day to do good, or to do harm? To save a life, or to kill? But they held their peace. [5] And when he	

it, and lift it out? [12] How much then is a man of more value than a sheep! Wherefore it is lawful to do good on the Sabbath day. [13] Then said he to the man, Stretch forth your hand. And he stretched it forth; and it was restored whole, as the other. [14] But the Pharisees went out, and took counsel against him, how they might destroy him.

had looked round about on them with anger, being grieved at the hardening of their heart,

he said unto the man, Stretch forth your hand. And he stretched it forth; and his hand was restored.

[6] And the Pharisees went out, and straightway with the Herodians took counsel against him, how they might destroy him.

looked round about on them all,

and said unto him, Stretch forth your hand. And he did <so>: and his hand was restored.

[11] But they were filled with madness; and communed one with another what they might do to Yeshua.

[§ 53]—14. Messiah's Authority to Heal

Matthew 12:15-21

[15] And Yeshua perceiving <it> withdrew from thence: and many followed him;

Mark 3:7-12

[7] And Yeshua with his disciples withdrew to the sea: and a great multitude from Galil followed; and from Yehudah, [8] and from Yerushalayim, and from Idumea, and beyond the Yarden, and about Tzor and Tzidon, a great multitude, hearing what great things he did, came unto him. [9] And he spoke to his disciples, that a little boat should wait on him because of the crowd, lest they should throng him:

and he healed them all,

[10] for he had healed many; insomuch that as many as had plagues pressed upon him that they might touch him. [11] And the unclean spirits, whensoever they beheld him, fell down before him, and cried, saying, You are the Son of God. [12] And he charged them much that they should not make him known.

[16] and charged them that they should not make him known: [17] that it might be fulfilled which was spoken through Yeshayahu the prophet, saying,

[18] Behold, my servant whom I have chosen; My beloved in whom my soul is well pleased: I will put my Spirit upon him, And he shall declare judgment to the Gentiles.

[19] He shall not strive, nor cry aloud; Neither shall anyone hear his voice in the streets.

[20] A bruised reed shall he not break, And smoking flax shall he not quench, Till he send forth judgment unto victory.

[21] And in his name shall the Gentiles hope.

[§ 54]—15. The Choosing of the Twelve

Mark 3:13-19a

[13] And he goes up into the mountain, and calls unto him whom he himself would; and they went unto him.

Luke 6:12-16

[12] And it came to pass in these days that he went out into the mountain to pray; and he continued all night in prayer to God. [13] And when it was

¹⁴ And he appointed twelve, that they might be with him, and that he might send them forth to preach, ¹⁵ and to have authority to cast out demons:
¹⁶ and Shimon he surnamed Peter; ¹⁷ and Yaakov the <son> of Zavdi, and Yochanan the brother of Yaakov; and them he surnamed Bnei Regesh, which is, Sons of thunder: ¹⁸ and Andrei, and Philip, and Bar Talmai, and Mattai, and Toma, and Yaakov the <son> of Chalphi, and Taddai, and Shimon the Cananaean, ¹⁹ and Yehudah Ish Kriyot, who also betrayed him.

day, he called his disciples; and he chose from them twelve, whom also he named apostles:

¹⁴ Shimon, whom he also named Peter, and Andrei his brother, and Yaakov and Yochanan, and Philip and Bar Talmai, ¹⁵ and Mattai and Toma, and Yaakov <the son> of Chalphi, and Shimon who was called the Zealot, ¹⁶ and Yehudah <the son> of Yaakov, and Yehudah Ish Kriyot, who became a traitor;

[§ 55]—16. Messiah's Authority to Interpret the Law

a. The Occasion

Matthew 5:1-2

¹ And seeing the multitudes, he went up into the mountain: and when he had sat down, his disciples came unto him: ² and he opened his mouth and taught them, saying,

Luke 6:17-20a

¹⁷ and he came down with them, and stood on a level place, and a great multitude of his disciples, and a great number of the people from all Yehudah and Yerushalayim, and the sea coast of Tzor and Tzidon, who came to hear him, and to be healed of their diseases; ¹⁸ and they that were troubled with unclean spirits were healed.
¹⁹ And all the multitude sought to touch him; for power came forth from him, and healed <them> all.

20a And he lifted up his eyes on his disciples, and said,

b. The Characteristics of True Righteousness

(1) Characteristics of Those Who Attain

Matthew 5:3-12	Luke 6:20b-23
3 Blessed are the poor in spirit: for theirs is the kingdom of heaven.	20b Blessed <are> ye poor: for yours is the kingdom of God.
4 Blessed are they that mourn: for they shall be comforted.	
5 Blessed are the meek: for they shall inherit the earth.	
6 Blessed are they that hunger and thirst after righteousness: for they shall be filled.	21 Blessed <are> ye that hunger now: for ye shall be filled.
7 Blessed are the merciful: for they shall obtain mercy.	Blessed <are> ye that weep now: for ye shall laugh.
8 Blessed are the pure in heart: for they shall see God.	
9 Blessed are the peacemakers: for they shall be called sons of God.	
10 Blessed are they that have been persecuted for righteousness' sake: for theirs is the kingdom of heaven.	
11 Blessed are ye when <men> shall reproach you, and persecute you, and say all manner of evil against you falsely, for my sake.	22 Blessed are ye, when men shall hate you, and when they shall separate you <from their company>, and reproach you, and cast out your name as evil, for the Son of man's sake.
12 Rejoice, and be exceeding glad: for great is your reward in heaven:	23 Rejoice in that day, and leap <for joy>: for behold, your reward is

for so persecuted they the prophets that were before you.

great in heaven; for in the same manner did their fathers unto the prophets.

(2) Characteristics of Those Who Fail

Luke 6:24-26

[24] But woe unto you that are rich! for ye have received your consolation. [25] Woe unto you, ye that are full now! for ye shall hunger. Woe <unto you>, ye that laugh now! for ye shall mourn and weep. [26] Woe <unto you>, when all men shall speak well of you! for in the same manner did their fathers to the false prophets.

(3) Characteristics in Relation to the World

Matthew 5:13-16

[13] Ye are the salt of the earth: but if the salt has lost its savor, wherewith shall it be salted? It is then good for nothing, but to be cast out and trodden under foot of men. [14] Ye are the light of the world. A city set on a hill cannot be hid. [15] Neither do <men> light a lamp, and put it under the bushel, but on the stand; and it shines unto all that are in the house. [16] Even so let your light shine before men; that they may see your good works, and glorify your Father who is in heaven.

c. The Code of True Righteousness

(1) Introduction

Matthew 5:17-20

[17] Think not that I came to destroy the law or the prophets: I came not to destroy, but to fulfill. [18] For verily I say unto you, Till heaven and earth pass

away, one jot[6] or one tittle[7] shall in no wise pass away from the law, till all things be accomplished. [19] Whosoever therefore shall break one of these least commandments, and shall teach men so, shall be called least in the kingdom of heaven: but whosoever shall do and teach them, he shall be called great in the kingdom of heaven. [20] For I say unto you, that except your righteousness shall exceed <the righteousness> of the scribes and Pharisees, ye shall in no wise enter into the kingdom of heaven.

(2) The Examples

i. The Law of Murder

Matthew 5:21-26

[21] Ye have heard that it was said to them of old time, You shall not kill; and whosoever shall kill shall be in danger of the judgment: [22] but I say unto you, that everyone who is angry with his brother shall be in danger of the judgment; and whosoever shall say to his brother, Raca, shall be in danger of the council; and whosoever shall say, You fool, shall be in danger of the hell of fire. [23] If therefore you are offering your gift at the altar, and there remember that your brother has something against you, [24] leave there your gift before the altar, and go your way, first be reconciled to your brother, and then come and offer your gift. [25] Agree with your adversary quickly, while you are with him in the way; lest haply the adversary deliver you to the judge, and the judge deliver you to the officer, and you be cast into prison. [26] Verily I say unto you, you shall by no means come out there, till you have paid the last farthing.

---

[6] Refers to *yod*, the tenth and smallest letter of the Hebrew alphabet.

[7] Refers to a small, distinguishing element of a Hebrew letter, such as a spur or a point.

ii. The Law of Adultery

Matthew 5:27-30

[27] Ye have heard that it was said, You shall not commit adultery: [28] but I say unto you, that everyone that looks on a woman to lust after her has committed adultery with her already in his heart. [29] And if your right eye causes you to stumble, pluck it out, and cast it from you: for it is profitable for you that one of your members should perish, and not your whole body be cast into hell. [30] And if your right hand causes you to stumble, cut it off, and cast it from you: for it is profitable for you that one of your members should perish, and not your whole body go into hell.

iii. The Law of Divorce

Matthew 5:31-32

[31] It was said also, Whosoever shall put away his wife, let him give her a writing of divorcement: [32] but I say unto you, that everyone that puts away his wife, saving for the cause of fornication, makes her an adulteress: and whosoever shall marry her when she is put away commits adultery.

iv. The Law of Oaths

Matthew 5:33-37

[33] Again, ye have heard that it was said to them of old time, You shall not forswear yourself, but shall perform unto the Lord your oaths: [34] but I say unto you, swear not at all; neither by the heaven, for it is the throne of God; [35] nor by the earth, for it is the footstool of his feet; nor by Yerushalayim, for it is the city of the great King. [36] Neither shall you swear by your head, for you cannot make one hair white or black. [37] But let your speech be, Yea, yea; Nay, nay: and whatsoever is more than these is of the evil <one>.

v. The Law of Non-Resistance

Matthew 5:38-42

[38] Ye have heard that it was said, An eye for an eye, and a tooth for a tooth: [39] but I say unto you, resist not him that is evil: but whosoever smites you

on your right cheek, turn to him the other also. [40] And if any man would go to law with you, and take away your coat, let him have your cloak also. [41] And whosoever shall compel you to go one mile, go with him two. [42] Give to him that asks you, and from him that would borrow from you turn not you away.

vi. The Law of Love

Matthew 5:43-48	Luke 6:27-30, 32-36
[43] Ye have heard that it was said, You shall love your neighbor, and hate your enemy:	
[44] but I say unto you, love your enemies, and pray for them that persecute you; [45] that ye may be sons of your Father who is in heaven: for he makes his sun to rise on the evil and the good, and sends rain on the just and the unjust.	[27] But I say unto you that hear, Love your enemies, do good to them that hate you, [28] bless them that curse you, pray for them that despitefully use you. [29] To him that smites you on the <one> cheek offer also the other; and from him that takes away your cloak withhold not your coat also. [30] Give to everyone that asks you; and of him that takes away your goods ask them not again.
[46] For if ye love them that love you, what reward have ye? Do not even the publicans the same? [47] And if ye salute your brethren only, what do ye more <than others>? do not even the Gentiles the same?	[32] And if ye love them that love you, what thank have ye? for even sinners love those that love them. [33] And if ye do good to them that do good to you, what thank have ye? for even sinners do the same. [34] And if ye lend to them of whom ye hope to receive, what thank have ye? even sinners lend to sinners, to receive again as much. [35] But love your enemies, and do <them> good, and lend, never despairing; and your reward shall be great, and ye shall

[48] Ye therefore shall be perfect, as your heavenly Father is perfect.

be sons of the Most High: for he is kind toward the unthankful and evil. [36] Be ye merciful, even as your Father is merciful.

d. The Conduct of True Righteousness

(1) Introduction

Matthew 6:1

[1] Take heed that ye do not your righteousness before men, to be seen of them: else ye have no reward with your Father who is in heaven.

(2) The Examples

i. The Giving of Alms

Matthew 6:2-4

[2] When therefore you do alms, sound not a trumpet before you, as the hypocrites do in the synagogues and in the streets, that they may have glory of men. Verily I say unto you, They have received their reward. [3] But when you do alms, let not your left hand know what your right hand does: [4] that your alms may be in secret: and your Father who sees in secret shall recompense you.

ii. Public Prayer

Matthew 6:5-15

[5] And when ye pray, ye shall not be as the hypocrites: for they love to stand and pray in the synagogues and in the corners of the streets, that they may be seen of men. Verily I say unto you, They have received their reward. [6] But you, when you pray, enter into your inner chamber, and having shut your door, pray to your Father who is in secret, and your Father who sees in secret shall recompense you. [7] And in praying use not vain repetitions, as

the Gentiles do: for they think that they shall be heard for their much speaking. [8] Be not therefore like unto them: for your Father knows what things ye have need of, before ye ask him. [9] After this manner therefore pray ye. Our Father who is in heaven, Hallowed be your name. [10] Your kingdom come. Your will be done, as in heaven, so on earth. [11] Give us this day our daily bread. [12] And forgive us our debts, as we also have forgiven our debtors. [13] And bring us not into temptation, but deliver us from the evil <one>. [14] For if ye forgive men their trespasses, your heavenly Father will also forgive you. [15] But if ye forgive not men their trespasses, neither will your Father forgive your trespasses.

iii. Fasting

Matthew 6:16-18

[16] Moreover when ye fast, be not, as the hypocrites, of a sad countenance: for they disfigure their faces, that they may be seen of men to fast. Verily I say unto you, They have received their reward. [17] But you, when you fast, anoint your head, and wash your face; [18] that you be not seen of men to fast, but of your Father who is in secret: and your Father, who sees in secret, shall recompense you.

e. The Practice of True Righteousness

(1) Concerning Money

Matthew 6:19-24

[19] Lay not up for yourselves treasures upon the earth, where moth and rust consume, and where thieves break through and steal: [20] but lay up for yourselves treasures in heaven, where neither moth nor rust does consume, and where thieves do not break through nor steal: [21] for where your treasure is, there will your heart be also. [22] The lamp of the body is the eye: if therefore your eye be single, your whole body shall be full of light. [23] But if your eye be evil, your whole body shall be full of darkness. If therefore the light that is in you be darkness, how great is the darkness! [24] No man can serve two

masters; for either he will hate the one, and love the other; or else he will hold to one, and despise the other. Ye cannot serve God and mammon.

(2) Concerning Anxiety

Matthew 6:25-34

[25] Therefore I say unto you, be not anxious for your life, what ye shall eat, or what ye shall drink; nor yet for your body, what ye shall put on. Is not the life more than the food, and the body than the raiment? [26] Behold the birds of the heaven, that they sow not, neither do they reap, nor gather into barns; and your heavenly Father feeds them. Are not ye of much more value then they? [27] And which of you by being anxious can add one cubit unto the measure of his life? [28] And why are ye anxious concerning raiment? Consider the lilies of the field, how they grow; they toil not, neither do they spin: [29] yet I say unto you, that even Shlomoh in all his glory was not arrayed like one of these. [30] But if God does so clothe the grass of the field, which today is, and tomorrow is cast into the oven, <shall he> not much more <clothe> you, O ye of little faith? [31] Be not therefore anxious, saying, What shall we eat? Or, What shall we drink? Or, Wherewithal shall we be clothed? [32] For after all these things do the Gentiles seek; for your heavenly Father knows that ye have need of all these things. [33] But seek ye first his kingdom, and his righteousness; and all these things shall be added unto you. [34] Be not therefore anxious for the morrow: for the morrow will be anxious for itself. Sufficient unto the day is the evil thereof.

(3) Concerning Judging

Matthew 7:1-6

[1] Judge not, that ye be not judged. [2] For with what judgment ye judge, ye shall be judged: and with what measure ye mete, it shall be measured unto you.

Luke 6:37-42

[37] And judge not, and ye shall not be judged: and condemn not, and ye shall not be condemned: release, and ye shall be released: [38] give, and it shall be given unto you; good measure, pressed down, shaken together, running over, shall they

give into your bosom. For with what measure ye mete it shall be measured to you again. [39] And he spoke also a parable unto them, Can the blind guide the blind? Shall they not both fall into a pit? [40] The disciple is not above his teacher: but everyone when he is perfected shall be as his teacher.

[3] And why behold you the mote that is in your brother's eye, but consider not the beam that is in your own eye? [4] Or how will you say to your brother, Let me cast out the mote out of your eye; and lo, the beam is in yours own eye?

[41] And why do you behold the mote that is in your brother's eye, but consider not the beam that is in your own eye? [42] Or how can you say to your brother, Brother, let me cast out the mote that is in your eye, when you yourself behold not the beam that is in your own eye?

[5] You hypocrite, cast out first the beam out of your own eye; and then shall you see clearly to cast out the mote out of your brother's eye. [6] Give not that which is holy unto the dogs, neither cast your pearls before the swine, lest haply they trample them under their feet, and turn and tear you.

You hypocrite, cast out first the beam out of your own eye, and then shall you see clearly to cast out the mote that is in your brother's eye.

(4) Concerning Prayer

Matthew 7:7-11

[7] Ask, and it shall be given you; seek, and ye shall find; knock, and it shall be opened unto you: [8] for everyone that asks receives; and he that seeks finds; and to him that knocks it shall be opened. [9] Or what man is there of you, who, if his son shall ask him for a loaf, will give him a stone; [10] or if he shall ask for a fish, will give him a serpent? [11] If ye then, being evil, know how to

give good gifts unto your children, how much more shall your Father who is in heaven give good things to them that ask him?

(5) The Core of Practice of True Righteousness

Matthew 7:12	Luke 6:31
[12] All things therefore whatsoever ye would that men should do unto you, even so do ye also unto them: for this is the law and the prophets.	[31] And as ye would that men should do to you, do ye also to them likewise.

f. The Warnings Concerning True Righteousness

(1) The Two Ways

Matthew 7:13-14

[13] Enter ye in by the narrow gate: for wide is the gate, and broad is the way, that leads to destruction, and many are they that enter in thereby. [14] For narrow is the gate, and straitened the way, that leads unto life, and few are they that find it.

(2) The Two Trees

Matthew 7:15-20	Luke 6:43-45
[15] Beware of false prophets, who come to you in sheep's clothing, but inwardly are ravening wolves. [16] By their fruits ye shall know them. Do <men> gather grapes of thorns, or figs of thistles? [17] Even so every good tree brings forth good fruit; but the corrupt tree brings forth evil fruit. [18] A good tree cannot bring	[43] For there is no good tree that brings forth corrupt fruit; nor again a corrupt tree that brings forth good fruit. [44] For each tree is known by its own fruit. For of thorns men do not gather figs, nor of a bramble bush gather they grapes. [45] The good man out of the good treasure of his heart brings forth that which is good; and

forth evil fruit, neither can a corrupt tree bring forth good fruit. [19] Every tree that brings not forth good fruit is hewn down, and cast into the fire. [20] Therefore by their fruits ye shall know them.

the evil <man> out of the evil <treasure> brings forth that which is evil: for out of the abundance of the heart his mouth speaks.

(3) The Two Professions

Matthew 7:21-23

[21] Not everyone that said unto me, Lord, Lord, shall enter into the kingdom of heaven; but he that does the will of my Father who is in heaven. [22] Many will say to me in that day, Lord, Lord, did we not prophesy by your name, and by your name cast out demons, and by your name do many mighty works? [23] And then will I profess unto them, I never knew you: depart from me, ye that work iniquity.

Luke 6:46

[46] And why call ye me, Lord, Lord, and do not the things which I say?

(4) The Two Builders

Matthew 7:24-27

[24] Everyone therefore that hears these words of mine, and does them,
shall be likened unto a wise man, who built his house upon the rock: [25] and the rain descended, and the floods came, and the winds blew, and beat upon that house; and it fell

Luke 6:47-49

[47] Everyone that comes unto me, and hears my words, and does them, I will show you to whom he is like: [48] he is like a man building a house, who digged and went deep, and laid a foundation upon the rock: and when a flood arose, the stream broke against that house, and could

not: for it was founded upon the rock. [26] And everyone that hears these words of mine, and does them not, shall be likened unto a foolish man, who built his house upon the sand: [27] and the rain descended, and the floods came, and the winds blew, and smote upon that house; and it fell: and great was the fall thereof.

not shake it: because it had been well built. [49] But he that hears, and does not, is like a man that built a house upon the earth without a foundation; against which the stream broke, and straightway it fell in; and the ruin of that house was great.

g. The Conclusion

Matthew 7:28-8:1

[28] And it came to pass, when Yeshua had finished these words, the multitudes were astonished at his teaching: [29] for he taught them as <one> having authority, and not as their scribes. [8:1] And when he was come down from the mountain, great multitudes followed him.

[§ 56]—17. Recognition of Authority in Kfar Nachum

Matthew 8:5-13

[5] And when he was entered into Kfar Nachum, there came unto him a centurion, beseeching him, [6] and saying, Lord, my servant lies in the house sick of the palsy, grievously tormented. [7] And he said unto him, I will come and heal him.

Luke 7:1-10

[1] After he had ended all his sayings in the ears of the people, he entered into Kfar Nachum. [2] And a certain centurion's servant, who was dear unto him, was sick and at the point of death. [3] And when he heard concerning Yeshua, he sent unto him elders of the Jews, asking him that he would come and save his servant. [4] And they, when they came to Yeshua, besought him earnestly, saying, He is worthy that you should do this for him; [5] for he loves our na-

[8] And the centurion answered and said,

Lord, I am not worthy that you should come under my roof; but only say the word, and my servant shall be healed. [9] For I also am a man under authority, having under myself soldiers: and I say to this one, Go, and he goes; and to another, Come, and he comes; and to my servant, Do this, and he does it.

[10] And when Yeshua heard it, he marveled, and said to them that followed,

Verily I say unto you, I have not found so great faith, no, not in Yisrael. [11] And I say unto you, that many shall come from the east and the west, and shall sit[8] down with Avraham, and Yitzchak, and Yaakov, in the kingdom of heaven: [12] but the sons of the kingdom shall be cast forth into the outer darkness: there shall be the weeping and the gnashing of teeth.

tion, and himself built us our synagogue. [6] And Yeshua went with them. And when he was now not far from the house, the centurion sent friends to him, saying unto him,

Lord, trouble not yourself; for I am not worthy that you should come under my roof: [7] Wherefore neither thought I myself worthy to come unto you: but say the word, and my servant shall be healed. [8] For I also am a man set under authority, having under myself soldiers: and I say to this one, Go, and he goes; and to another, Come, and he comes; and to my servant, Do this, and he does it.

[9] And when Yeshua heard these things, he marveled at him, and turned and said unto the multitude that followed him,

I say unto you, I have not found so great faith, no, not in Yisrael.

---

[8] Greek: *recline.*

¹³ And Yeshua said unto the centurion, Go your way; as you have believed, <so> be it done unto you. And the servant was healed in that hour.

¹⁰ And they that were sent, returning to the house, found the servant whole.

[§ 57]—18. Recognition of Authority Throughout the Land

Luke 7:11-17

¹¹ And it came to pass soon afterwards, that he went to a city called Nayim; and his disciples went with him, and a great multitude. ¹² Now when he drew near to the gate of the city, behold, there was carried out one that was dead, the only son of his mother, and she was a widow: and much people of the city was with her. ¹³ And when the Lord saw her, he had compassion on her, and said unto her, Weep not. ¹⁴ And he came near and touched the bier: and the bearers stood still. And he said, Young man, I say unto you, Arise. ¹⁵ And he that was dead sat up, and began to speak. And he gave him to his mother. ¹⁶ And fear took hold on all: and they glorified God, saying, A great prophet is arisen among us: and, God has visited his people. ¹⁷ And this report went forth concerning him in the whole of Yehudah, and all the region round about.

III. The Controversy over the King
— §§ 58–73 —

[§ 58]—A. The Rejection of the Herald

Matthew 11:2-19	Luke 7:18-35
[2] Now when Yochanan heard in the prison the works of the Messiah, he sent by his disciples [3] and said unto him, Are you he that comes, or look we for another?	[18] And the disciples of Yochanan told him of all these things. [19] And Yochanan calling unto him two of his disciples sent them to the Lord, saying, Are you he that comes, or look we for another? [20] And when the men were come unto him, they said, Yochanan the Baptizer has sent

[4] And Yeshua answered and said unto them, Go and tell Yochanan the things which ye hear and see: [5] the blind receive their sight, and the lame walk, the lepers are cleansed, and the deaf hear, and the dead are raised up, and the poor have good tidings preached to them. [6] And blessed is he, whosoever shall find no occasion of stumbling in me. [7] And as these went their way, Yeshua began to say unto the multitudes concerning Yochanan, What went ye out into the wilderness to behold? A reed shaken with the wind? [8] But what went ye out to see? A man clothed in soft <raiment>? Behold, they that wear soft <raiment> are in kings' houses.

[9] But wherefore went ye out? To see a prophet? Yea, I say unto you, and much more than a prophet. [10] This is he, of whom it is written, Behold, I send my messenger before your face, Who shall prepare your way before you.

[11] Verily I say unto you, Among them that are born of women there has not arisen a greater than Yochanan

us unto you, saying, Are you he that comes, or look we for another? [21] In that hour he cured many of diseases and plagues and evil spirits; and on many that were blind he bestowed sight.

[22] And he answered and said unto them, Go and tell Yochanan the things which ye have seen and heard; the blind receive their sight, the lame walk, the lepers are cleansed, and the deaf hear, the dead are raised up, the poor have good tidings preached to them. [23] And blessed is he, whosoever shall find no occasion of stumbling in me.

[24] And when the messengers of Yochanan were departed, he began to say unto the multitudes concerning Yochanan, What went ye out into the wilderness to behold? A reed shaken with the wind? [25] But what went ye out to see? A man clothed in soft raiment? Behold, they that are gorgeously appareled, and live delicately, are in kings' courts.

[26] But what went ye out to see? A prophet? Yea, I say unto you, and much more than a prophet. [27] This is he of whom it is written, Behold, I send my messenger before your face, Who shall prepare your way before you.

[28] I say unto you, Among them that are born of women there is none greater than Yochanan: yet he that

the Baptizer: yet he that is but little in the kingdom of heaven is greater than he. [12] And from the days of Yochanan the Baptizer until now the kingdom of heaven suffers violence, and men of violence take it by force. [13] For all the prophets and the law prophesied until Yochanan. [14] And if ye are willing to receive <it>, this is Eliyahu that is to come. [15] He that has ears to hear, let him hear.

is but little in the kingdom of God is greater than he.

[29] And all the people when they heard, and the publicans, justified God, being baptized with the baptism of Yochanan. [30] But the Pharisees and the lawyers rejected for themselves the counsel of God, being not baptized of him.

[16] But whereunto shall I liken this generation? It is like unto children sitting in the marketplaces, who call unto their fellows [17] and say, We piped unto you, and ye did not dance; we wailed, and ye did not mourn.

[31] Whereunto then shall I liken the men of this generation, and to what are they like? [32] They are like unto children that sit in the marketplace, and call one to another; who say, We piped unto you, and ye did not dance; we wailed, and ye did not weep.

[18] For Yochanan came neither eating nor drinking, and they say, He has a demon. [19] The Son of man came eating and drinking, and they say, Behold, a gluttonous man and a winebibber, a friend of publicans and sinners! And wisdom is justified by her works.

[33] For Yochanan the Baptizer is come eating no bread nor drinking wine; and ye say, He has a demon. [34] The Son of man is come eating and drinking; and ye say, Behold, a gluttonous man, and a winebibber, a friend of publicans and sinners! [35] And wisdom is justified of all her children.

[§ 59]—B. Curses on Cities of Galil

1. The Condemnation for Unbelief

Matthew 11:20-24

[20] Then began he to upbraid the cities wherein most of his mighty works were done, because they repented not. [21] Woe unto you, Korazin! woe unto you, Beit Tzaida! For if the mighty works had been done in Tzor and Tzidon which were done in you, they would have repented long ago in sackcloth and ashes. [22] But I say unto you, it shall be more tolerable for Tzor and Tzidon in the day of judgment than for you. [23] And you, Kfar Nachum, shall you be exalted unto heaven? You shall go down unto Hades: for if the mighty works had been done in Sedom which were done in you, it would have remained until this day. [24] But I say unto you that it shall be more tolerable for the land of Sedom in the day of judgment, than for you.

2. The Explanation of Unbelief

Matthew 11:25-27

[25] At that season Yeshua answered and said, I thank you, O Father, Lord of heaven and earth, that you did hide these things from the wise and understanding, and did reveal them unto babes: [26] yea, Father, for so it was well-pleasing in your sight. [27] All things have been delivered unto me of my Father: and no one knows the Son, save the Father; neither does any know the Father, save the Son, and he to whomsoever the Son wills to reveal <him>.

3. The Invitation to Belief and Discipleship

Matthew 11:28-30

[28] Come unto me, all ye that labor and are heavy laden, and I will give you rest. [29] Take my yoke upon you, and learn of me; for I am meek and lowly in

heart: and ye shall find rest unto your souls. [30] For my yoke is easy, and my burden is light.

[§ 60]—C. The Reception by a Sinner

Luke 7:36-50

[36] And one of the Pharisees desired him that he would eat with him. And he entered into the Pharisee's house, and sat down to meat. [37] And behold, a woman who was in the city, a sinner; and when she knew that he was sitting at meat in the Pharisee's house, she brought an alabaster cruse of ointment, [38] and standing behind at his feet, weeping, she began to wet his feet with her tears, and wiped them with the hair of her head, and kissed his feet, and anointed them with the ointment. [39] Now when the Pharisee that had bidden him saw it, he spoke within himself, saying, This man, if he were a prophet, would have perceived who and what manner of woman this is that touches him, that she is a sinner. [40] And Yeshua answering said unto him, Shimon, I have somewhat to say unto you. And he said, Teacher, say on. [41] A certain lender had two debtors: the one owed five hundred shillings, and the other fifty. [42] When they had not <wherewith> to pay, he forgave them both. Which of them therefore will love him most? [43] Shimon answered and said, He, I suppose, to whom he forgave the most. And he said unto him, You have rightly judged. [44] And turning to the woman, he said unto Shimon, Do you see this woman? I entered into your house, you gave me no water for my feet: but she has wetted my feet with her tears, and wiped them with her hair. [45] You gave me no kiss: but she, since the time I came in, has not ceased to kiss my feet. [46] My head with oil you did not anoint: but she has anointed my feet with ointment. [47] Wherefore I say unto you, Her sins, which are many, are forgiven; for she loved much: but to whom little is forgiven, <the same> loves little. [48] And he said unto her, Your sins are forgiven. [49] And they that sat at meat with him began to say within themselves, Who is this that even forgives sins? [50] And he said unto the woman, Your faith has saved you; go in peace.

[§ 61]—D. The Witness of the King to Women

Luke 8:1-3

[1] And it came to pass soon afterwards, that he went about through cities and villages, preaching and bringing the good tidings of the kingdom of God, and with him the twelve, [2] and certain women who had been healed of evil spirits and infirmities: Miriam that was called Magdalit, from whom seven demons had gone out, [3] and Yochanah the wife of Kuza Herod's steward, and Shoshanah, and many others, who ministered unto them of their substance.

[§§ 62–63]—
E. The Rejection of the King by the Leaders

[§ 62]—1. The Unpardonable Sin

a. The Rejection

Matthew 12:22-24	Mark 3:19b-22
	[19b] And he came into a house. [20] And the multitude came together again, so that they could not so much as eat bread. [21] And when his friends heard it, they went out to lay hold on him: for they said, He is beside himself.
[22] Then was brought unto him one possessed with a demon, blind and dumb: and he healed him, insomuch that the dumb man spoke and saw. [23] And all the multitudes were amazed, and said, Can this be the son of David? [24] But when the Phari-	

sees heard it, they said, This man does not cast out demons, but by Beelzebub[1] the prince of the demons.

²² And the scribes that came down from Yerushalayim said, He has Beelzebub, and, By the prince of the demons casts he out the demons.

b. The Defense

Matthew 12:25-29

²⁵ And knowing their thoughts he said unto them, Every kingdom divided against itself is brought to desolation; and every city or house divided against itself shall not stand: ²⁶ and if Satan casts out Satan, he is divided against himself; how then shall his kingdom stand? ²⁷ And if I by Beelzebub cast out demons, by whom do your sons cast them out? Therefore shall they be your judges. ²⁸ But if I by the Spirit of God cast out demons, then is the kingdom of God come upon you.

²⁹ Or how can one enter into the house of the strong <man>, and spoil his goods, except he first bind the strong <man>? And then he will spoil his house.

Mark 3:23-27

²³ And he called them unto him, and said unto them in parables, How can Satan cast out Satan? ²⁴ And if a kingdom be divided against itself, that kingdom cannot stand. ²⁵ And if a house be divided against itself, that house will not be able to stand. ²⁶ And if Satan has risen up against himself, and is divided, he cannot stand, but has an end.

²⁷ But no one can enter into the house of the strong <man>, and spoil his goods, except he first bind the strong <man>; and then he will spoil his house.

---

[1] Greek: *Beelzebul*; Hebrew: *Baal Zevul* or *Baal Zvuv*.

c. The Judgment

Matthew 12:30-37

[30] He that is not with me is against me, and he that gathers not with me scatters. [31] Therefore I say unto you, Every sin and blasphemy shall be forgiven unto men; but the blasphemy against the Spirit shall not be forgiven. [32] And whosoever shall speak a word against the Son of man, it shall be forgiven him; but whosoever shall speak against the Holy Spirit, it shall not be forgiven him, neither in this world, nor in that which is to come. [33] Either make the tree good, and its fruit good; or make the tree corrupt, and its fruit corrupt: for the tree is known by its fruit. [34] Ye offspring of vipers, how can ye, being evil, speak good things? For out of the abundance of the heart the mouth speaks. [35] The good man out of his good treasure brings forth good things: and the evil man out of his evil treasure brings forth evil things. [36] And I say unto you, that every idle word that men shall speak, they shall give account thereof in the day of judgment. [37] For by your words you shall be justified, and by your words you shall be condemned.

Mark 3:28-30

[28] Verily I say unto you, All their sins shall be forgiven unto the sons of men, and their blasphemies wherewith soever they shall blaspheme: [29] but whosoever shall blaspheme against the Holy Spirit has never forgiveness, but is guilty of an eternal sin: [30] because they said, He has an unclean spirit.

[§ 63]—2. The New Policy Concerning Signs

a. The Sign for that Generation

Matthew 12:38-40

[38] Then certain of the scribes and Pharisees answered him, saying, Teacher, we would see a sign from you. [39] But he answered and said unto them, An evil and adulterous generation seeks after a sign; and there shall no sign be given it but the sign of Yonah the prophet: [40] for as Yonah was three days and three nights in the belly of the whale; so shall the Son of man be three days and three nights in the heart of the earth.

b. The Judgment of that Generation

Matthew 12:41-45

[41] The men of Nineveh shall stand up in the judgment with this generation, and shall condemn it: for they repented at the preaching of Yonah; and behold, a greater than Yonah is here. [42] The queen of the south shall rise up in the judgment with this generation, and shall condemn it: for she came from the ends of the earth to hear the wisdom of Shlomoh; and behold, a greater than Shlomoh is here. [43] But the unclean spirit, when he is gone out of the man, passes through waterless places, seeking rest, and finds it not. [44] Then he said, I will return into my house from where I came out; and when he is come, he finds it empty, swept, and garnished. [45] Then goes he, and takes with himself seven other spirits more evil than himself, and they enter in and dwell there: and the last state of that man becomes worse than the first. Even so shall it be also unto this evil generation.

[§§ 64–70]—F. Revelation in View of Rejection

[§ 64]—1. The Course of the Kingdom Program
in the Present Age

— Public Parables —

a. Introduction

Matthew 13:1-3a	Mark 4:1-2	Luke 8:4
[1] On that day went Yeshua out of the house, and sat by the seaside.	[1] And again he began to teach by the seaside.	
[2] And there were gathered unto him great multitudes, so that he entered into a boat, and sat; and all the multitude stood on the beach. [3a] And he spoke to them many things in parables, saying,	And there is gathered unto him a very great multitude, so that he entered into a boat, and sat in the sea; and all the multitude were by the sea on the land. [2] And he taught them many things in parables, and said unto them in his teaching,	[4] And when a great multitude came together, and they of every city resorted unto him, he spoke by a parable:

b. Parable of the Sower

Matthew 13:3b-23	Mark 4:3-25	Luke 8:5-18
[3b] Behold, the sower went forth to sow; [4] and as he sowed, some <seeds> fell by	[3] Hearken: Behold, the sower went forth to sow: [4] and it came to pass, as he sowed,	[5] The sower went forth to sow his seed: and as he sowed, some fell by the way side; and it

the way side, and the birds came and devoured them: [5] and others fell upon the rocky places, where they had not much earth: and straightway they sprang up, because they had no deepness of earth: [6] and when the sun was risen, they were scorched; and because they had no root, they withered away.

[7] And others fell upon the thorns; and the thorns grew up and choked them:

[8] and others fell upon the good ground, and yielded fruit, some a hundredfold, some sixty, some thirty.

[9] He that has ears, let him hear.

[10] And the disciples came, and said unto him, Why do you speak unto them in parables?

[11] And he answered and said unto them,

some <seed> fell by the way side, and the birds came and devoured it. [5] And other fell on the rocky <ground>, where it had not much earth; and straightway it sprang up, because it had no deepness of earth: [6] and when the sun was risen, it was scorched; and because it had no root, it withered away.

[7] And other fell among the thorns, and the thorns grew up, and choked it, and it yielded no fruit.

[8] And others fell into the good ground, and yielded fruit, growing up and increasing; and brought forth, thirtyfold, and sixtyfold, and a hundredfold.

[9] And he said,

Who has ears to hear, let him hear.

[10] And when he was alone, they that were about him with the twelve asked of him the parables. [11] And he said unto them, Unto

was trodden under foot, and the birds of the heaven devoured it. [6] And other fell on the rock; and as soon as it grew, it withered away, because it had no moisture.

[7] And other fell amidst the thorns; and the thorns grew with it, and choked it.

[8] And other fell into the good ground, and grew, and brought forth fruit a hundredfold.

As he said these things, he cried,

He that has ears to hear, let him hear.

[9] And his disciples asked him what this parable might be.

[10] And he said, Unto you it is given to know

Unto you it is given to know the mysteries of the kingdom of heaven, but to them it is not given. [12] For whosoever has, to him shall be given, and he shall have abundance: but whosoever has not, from him shall be taken away even that which he has. [13] Therefore speak I to them in parables; because seeing they see not, and hearing they hear not, neither do they understand.

[14] And unto them is fulfilled the prophecy of Yeshayahu, which says,

> By hearing ye shall hear, and shall in no wise understand; And seeing ye shall see, and shall in no wise perceive: [15] For this people's heart is waxed gross, And their ears are dull of

you is given the mystery of the kingdom of God: but unto them that are without, all things are done in parables:

[12] that seeing they may see, and not perceive; and hearing they may hear, and not understand; lest haply they should turn again, and it should be forgiven them.

the mysteries of the kingdom of God: but to the rest in parables;

that seeing they may not see, and hearing they may not understand.

hearing, And their eyes they have closed; Lest haply they should perceive with their eyes, And hear with their ears, And understand with their heart, And should turn again, And I should heal them.

[16] But blessed are your eyes, for they see; and your ears, for they hear. [17] For verily I say unto you, that many prophets and righteous men desired to see the things which ye see, and saw them not; and to hear the things which ye hear, and heard them not.

[18] Hear then ye the parable of the sower. [19] When anyone hears the word of the kingdom, and understands it not, <then> comes the evil <one>, and snatches away that which has been sown in his heart. This is he that was sown by the way side.

[13] And he said unto them, Know ye not this parable? And how shall ye know all the parables?

[14] The sower sows the word. [15] And these are they by the way side, where the word is sown; and when they have heard, straightway comes Satan, and takes away the word which has been sown in them. [16] And these in like manner are they that are sown upon the rocky <places>, who,

[11] Now the parable is this: The seed is the word of God. [12] And those by the way side are they that have heard; then comes the devil, and takes away the word from their heart, that they may not believe and be saved.

20 And he that was sown upon the rocky places, this is he that hears the word, and straightway with joy receives it; 21 yet has he not root in himself, but endures for a while; and when tribulation or persecution arises because of the word, straightway he stumbles.

22 And he that was sown among the thorns, this is he that hears the word; and the care of the world, and the deceitfulness of riches, choke the word, and he becomes unfruitful.

23 And he that was sown upon the good ground, this is he that hears the word, and understands it; who verily bears fruit, and brings forth, some a hundredfold, some sixty, some thirty.

when they have heard the word, straightway receive it with joy; 17 and they have no root in themselves, but endure for a while; then, when tribulation or persecution arises because of the word, straightway they stumble. 18 And others are they that are sown among the thorns; these are they that have heard the word, 19 and the cares of the world, and the deceitfulness of riches, and the lusts of other things entering in, choke the word, and it becomes unfruitful. 20 And those are they that were sown upon the good ground; such as hear the word, and accept it, and bear fruit, thirtyfold, and sixtyfold, and a hundredfold.

21 And he said unto them, Is the lamp brought to be put under the bushel, or under the bed, <and>

13 And those on the rock <are> they who, when they have heard, receive the word with joy; and these have no root, who for a while believe, and in time of temptation fall away.

14 And that which fell among the thorns, these are they that have heard, and as they go on their way they are choked with cares and riches and pleasures of <this> life, and bring no fruit to perfection. 15 And that in the good ground, these are such as in an honest and good heart, having heard the word, hold it fast, and bring forth fruit with patience. 16 And no man, when he has lighted a lamp, covers it with a vessel, or puts it under a bed; but puts it on a stand,

not to be put on the stand? ²² For there is nothing hid, save that it should be manifested; neither was <anything> made secret, but that it should come to light. ²³ If any man has ears to hear, let him hear. ²⁴ And he said unto them, Take heed what ye hear: with what measure ye mete it shall be measured unto you; and more shall be given unto you. ²⁵ For he that has, to him shall be given: and he that has not, from him shall be taken away even that which he has.	that they that enter in may see the light. ¹⁷ For nothing is hid, that shall not be made manifest; nor <anything> secret, that shall not be known and come to light. ¹⁸ Take heed therefore how ye hear: for whosoever has, to him shall be given; and whosoever has not, from him shall be taken away even that which he thinks he has.

c. Parable of the Seed

Mark 4:26-29

²⁶ And he said, So is the kingdom of God, as if a man should cast seed upon the earth; ²⁷ and should sleep and rise night and day, and the seed should spring up and grow, he knows not how. ²⁸ The earth bears fruit of herself; first the blade, then the ear, then the full grain in the ear. ²⁹ But when the fruit is ripe, straightway he puts forth the sickle, because the harvest is come.

d. Parable of the Tares

Matthew 13:24-30

[24] Another parable set he before them, saying, The kingdom of heaven is likened unto a man that sowed good seed in his field: [25] but while men slept, his enemy came and sowed tares[2] also among the wheat, and went away. [26] But when the blade sprang up and brought forth fruit, then appeared the tares also. [27] And the servants of the householder came and said unto him, Sir, did you not sow good seed in your field? From where then has it tares? [28] And he said unto them, An enemy has done this. And the servants say unto him, Will you then that we go and gather them up? [29] But he said, Nay; lest haply while ye gather up the tares, ye root up the wheat with them. [30] Let both grow together until the harvest: and in the time of the harvest I will say to the reapers, Gather up first the tares, and bind them in bundles to burn them; but gather the wheat into my barn.

e. Parable of the Mustard Seed

Matthew 13:31-32	Mark 4:30-32
[31] Another parable set he before them, saying,	[30] And he said, How shall we liken the kingdom of God? Or in what parable shall we set it forth?
The kingdom of heaven is like unto a grain of mustard seed, which a man took, and sowed in his field: [32] which indeed is less than all seeds; but when it is grown, it is greater than the herbs, and becomes a tree, so that the birds of the heaven come and lodge in the branches thereof.	[31] It is like a grain of mustard seed, which, when it is sown upon the earth, though it be less than all the seeds that are upon the earth, [32] yet when it is sown, grows up, and becomes greater than all the herbs, and puts out great branches; so that the birds of the heaven can lodge under the shadow thereof.

---

[2] Or, *darnel.*

f. Parable of the Leaven

Matthew 13:33-35	Mark 4:33-34
[33] Another parable spoke he unto them; The kingdom of heaven is like unto leaven, which a woman took, and hid in three measures of meal, till it was all leavened. [34] All these things spoke Yeshua in parables unto the multitudes; and without a parable spoke he nothing unto them: [35] that it might be fulfilled which was spoken through the prophet, saying, I will open my mouth in parables; I will utter things hidden from the foundation of the world.	[33] And with many such parables spoke he the word unto them, as they were able to hear it; [34] and without a parable spoke he not unto them: but privately to his own disciples he expounded all things.

[§ 65]—2. The Repudiation of all Earthly Relations

Matthew 12:46-50	Mark 3:31-35	Luke 8:19-21
[46] While he was yet speaking to the multitudes, behold, his mother and his brethren stood without, seeking to speak to him. [47] And one said unto him, Behold, your mother and your brethren stand without, seeking to speak to you. [48] But he answered and said unto him that told	[31] And there come his mother and his brethren; and, standing without, they sent unto him, calling him. [32] And a multitude was sitting about him; and they say unto him, Behold, your mother and your brethren without seek for you. [33] And he answered them, and said, Who is	[19] And there came to him his mother and brethren, and they could not come at him for the crowd. [20] And it was told him, Your mother and your brethren stand without, desiring to see you. [21] But he answered and said unto them,

him, Who is my mother? And who are my brethren?
⁴⁹ And he stretched forth his hand towards his disciples, and said, Behold, my mother and my brethren!
⁵⁰ For whosoever shall do the will of my Father who is in heaven, he is my brother, and sister, and mother.

my mother and my brethren?

³⁴ And looking round on them that sat round about him, he said, Behold, my mother and my brethren!
³⁵ For whosoever shall do the will of God, the same is my brother, and sister, and mother.

My mother and my brethren are these that hear the word of God, and do it.

[§ 66]—3. The Course of the Kingdom Program in the Present Age

— Private Parables —

a. Explanation of the Parable of the Tares

Matthew 13:36-43

³⁶ Then he left the multitudes, and went into the house: and his disciples came unto him, saying, Explain unto us the parable of the tares of the field. ³⁷ And he answered and said, He that sows the good seed is the Son of man; ³⁸ and the field is the world; and the good seed, these are the sons of the kingdom; and the tares are the sons of the evil <one>; ³⁹ and the enemy that sowed them is the devil: and the harvest is the end of the world[3]; and the reapers are angels. ⁴⁰ As therefore the tares are gathered up and burned with fire; so shall it be in the end of the world. ⁴¹ The Son of man shall send forth his angels, and they shall gather out of his kingdom all

---

[3] Or, *the consummation of the age.*

things that cause stumbling, and them that do iniquity, [42] and shall cast them into the furnace of fire: there shall be the weeping and the gnashing of teeth. [43] Then shall the righteous shine forth as the sun in the kingdom of their Father. He that has ears, let him hear.

b. The Parable of the Hidden Treasure

Matthew 13:44

[44] The kingdom of heaven is like unto a treasure hidden in the field; which a man found, and hid; and in his joy he goes and sells all that he has, and buys that field.

c. The Parable of the Pearl of Great Price

Matthew 13:45-46

[45] Again, the kingdom of heaven is like unto a man that is a merchant seeking goodly pearls: [46] and having found one pearl of great price, he went and sold all that he had, and bought it.

d. The Parable of the Net

Matthew 13:47-50

[47] Again, the kingdom of heaven is like unto a net, that was cast into the sea, and gathered of every kind: [48] which, when it was filled, they drew up on the beach; and they sat down, and gathered the good into vessels, but the bad they cast away. [49] So shall it be in the end of the world[4]: the angels shall come forth, and sever the wicked from among the righteous, [50] and shall cast them into the furnace of fire: there shall be the weeping and the gnashing of teeth.

---

[4] Or, *the consummation of the age.*

e. The Parable of the Householder

Matthew 13:51-53

[51] Have ye understood all these things? They say unto him, Yea. [52] And he said unto them, Therefore every scribe who has been made a disciple to the kingdom of heaven is like unto a man that is a householder, who brings forth out of his treasure things new and old. [53] And it came to pass, when Yeshua had finished these parables, he departed thence.

[§ 67]—4. Power over Nature

Mt. 8:18, 23-27	Mark 4:35-41	Luke 8:22-25
[18] Now when Yeshua saw great multitudes about him, he gave commandment to depart unto the other side. [23] And when he was entered into a boat, his disciples followed him.	[35] And on that day, when even was come, he said unto them, Let us go over unto the other side. [36] And leaving the multitude, they take him with them, even as he was, in the boat. And other boats were with him.	[22] Now it came to pass on one of those days, that he entered into a boat, himself and his disciples; and he said unto them, Let us go over unto the other side of the lake: and they launched forth. [23] But as they sailed he fell asleep:
[24] And behold, there arose a great tempest in the sea, insomuch that the boat was covered with the waves: but he was asleep.	[37] And there arose a great storm of wind, and the waves beat into the boat, insomuch that the boat was now filling. [38] And he himself was in the stern, asleep on the cushion: and they awake him, and say unto him, Teacher, care you not that we	and there came down a storm of wind on the lake; and they were filling <with water>, and were in jeopardy.
[25] And they came to him, and awoke him, saying, Save, Lord; we perish. [26] And he said		[24] And they came to him, and awoke him, saying, Master, master, we perish.

unto them, Why are ye fearful, O ye of little faith? Then he arose, and rebuked the winds and the sea; and there was a great calm.	perish? [39] And he awoke, and rebuked the wind, and said unto the sea, Peace, be still. And the wind ceased, and there was a great calm. [40] And he said unto them, Why are ye fearful? Have ye not yet faith?	And he awoke, and rebuked the wind and the raging of the water: and they ceased, and there was a calm. [25] And he said unto them, Where is your faith?
[27] And the men marveled, saying,

What manner of man is this, that even the winds and the sea obey him? | [41] And they feared exceedingly, and said one to another,

Who then is this, that even the wind and the sea obey him? | And being afraid they marveled, saying one to another,

Who then is this, that he commands even the winds and the water, and they obey him? |

[§ 68]—5. Power over Demons

Matthew 8:28-34	Mark 5:1-20	Luke 8:26-39
[28] And when he was come to the other side into the country of the Gadarenes,	[1] And they came to the other side of the sea, into the country of the Gerasenes. [2] And when he was come out of the boat, straightway	[26] And they arrived at the country of the Gerasenes, which is over against Galil. [27] And when he was come forth upon the land,
there met him two possessed with demons, coming forth out of the tombs, exceeding fierce, so that no man could pass by that way.	there met him out of the tombs a man with an unclean spirit, [3] who had his dwelling in the tombs: and no man could any more bind him, no, not with a	there met him a certain man out of the city, who had demons; and for a long time he had worn no clothes, and abode not in <any> house, but in the tombs.

chain; [4] because that he had been often bound with fetters and chains, and the chains had been rent asunder by him, and the fetters broken in pieces: and no man had strength to tame him. [5] And always, night and day, in the tombs and in the mountains, he was crying out, and cutting himself with stones. [6] And when he saw Yeshua from afar, he ran and worshipped him; [7] and crying out with a loud voice, he said, What have I to do with you, Yeshua, you Son of the Most High God? I adjure you by God, torment me not.

[8] For he said unto him, Come forth, you unclean spirit, out of the man.

[29] And behold, they cried out, saying, What have we to do with you, you Son of God? Are you come hither to torment us before the time?

[28] And when he saw Yeshua,

he cried out, and fell down before him, and with a loud voice said, What have I to do with you, Yeshua, you Son of the Most High God? I beseech you, torment me not.

[29] For he was commanding the unclean spirit to come out from the man. For oftentimes it had seized him: and he was kept under guard, and bound with chains and fetters; and breaking the bands asunder, he was driven of the demon into the deserts.

[9] And he asked him, What is your name? And he said unto him, My name is Legion; for we are many.

[10] And he besought him much that he would not send them away out of the country. [11] Now there was there on the mountainside a great herd of swine feeding. [12] And they besought him, saying, Send us into the swine, that we may enter into them. [13] And he gave them leave. And the unclean spirits came out, and entered into the swine: and the herd rushed down the steep into the sea, <in number> about two thousand; and they were drowned in the sea. [14] And they that fed them fled, and told it in the city, and in the country. And they came to see what it was that had come to pass.

[15] And they come to Yeshua, and behold him that was pos-

[30] Now there was afar off from them a herd of many swine feeding. [31] And the demons besought him, saying, If you cast us out, send us away into the herd of swine. [32] And he said unto them, Go. And they came out, and went into the swine: and behold, the whole herd rushed down the steep into the sea, and perished in the waters.

[33] And they that fed them fled, and went away into the city, and told everything, and what was befallen to them that were possessed with demons. [34] And behold, all the city came out to meet Yeshua:

[30] And Yeshua asked him, What is your name? And he said, Legion; for many demons were entered into him. [31] And they entreated him that he would not command them to depart into the abyss. [32] Now there was there a herd of many swine feeding on the mountain: and they entreated him that he would give them leave to enter into them. And he gave them leave. [33] And the demons came out from the man, and entered into the swine: and the herd rushed down the steep into the lake, and were drowned.

[34] And when they that fed them saw what had come to pass, they fled, and told it in the city and in the country. [35] And they went out to see what had come to pass; and they came to Yeshua, and found the man, from whom the

sessed with demons sitting, clothed and in his right mind, <even> him that had the legion: and they were afraid.

and when they saw him,

they besought <him> that he would depart from their borders.

16 And they that saw it declared unto them how it befell him that was possessed with demons, and concerning the swine. 17 And they began to beseech him to depart from their borders.

18 And as he was entering into the boat, he that had been possessed with demons besought him that he might be with him. 19 And he suffered him not, but said unto him, Go to your house unto your friends, and tell them how great things the Lord has done for you, and <how> he had mercy on you.

demons were gone out, sitting, clothed and in his right mind, at the feet of Yeshua: and they were afraid.

36 And they that saw it told them how he that was possessed with demons was made whole.

37 And all the people of the country of the Gerasenes round about asked him to depart from them, for they were holden with great fear: and he entered into a boat, and returned. 38 But the man from whom the demons were gone out prayed him that he might be with him:

but he sent him away, saying, 39 Return to your house, and declare how great things God has done for you.

[20] And he went his way, and began to publish in Decapolis how great things Yeshua had done for him: and all men marveled.	And he went his way, publishing throughout the whole city how great things Yeshua had done for him.

[§ 69]—6. Power over Disease and Death

Matthew 9:18-26	Mark 5:21-43	Luke 8:40-56
[18] While he spoke these things unto them,	[21] And when Yeshua had crossed over again in the boat unto the other side, a great multitude was gathered unto him; and he was by the sea.	[40] And as Yeshua returned, the multitude welcomed him; for they were all waiting for him.
behold, there came a ruler, and worshipped him, saying,	[22] And there comes one of the rulers of the synagogue, Yair by name; and seeing him, he falls at his feet, [23] and beseeches him much, saying,	[41] And behold, there came a man named Yair, and he was a ruler of the synagogue: and he fell down at Yeshua's feet, and besought him to come into his house; [42] for he
My daughter is even now dead: but come and lay your hand upon her, and she shall live.	My little daughter is at the point of death: <I pray you>, that you come and lay your hands on her, that she may be made whole, and live.	had an only daughter, about twelve years of age, and she was dying.
[19] And Yeshua arose, and followed him, and <so did> his disciples.	[24] And he went with him; and a great multitude followed him, and they thronged him.	But as he went the multitudes thronged him.

[20] And behold, a woman, who had an issue of blood twelve years, came behind him, and touched the border of his garment: [21] for she said within herself, If I do but touch his garment, I shall be made whole.

[25] And a woman, who had an issue of blood twelve years, [26] and had suffered many things of many physicians, and had spent all that she had, and was nothing bettered, but rather grew worse, [27] having heard the things concerning Yeshua, came in the crowd behind, and touched his garment. [28] For she said, If I touch but his garments, I shall be made whole. [29] And straightway the fountain of her blood was dried up; and she felt in her body that she was healed of her plague. [30] And straightway Yeshua, perceiving in himself that the power <proceeding> from him had gone forth, turned him about in the crowd, and said, Who touched my garments? [31] And his disciples said unto him, You see the multitude thronging you, and you say, Who touched me?

[43] And a woman having an issue of blood twelve years, who had spent all her living upon physicians, and could not be healed of any, [44] came behind him, and touched the border of his garment:

and immediately the issue of her blood stanched.

[45] And Yeshua said, Who is it that touched me? And when all denied, Peter said, and they that were with him, Master, the multitudes press you and crush

²² But Yeshua turning and seeing her said, Daughter, be of good cheer; your faith has made you whole. And the woman was made whole from that hour.

²³ And when Yeshua came into the ruler's house, and saw the fluteplayers, and the crowd making a tumult,

³² And he looked round about to see her that had done this thing. ³³ But the woman fearing and trembling, knowing what had been done to her, came and fell down before him, and told him all the truth.

³⁴ And he said unto her,
Daughter, your faith has made you whole; go in peace, and be whole of your plague.
³⁵ While he yet spoke, they come from the ruler of the synagogue's <house> saying, Your daughter is dead: why trouble you the Teacher any further? ³⁶ But Yeshua, not heeding the word spoken, said unto the ruler of the synagogue, Fear not, only believe. ³⁷ And he suffered no man to follow with him, save Peter, and

<you>. ⁴⁶ But Yeshua said, Someone did touch me; for I perceived that power had gone forth from me.
⁴⁷ And when the woman saw that she was not hid, she came trembling, and falling down before him declared in the presence of all the people for what cause she touched him, and how she was healed immediately.
⁴⁸ And he said unto her,
Daughter, your faith has made you whole; go in peace.

⁴⁹ While he yet spoke, there comes one from the ruler of the synagogue's <house>, saying, Your daughter is dead; trouble not the Teacher. ⁵⁰ But Yeshua hearing it, answered him, Fear not: only believe, and she shall be made whole.

⁵¹ And when he came to the house, he suffered not any man to

Yaakov, and Yochanan the brother of Yaakov. [38] And they come to the house of the ruler of the synagogue; and he beholds a tumult, and <many> weeping and wailing greatly. [39] And when he was entered in, he said unto them,

enter in with him, save Peter, and Yochanan, and Yaakov, and the father of the maiden and her mother. [52] And all were weeping, and bewailing her:

[24] he said, Give place: for the damsel is not dead, but sleeps. And they laughed him to scorn.

Why make ye a tumult, and weep? The child is not dead, but sleeps. [40] And they laughed him to scorn.

but he said,

Weep not; for she is not dead, but sleeps.

[53] And they laughed him to scorn, knowing that she was dead.

[25] But when the crowd was put forth, he entered in,

But he, having put them all forth, takes the father of the child and her mother and them that were with him, and goes in where the child was.

and took her by the hand;

[41] And taking the child by the hand, he said unto her, Talyeta kumi; which is, being interpreted, Damsel, I say unto you, Arise. [42] And straightway the damsel rose up, and walked; for she was twelve years old. And they were amazed straightway with a great amazement.

[54] But he, taking her by the hand, called, saying, Maiden, arise.

and the damsel arose.

[55] And her spirit returned, and she rose up immediately: and he commanded that <something> be given her to eat. [56] And her parents were amazed: but he charged them

[26] And the fame hereof went forth into all that land.	[43] And he charged them much that no man should know this: and he commanded that \<something\> should be given her to eat.	to tell no man what had been done.

[§ 70]—7. Power over Blindness

Matthew 9:27-34

[27] And as Yeshua passed by from thence, two blind men followed him, crying out, and saying, Have mercy on us, you son of David. [28] And when he was come into the house, the blind men came to him: and Yeshua said unto them, Believe ye that I am able to do this? They say unto him, Yea, Lord. [29] Then touched he their eyes, saying, According to your faith be it done unto you. [30] And their eyes were opened. And Yeshua strictly charged them, saying, See that no man know it. [31] But they went forth, and spread abroad his fame in all that land. [32] And as they went forth, behold, there was brought to him a dumb man possessed with a demon. [33] And when the demon was cast out, the dumb man spoke: and the multitudes marveled, saying, It was never so seen in Yisrael. [34] But the Pharisees said, By the prince of the demons casts he out demons.

[§ 71]—G. The Final Rejection in Natzeret

Matthew 13:54-58	Mark 6:1-6a
[54] And coming into his own country he taught them in their synagogue, insomuch that they were astonished, and said,	[1] And he went out from thence; and he comes into his own country; and his disciples follow him. [2] And when the Sabbath was come, he began to teach in the synagogue: and many hearing him were astonished, saying,

Whence has this man this wisdom, and these mighty works?

Whence has this man these things? And, What is the wisdom that is given unto this man, and <what mean> such mighty works wrought by his hands?

55 Is not this the carpenter's son? Is not his mother called Miriam? And his brethren, Yaakov, and Yoseph, and Shimon, and Yehudah? 56 And his sisters, are they not all with us? Whence then has this man all these things? 57 And they were offended in him.

3 Is not this the carpenter, the son of Miriam, and brother of Yaakov, and Yosei, and Yehudah, and Shimon? And are not his sisters here with us? And they were offended in him.

But Yeshua said unto them, A prophet is not without honor, save in his own country, and in his own house. 58 And he did not many mighty works there because of their unbelief.

4 And Yeshua said unto them, A prophet is not without honor, save in his own country, and among his own kin, and in his own house. 5 And he could there do no mighty work, save that he laid his hands upon a few sick folk, and healed them. 6a And he marveled because of their unbelief.

[§ 72]—H. Witness in View of Rejection

1. Introduction

Matthew 9:35–10:4	Mark 6:6b-7	Luke 9:1-2
35 And Yeshua went about all the cities and the villages, teaching in their synagogues, and preaching the gospel of the kingdom, and	6b And he went round about the villages teaching.	

healing all manner of disease and all manner of sickness. [36] But when he saw the multitudes, he was moved with compassion for them, because they were distressed and scattered, as sheep not having a shepherd. [37] Then said he unto his disciples, The harvest indeed is plenteous, but the laborers are few. [38] Pray ye therefore the Lord of the harvest, that he send forth laborers into his harvest. [10:1] And he called unto him his twelve disciples, and gave them authority over unclean spirits, to cast them out, and to heal all manner of disease and all manner of sickness.

[7] And he calls unto him the twelve, and began to send them forth by two and two; and he gave them authority over the unclean spirits;

[1] And he called the twelve together, and gave them power and authority over all demons, and to cure diseases. [2] And he sent them forth to preach the kingdom of God, and to heal the sick.

Mt. cont.: [2] Now the names of the twelve apostles are these: The first, Shimon, who is called Peter, and Andrei his brother; Yaakov the <son> of Zavdi, and Yochanan his brother; [3] Philip, and Bar Talmai; Toma, and Mattai the publican; Yaakov the <son> of Chalphi, and Taddai; [4] Shimon the Cananaean, and Yehudah Ish Kriyot, who also betrayed him.

2. Practical Instructions for the Mission

Matthew 10:5-15

[5] These twelve Yeshua sent forth, and charged them, saying, Go not into <any> way of the Gentiles, and enter not into any city of the Samaritans: [6] but go rather to the lost sheep of the house of Yisrael. [7] And as ye go, preach, saying, The kingdom of heaven is at hand. [8] Heal the sick, raise the dead, cleanse the lepers, cast out demons: freely ye received, freely give.

Mt. cont.	Mark 6:8-11	Luke 9:3-5
[9] Get you no gold, nor silver, nor brass in your purses; [10] no wallet for <your> journey, neither two coats, nor shoes, nor staff: for the laborer is worthy of his food.	[8] and he charged them that they should take nothing for <their> journey, save a staff only; no bread, no wallet, no money in their purse; [9] but <to go> shod with sandals: and, <said he>, put not on two coats.	[3] And he said unto them, Take nothing for your journey, neither staff, nor wallet, nor bread, nor money; neither have two coats.
[11] And into whatsoever city or village ye shall enter, search out who in it is worthy; and there abide till ye go forth. [12] And as ye enter into the house, salute it. [13] And if the house be worthy, let your peace come upon it: but if it be not worthy, let your peace return to you. [14] And whosoever shall not receive you, nor	[10] And he said unto them, Wheresoever ye enter into a house, there abide till ye depart thence.	[4] And into whatsoever house ye enter, there abide, and thence depart.
	[11] And whatsoever place shall not receive	[5] And as many as receive you not, when ye

hear your words, as ye go forth out of that house or that city, shake off the dust of your feet. [15] Verily I say unto you, It shall be more tolerable for the land of Sedom and Gomorrah in the day of judgment, than for that city.

you, and they hear you not, as ye go forth thence, shake off the dust that is under your feet for a testimony unto them.

depart from that city, shake off the dust from your feet for a testimony against them.

3. Instructions in View of the Coming Persecution

Matthew 10:16-23

[16] Behold, I send you forth as sheep in the midst of wolves: be ye therefore wise as serpents, and harmless as doves. [17] But beware of men: for they will deliver you up to councils, and in theirs synagogues they will scourge you; [18] yea and before governors and kings shall ye be brought for my sake, for a testimony to them and to the Gentiles. [19] But when they deliver you up, be not anxious how or what ye shall speak: for it shall be given you in that hour what ye shall speak. [20] For it is not ye that speak, but the Spirit of your Father that speaks in you. [21] And brother shall deliver up brother to death, and the father his child: and children shall rise up against parents, and cause them to be put to death. [22] And ye shall be hated of all men for my name's sake: but he that endures to the end, the same shall be saved. [23] But when they persecute you in this city, flee into the next: for verily I say unto you, Ye shall not have gone through the cities of Yisrael, till the Son of man be come.

4. Instruction in View of Rejection

Matthew 10:24-33

[24] A disciple is not above his teacher, nor a servant above his lord. [25] It is enough for the disciple that he be as his teacher, and the servant as his lord. If they have called the master of the house Beelzebub, how much more them of his household! [26] Fear them not therefore: for there is nothing covered, that shall not be revealed; and hid, that shall not be known. [27] What I tell you in the darkness, speak ye in the light; and what ye hear in the ear, proclaim upon the housetops. [28] And be not afraid of them that kill the body, but are not able to kill the soul: but rather fear him who is able to destroy both soul and body in hell. [29] Are not two sparrows sold for a penny? And not one of them shall fall on the ground without your Father: [30] but the very hairs of your head are all numbered. [31] Fear not therefore: ye are of more value than many sparrows. [32] Everyone therefore who shall confess me before men, him will I also confess before my Father who is in heaven. [33] But whosoever shall deny me before men, him will I also deny before my Father who is in heaven.

5. The Results of the Rejection

Matthew 10:34-39

[34] Think not that I came to send peace on the earth: I came not to send peace, but a sword. [35] For I came to set a man at variance against his father, and the daughter against her mother, and the daughter in law against her mother in law: [36] and a man's foes <shall be> they of his own household. [37] He that loves father or mother more than me is not worthy of me; and he that loves son or daughter more than me is not worthy of me. [38] And he that does not take his cross and follow after me, is not worthy of me. [39] He that finds his life shall lose it; and he that loses his life for my sake shall find it.

6. Rewards for Individuals Who Accept

Matthew 10:40-42

[40] He that receives you receives me, and he that receives me receives him that sent me. [41] He that receives a prophet in the name of a prophet shall receive a prophet's reward: and he that receives a righteous man in the name of a righteous man shall receive a righteous man's reward. [42] And whosoever shall give to drink unto one of these little ones a cup of cold water only, in the name of a disciple, verily I say unto you he shall in no wise lose his reward.

7. The Fulfillment

Matthew 11:1	Mark 6:12-13	Luke 9:6
[1] And it came to pass when Yeshua had finished commanding his twelve disciples, he departed thence to teach and preach in their cities.	[12] And they went out, and preached that <men> should repent. [13] And they cast out many demons, and anointed with oil many that were sick, and healed them.	[6] And they departed, and went throughout the villages, preaching the gospel, and healing everywhere.

[§ 73]—I. The Death of the Herald

Matthew 14:1-12	Mark 6:14-29	Luke 9:7-9
[1] At that season Herod[5] the tetrarch heard the report concerning Yeshua, [2] and said unto	[14] And king Herod heard <thereof>; for his name had become known: and he said,	[7] Now Herod the tetrarch heard of all that was done: and he was much perplexed, be-

---

[5] The Hebrew form of the name Herod is *Hordos*.

his servants, This is Yochanan the Baptizer; he is risen from the dead; and therefore do these powers work in him.

[3] For Herod had laid hold on Yochanan, and bound him, and put him in prison for the sake of Herodias[6], his brother Philip's wife.

Yochanan the Baptizer is risen from the dead, and therefore do these powers work in him.

[15] But others said, It is Eliyahu. And others said, <It is> a prophet, <even> as one of the prophets. [16] But Herod, when he heard <thereof>, said, Yochanan, whom I beheaded, he is risen.

[17] For Herod himself had sent forth and laid hold upon Yochanan, and bound him in prison for the sake of Herodias, his brother Philip's wife; for he had married her.

cause that it was said by some, that Yochanan was risen from the dead;

[8] and by some, that Eliyahu had appeared; and by others, that one of the old prophets was risen again. [9] And Herod said, Yochanan I beheaded: but who is this, about whom I hear such things? And he sought to see him.

Mt. cont. [4] For Yochanan said unto him, It is not lawful for you to have her.

[5] And when he would have put him to death, he feared the multitude,

Mk. cont. [18] For Yochanan said unto Herod, It is not lawful for you to have your brother's wife. [19] And Herodias set herself against him, and desired to kill him; and she could not; [20] for Herod feared Yochanan, knowing that he was a righteous

---

[6] The Hebrew form of the name Herodias is *Horodyah*.

because they counted him as a prophet.

[6] But when Herod's birthday came, the daughter of Herodias danced in the midst, and pleased Herod.

and holy man, and kept him safe. And when he heard him, he was much perplexed; and he heard him gladly.

[21] And when a convenient day was come, that Herod on his birthday made a supper to his lords, and the high captains, and the chief men of Galil;

[22] and when the daughter of Herodias herself came in and danced, she pleased Herod and them that sat at meat with him; and the king said unto the damsel, Ask of me whatsoever you will, and I will give it to you.

[23] And he sware unto her, Whatsoever you shall ask of me, I will give it to you, unto the half of my kingdom.

[7] Whereupon he promised with an oath to give her whatsoever she should ask.

[24] And she went out, and said unto her mother, What shall I ask? And she said, The head of Yochanan the Baptizer.

[25] And she came in straightway with haste unto the king, and asked, saying,

I will that you forthwith give me on a platter the head of Yochanan the Baptizer.

[8] And she, being put forward by her mother, said,

Give me here on a platter the head of Yochanan the Baptizer.

[9] And the king was grieved; but for the sake of his oaths, and of them that sat at meat with him, he commanded it to be given; [10] and he sent and beheaded Yochanan in the prison.

[26] And the king was exceeding sorry; but for the sake of his oaths, and of them that sat at meat, he would not reject her. [27] And straightway the king sent forth a soldier of his guard, and commanded to bring his head: and he went and beheaded him in the prison,

[11] And his head was brought on a platter, and given to the damsel: and she brought it to her mother.

[12] And his disciples came, and took up the corpse, and buried him; and they went and told Yeshua.

[28] and brought his head on a platter, and gave it to the damsel; and the damsel gave it to her mother.

[29] And when his disciples heard <thereof>, they came and took up his corpse, and laid it in a tomb.[7]

---

[7] Josephus (*Antiquities of the Jews*, Book XVIII, v. 2) says of Yochanan that Herod "thought it best, by putting him to death, to prevent any mischief he might cause, and not bring himself into difficulties, by sparing a man who might make him repent of it when it should be too late." Josephus in no wise controverts the picture in Mark where Herodias appears as the one who prods Antipas to execute Yochanan to satisfy her resentment against him for his rebuke of her adulterous marriage. Josephus merely presents the public and political aspects of the imprisonment and death of the Baptizer.

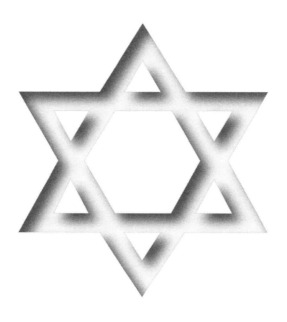

IV. THE TRAINING OF THE TWELVE BY THE KING
— §§ 74–98 —

[§ 74]—A. The Feeding of the Five Thousand

Mt. 14:13-21	Mark 6:30-44	Luke 9:10-17	John 6:1-13
	[30] And the apostles gather themselves together unto Yeshua; and they told him all things, whatsoever they had	[10] And the apostles, when they were returned, declared unto him what things they had done.	

done, and whatsoever they had taught.

13 Now when Yeshua heard <it>, he withdrew from thence in a boat, to a desert place apart: and when the multitudes heard <thereof>, they followed him on foot from the cities. 14 And he came forth, and saw a great multitude, and he had compassion on them, and healed their sick.

31 And he said unto them, Come ye yourselves apart into a desert place, and rest a while. For there were many coming and going, and they had no leisure so much as to eat. 32 And they went away in the boat to a desert place apart. 33 And <the people> saw them going, and many knew <them>, and they ran together there on foot from all the cities, and outwent them.

And he took them, and withdrew apart to a city called Beit Tzaida. 11 But the multitudes perceiving it followed him: and he welcomed them, and spoke to them of the kingdom of God, and them that had need of healing he cured.

1 After these things Yeshua went away to the other side of the sea of Galil, which is <the sea> of Tverya. 2 And a great multitude followed him, because they beheld the signs which he did on them that were sick.

15 And when even was come, the disciples came to him, saying, The place is desert, and the time is already past;

34 And he came forth and saw a great multitude, and he had compassion on them, because they were as sheep not having a shepherd:

12 And the day began to wear away; and the twelve came, and said unto him,

3 And Yeshua went up into the mountain, and there he sat with his disciples. 4 Now the Passover, the feast of the Jews, was at hand.

send the multitudes away, that they may go into the villages, and buy themselves food.

and he began to teach them many things. ³⁵ And when the day was now far spent, his disciples came unto him, and said, The place is desert, and the day is now far spent;

Send the multitude away, that they may go into the villages and country round about, and lodge, and get provisions: for we are here in a desert place.

¹⁶ But Yeshua said unto them, They have no need to go away; give ye them to eat.

³⁶ send them away, that they may go into the country and villages round about, and buy themselves somewhat to eat. ³⁷ But he answered and said unto them, Give ye them to eat. And they say unto him, Shall we go and buy two hundred shillings' worth of bread, and give them to eat? ³⁸ And he said unto them, How many loaves have ye? Go <and> see.

¹³ But he said unto them, Give ye them to eat.

⁵ Yeshua therefore lifting up his eyes, and seeing that a great multitude comes unto him, said unto Philip, Whence are we to buy bread, that these may eat? ⁶ And this he said to prove him: for he himself knew what he would do. ⁷ Philip answered him, Two hundred shillings' worth of bread is not sufficient for them, that everyone may take a little.

¹⁷ And they say unto him, We have here but five loaves, and two fishes. ¹⁸ And he said, Bring them hither to me.

And they said, We have no more than five loaves and two fishes; except we should go and buy food for all this people. ¹⁴ For they were about five thousand men.

And when they knew, they say, Five, and two fishes.

19 And he commanded the multitudes to sit down on the grass;

and he took the five loaves, and the two fishes, and looking up to heaven, he blessed, and broke and gave the loaves to the disciples, and the disciples to the multitudes.

39 And he commanded them that all should sit down by companies upon the green grass. 40 And they sat down in ranks, by hundreds, and by fifties. 41 And he took the five loaves and the two fishes, and looking up to heaven, he blessed, and broke the loaves; and he gave to the disciples to set before them; and the two fishes divided he among them all.

And he said unto his disciples, Make them sit down in companies, about fifty each. 15 And they did so, and made them all sit down. 16 And he took the five loaves and the two fishes, and looking up to heaven, he blessed them, and broke; and gave to the disciples to set before the multitude.

8 One of his disciples, Andrei, Shimon Peter's brother, said unto him, 9 There is a lad here, who has five barley loaves, and two fishes: but what are these among so many? 10 Yeshua said, Make the people sit down. Now there was much grass in the place. So the men sat down, in number about five thousand. 11 Yeshua therefore took the loaves; and having given thanks, he distributed to them that were set down; likewise also of the fishes as much as they would.

²⁰ And they all ate, and were filled: and they took up that which remained over of the broken pieces, twelve baskets full. ²¹ And they that did eat were about five thousand men, besides women and children.

⁴² And they all ate, and were filled. ⁴³ And they took up broken pieces, twelve basketfuls, and also of the fishes. ⁴⁴ And they that ate the loaves were five thousand men.

¹⁷ And they ate, and were all filled: and there was taken up that which remained over to them of broken pieces, twelve baskets.

¹² And when they were filled, he said unto his disciples, Gather up the broken pieces which remain over, that nothing be lost. ¹³ So they gathered them up, and filled twelve baskets with broken pieces from the five barley loaves, which remained over unto them that had eaten.

[§ 75]—B. Messiah's Rejection of the Galileans' Offer to Make Him King

Matthew 14:22-23	Mark 6:45-46	John 6:14-15
²² And straightway he constrained the disciples to enter into the boat, and to go before him unto the other side, till he should send the multitudes away.	⁴⁵ And straightway he constrained his disciples to enter into the boat, and to go before <him> unto the other side to Beit Tzaida, while he himself sent the multitude away.	¹⁴ When therefore the people saw the sign which he did, they said, This is of a truth the prophet that comes into the world.
²³ And after he had sent the multitudes	⁴⁶ And after he had taken leave of them,	¹⁵ Yeshua therefore perceiving that they

away, he went up into the mountain apart to pray: and when even was come, he was there alone.	he departed into the mountain to pray.	were about to come and take him by force, to make him king, withdrew again into the mountain himself alone.

[§ 76]—C. The Training through the Storm

Matthew 14:24-33	Mark 6:47-52	John 6:16-21
[24] But the boat was now in the midst of the sea, distressed by the waves; for the wind was contrary.	[47] And when even was come, the boat was in the midst of the sea, and he alone on the land. [48] And seeing them distressed in rowing, for the wind was contrary unto them,	[16] And when evening came, his disciples went down unto the sea; [17] and they entered into a boat, and were going over the sea unto Kfar Nachum. And it was now dark, and Yeshua had not yet come to them. [18] And the sea was rising by reason of a great wind that blew.
[25] And in the fourth watch of the night he came unto them, walking upon the sea.	about the fourth watch of the night he comes unto them, walking on the sea; and he would have passed by them:	[19] When therefore they had rowed about five and twenty or thirty furlongs,
[26] And when the disciples saw him walking on the sea, they were troubled, saying, It is a ghost; and they cried out for fear.	[49] but they, when they saw him walking on the sea, supposed that it was a ghost, and cried out; [50] for they all saw him, and were trou-	they behold Yeshua walking on the sea, and drawing near unto the boat: and they were afraid.

²⁷ But straightway Yeshua spoke unto them, saying Be of good cheer; it is I; be not afraid. ²⁸ And Peter answered him and said, Lord, if it be you, bid me come unto you upon the waters. ²⁹ And he said, Come. And Peter went down from the boat, and walked upon the waters to come to Yeshua. ³⁰ But when he saw the wind, he was afraid; and beginning to sink, he cried out, saying, Lord, save me. ³¹ And immediately Yeshua stretched forth his hand, and took hold of him, and said unto him, O you of little faith, wherefore did you doubt? ³² And when they were gone up into the boat, the wind ceased. ³³ And they that were in the boat worshipped him, saying, Of a truth you are the Son of God.

bled. But he straightway spoke with them, and said unto them, Be of good cheer: it is I; be not afraid. ⁵¹ And he went up unto them into the boat; and the wind ceased: and they were sore amazed in themselves; ⁵² for they understood not concerning the loaves, but their heart was hardened.

²⁰ But he said unto them, It is I; be not afraid. ²¹ They were willing therefore to receive him into the boat: and straightway the boat was at the land whither they were going.

[§ 77]—D. The Reception in Ginosar

Matthew 14:34-36	Mark 6:53-56
[34] And when they had crossed over, they came to the land, unto Ginosar.	[53] And when they had crossed over, they came to the land unto Ginosar, and moored to the shore.
[35] And when the men of that place knew him, they sent into all that region round about, and brought unto him all that were sick,	[54] And when they were come out of the boat, straightway <the people> knew him, [55] and ran round about that whole region, and began to carry about on their beds those that were sick, where they heard he was. [56] And wheresoever he entered, into villages, or into cities, or into the country, they laid the sick in the marketplaces,
[36] and they besought him that they might only touch the border of his garment: and as many as touched were made whole.	and besought him that they might touch if it were but the border of his garment: and as many as touched him were made whole.

[§ 78]—E. Instruction Concerning the Bread of Life

John 6:22-71

[22] On the morrow the multitude that stood on the other side of the sea saw that there was no other boat there, save one, and that Yeshua entered not with his disciples into the boat, but <that> his disciples went away alone [23] (howbeit there came boats from Tverya near unto the place where they ate the bread after the Lord had given thanks): [24] when the multitude therefore saw that Yeshua was not there, neither his disciples, they themselves got into the boats, and came to Kfar Nachum, seeking Yeshua. [25] And when they found him on the other side of the sea, they said unto him, Rabbi, when came you here? [26] Yeshua answered them and said, Verily, verily, I say unto you, Ye seek me, not because ye saw signs, but because

ye ate of the loaves, and were filled. [27] Work not for the food which perishes, but for the food which abides unto eternal life, which the Son of man shall give unto you: for him the Father, even God, has sealed. [28] They said therefore unto him, What must we do, that we may work the works of God? [29] Yeshua answered and said unto them, This is the work of God, that ye believe on him whom he has sent. [30] They said therefore unto him, What then do you for a sign, that we may see, and believe you? What work will you do? [31] Our fathers ate the manna in the wilderness; as it is written, He gave them bread out of heaven to eat. [32] Yeshua therefore said unto them, Verily, verily, I say unto you, It was not Mosheh that gave you the bread out of heaven; but my Father gives you the true bread out of heaven. [33] For the bread of God is that which comes down out of heaven, and gives life unto the world. [34] They said therefore unto him, Lord, evermore give us this bread. [35] Yeshua said unto them. I am the bread of life: he that comes to me shall not hunger, and he that believes on me shall never thirst. [36] But I said unto you, that ye have seen me, and yet believe not. [37] All that which the Father gives me shall come unto me; and him that comes to me I will in no wise cast out. [38] For I am come down from heaven, not to do mine own will, but the will of him that sent me. [39] And this is the will of him that sent me, that of all that which he has given me I should lose nothing, but should raise it up at the last day. [40] For this is the will of my Father, that everyone that beholds the Son, and believes on him, should have eternal life; and I will raise him up at the last day.

[41] The Jews therefore murmured concerning him, because he said, I am the bread which came down out of heaven. [42] And they said, Is not this Yeshua, the son of Yoseph, whose father and mother we know? How does he now say, I am come down out of heaven? [43] Yeshua answered and said unto them, Murmur not among yourselves. [44] No man can come to me, except the Father that sent me draw him: and I will raise him up in the last day. [45] It is written in the prophets, And they shall all be taught of God. Every one that has heard from the Father, and has learned, comes unto me. [46] Not that any man has seen the Father, save he that is from God, he has seen the Father. [47] Verily, verily, I say unto you, He that believes has eternal life. [48] I am the bread of life. [49] Your fathers ate the manna in the wilderness, and they died. [50] This is the bread which comes down out of heaven, that a man may eat thereof, and not die. [51] I am the living bread which came down out

of heaven: if any man eat of this bread, he shall live forever: yea and the bread which I will give is my flesh, for the life of the world.

[52] The Jews therefore strove one with another, saying, How can this man give us his flesh to eat? [53] Yeshua therefore said unto them, Verily, verily, I say unto you, Except ye eat the flesh of the Son of man and drink his blood, ye have not life in yourselves. [54] He that eats my flesh and drinks my blood has eternal life: and I will raise him up at the last day. [55] For my flesh is meat indeed, and my blood is drink indeed. [56] He that eats my flesh and drinks my blood abides in me, and I in him. [57] As the living Father sent me, and I live because of the Father; so he that eats me, he also shall live because of me. [58] This is the bread which came down out of heaven: not as the fathers ate, and died; he that eats this bread shall live forever. [59] These things said he in the synagogue, as he taught in Kfar Nachum.

[60] Many therefore of his disciples, when they heard <this>, said, This is a hard saying; who can hear it? [61] But Yeshua knowing in himself that his disciples murmured at this, said unto them, Does this cause you to stumble? [62] <What> then if ye should behold the Son of man ascending where he was before? [63] It is the spirit that gives life; the flesh profits nothing: the words that I have spoken unto you are spirit, and are life. [64] But there are some of you that believe not. For Yeshua knew from the beginning who they were that believed not, and who it was that should betray him. [65] And he said, For this cause have I said unto you, that no man can come unto me, except it be given unto him of the Father.

[66] Upon this many of his disciples went back, and walked no more with him. [67] Yeshua said therefore unto the twelve, Would ye also go away? [68] Shimon Peter answered him, Lord, to whom shall we go? You have the words of eternal life. [69] And we have believed and know that you are the Holy One of God. [70] Yeshua answered them, Did not I choose you the twelve, and one of you is a devil? [71] Now he spoke of Yehudah <the son> of Shimon Ish Kriyot, for he it was that should betray him, <being> one of the twelve.

[§ 79]—F. Instruction Concerning Defilement

John 7:1

[1] And after these things Yeshua walked in Galil: for he would not walk in Yehudah, because the Jews sought to kill him.

Matthew 15:1-20	Mark 7:1-23
[1] Then there come to Yeshua from Yerushalayim Pharisees and scribes, saying,	[1] And there are gathered together unto him the Pharisees, and certain of the scribes, who had come from Yerushalayim, [2] and had seen that some of his disciples ate their bread with defiled, that is, unwashen, hands. [3] (For the Pharisees, and all the Jews, except they wash their hands diligently[1], eat not, holding the tradition of the elders; [4] and <when they come> from the marketplace, except they bathe themselves, they eat not; and many other things there are, which they have received to hold, washings of cups, and pots, and brazen vessels.) [5] And the Pharisees and the scribes ask him, Why walk not your disciples according to the tradition of the elders, but eat their bread with defiled hands?
[2] Why do your disciples transgress the tradition of the elders? For they wash not their hands when they eat bread.	[6] And he said unto them, Well did Yeshayahu prophesy of you hypocrites, as it is written, This people
[7] Ye hypocrites, well did Yeshayahu prophesy of you, saying, [8] This people honors me with their lips; But	

---

[1] Greek: *up to elbow.*

their heart is far from me. [9] But in vain do they worship me, Teaching <as their> doctrines the precepts of men.

[3] And he answered and said unto them,
Why do ye also transgress the commandment of God because of your tradition?

[4] For God said, Honor your father and your mother: and, He that speaks evil of father or mother, let him die the death.
[5] But ye say, whosoever shall say to his father or his mother, That wherewith you might have been profited by me is given <to God>;
[6] he shall not honor his father.

And ye have made void the word of God because of your tradition.

[10] And he called to him the multitude, and said unto them, Hear, and understand: [11] Not that which enters into the mouth defiles the man; but that which proceeds out of the mouth, this defiles the man.

honors me with their lips, But their heart is far from me. [7] But in vain do they worship me, Teaching <as their> doctrines the precepts of men.

[8] Ye leave the commandment of God, and hold fast the tradition of men.
[9] And he said unto them, Full well do ye reject the commandment of God, that ye may keep your tradition.
[10] For Mosheh said, Honor your father and your mother; and, He that speaks evil of father or mother, let him die the death:
[11] but ye say, If a man shall say to his father or his mother, That wherewith you might have been profited by me is Corban, that is to say, Given <to God>; [12] ye no longer suffer him to do anything for his father or his mother;
[13] making void the word of God by your tradition, which ye have delivered: and many such like things ye do.
[14] And he called to him the multitude again, and said unto them, Hear me all of you, and understand:
[15] there is nothing from without the man, that going into him can defile him; but the things which proceed out of the man are those that defile the man. [16] <If any man has ears to hear, let him hear.>

[12] Then came the disciples, and said unto him, Do you know that the Pharisees were offended, when they heard this saying? [13] But he answered and said, Every plant which my heavenly Father planted not, shall be rooted up. [14] Let them alone: they are blind guides. And if the blind guide the blind, both shall fall into a pit. [15] And Peter answered and said unto him, Declare unto us the parable.

[16] And he said, Are ye also even yet without understanding? [17] Perceive ye not, that whatsoever goes into the mouth passes into the belly, and is cast out into the draught?

[18] But the things which proceed out of the mouth come forth out of the heart; and they defile the man.
[19] For out of the heart come forth evil thoughts, murders, adulteries, fornications, thefts, false witness, railings:

[20] these are the things which defile the man; but to eat with unwashen hands defiles not the man.

[17] And when he was entered into the house from the multitude, his disciples asked of him the parable.
[18] And he said unto them, Are ye so without understanding also? Perceive ye not, that whatsoever from without goes into the man, <it> cannot defile him; [19] because it goes not into his heart, but into his belly, and goes out into the draught? <This he said>, making all meats clean.
[20] And he said, That which proceeds out of the man, that defiles the man.
[21] For from within, out of the heart of men, evil thoughts proceed, fornications, thefts, murders, adulteries, [22] covetings, wickednesses, deceit, lasciviousness, an evil eye, railing, pride, foolishness: [23] all these evil things proceed from within, and defile the man.

[§ 80]—G. The Reception in Tzor and Tzidon

Matthew 15:21-28	Mark 7:24-30
[21] And Yeshua went out thence, and withdrew into the parts of Tzor and Tzidon.	[24] And from thence he arose, and went away into the borders of Tzor and Tzidon. And he entered into a house, and would have no man know it; and he could not be hid.
[22] And behold, a Canaanitish woman came out from those borders, and cried, saying,	[25] But straightway a woman, whose little daughter had an unclean spirit, having heard of him, came and fell down at his feet. [26] Now the woman was a Greek, a Syro-Phoenician by race.
Have mercy on me, O Lord, you son of David; my daughter is grievously vexed with a demon. [23] But he answered her not a word. And his disciples came and besought him, saying, Send her away; for she cries after us. [24] But he answered and said, I was not sent but unto the lost sheep of the house of Yisrael.	
[25] But she came and worshipped him, saying, Lord, help me.	And she besought him that he would cast forth the demon out of her daughter.
[26] And he answered and said, It is not meet to take the children's bread and cast it to the dogs. [27] But she said, Yea, Lord: for even the dogs eat of the crumbs which fall from their masters' table.	[27] And he said unto her, Let the children first be filled: for it is not meet to take the children's bread and cast it to the dogs. [28] But she answered and said unto him, Yea, Lord; even the dogs under the table eat of the children's crumbs.
[28] Then Yeshua answered and said unto her, O woman, great is your	[29] And he said unto her, For this saying go your way; the demon is

faith: be it done unto you even as you will. And her daughter was healed from that hour.

gone out of your daughter. [30] And she went away unto her house, and found the child laid upon the bed, and the demon gone out.

[§ 81]—H. The Reception in Decapolis

Matthew 15:29-38

[29] And Yeshua departed thence, and came near unto the sea of Galil; and he went up into the mountain, and sat there.

[30] And there came unto him great multitudes, having with them the lame, blind, dumb, maimed, and many others, and they cast them down at his feet; and he healed them:

[31] insomuch that the multitude wondered, when they saw the

Mark 7:31-8:9

[31] And again he went out from the borders of Tzor, and came through Tzidon unto the sea of Galil, through the midst of the borders of Decapolis.

[32] And they bring unto him one that was deaf, and had an impediment in his speech; and they beseech him to lay his hand upon him. [33] And he took him aside from the multitude privately, and put his fingers into his ears, and he spat, and touched his tongue; [34] and looking up to heaven, he sighed, and said unto him, Ephphatha,[2] that is, Be opened. [35] And his ears were opened, and the bond of his tongue was loosed, and he spoke plain. [36] And he charged them that they should tell no man: but the more he charged them, so much the more a great deal they published it. [37] And they were beyond measure astonished, saying, He has done all

---

[2] Hebrew: *hipatach.*

dumb speaking, the maimed whole, and lame walking, and the blind seeing: and they glorified the God of Yisrael.

[32] And Yeshua called unto him his disciples, and said, I have compassion on the multitude, because they continue with me now three days and have nothing to eat: and I would not send them away fasting, lest haply they faint on the way.

[33] And the disciples say unto him, Whence should we have so many loaves in a desert place as to fill so great a multitude? [34] And Yeshua said unto them, How many loaves have ye? And they said, Seven, and a few small fishes. [35] And he commanded the multitude to sit down on the ground; [36] and he took the seven loaves and the fishes; and he gave thanks and broke, and gave to the disciples, and the disciples to the multitudes.

[37] And they all ate, and were filled: and they took up that which remained over of the broken pieces, seven baskets full. [38] And they that did eat were four thousand men, besides women and children.

things well; he makes even the deaf to hear, and the dumb to speak.

[8:1] In those days, when there was again a great multitude, and they had nothing to eat, he called unto him his disciples, and said unto them, [2] I have compassion on the multitude, because they continue with me now three days, and have nothing to eat: [3] and if I send them away fasting to their home, they will faint on the way; and some of them are come from far.

[4] And his disciples answered him, Whence shall one be able to fill these men with bread here in a desert place? [5] And he asked them, How many loaves have ye? And they said, Seven.

[6] And he commanded the multitude to sit down on the ground: and he took the seven loaves, and having given thanks, he broke, and gave to his disciples, to set before them; and they set them before the multitude. [7] And they had a few small fishes: and having blessed them, he commanded to set these also before them. [8] And they ate, and were filled: and they took up, of broken pieces that remained over, seven baskets. [9] And they were about four thousand: and he sent them away.

[§ 82]—I. The Rejection in Magadan

Matthew 15:39-16:4	Mark 8:10-12
[39] And he sent away the multitudes, and entered into the boat, and came into the borders of Magadan. [16:1] And the Pharisees and Sadducees came, and trying him asked him to show them a sign from heaven. [2] But he answered and said unto them, When it is evening, ye say, <It will be> fair weather: for the heaven is red. [3] And in the morning, <It will be> foul weather today: for the heaven is red and lowering. Ye know how to discern the face of the heaven; but ye cannot <discern> the signs of the times. [4] An evil and adulterous generation seeks after a sign;	[10] And straightway he entered into the boat with his disciples, and came into the parts of Dalmanuta. [11] And the Pharisees came forth, and began to question with him, seeking of him a sign from heaven, trying him. [12] And he sighed deeply in his spirit, and said, Why does this generation seek a sign?
and there shall no sign be given unto it, but the sign of Yonah. And he left them, and departed.	Verily I say unto you, There shall no sign be given unto this generation.

[§ 83]—J. The Warning against Rejection

Matthew 16:5-12	Mark 8:13-21
[5] And the disciples came to the other side and forgot to take bread.	[13] And he left them, and again entering into <the boat> departed to the other side. [14] And they forgot to take bread; and they had not in the boat with them more than one loaf.

[6] And Yeshua said unto them, Take heed and beware of the leaven of the Pharisees and Sadducees. [7] And they reasoned among themselves, saying, We took no bread.

[8] And Yeshua perceiving it said, O ye of little faith, why reason ye among yourselves, because ye have no bread?

[9] Do ye not yet perceive, neither remember the five loaves of the five thousand, and how many baskets ye took up? [10] Neither the seven loaves of the four thousand, and how many baskets ye took up?

[11] How is it that ye do not perceive that I spoke not to you concerning bread? But beware of the leaven of the Pharisees and Sadducees. [12] Then understood they that he bade them not beware of the leaven of bread, but of the teaching of the Pharisees and Sadducees.

[15] And he charged them, saying, Take heed, beware of the leaven of the Pharisees and the leaven of Herod.

[16] And they reasoned one with another, saying, We have no bread.

[17] And Yeshua perceiving it said unto them, Why reason ye, because ye have no bread? Do ye not yet perceive, neither understand? Have ye your heart hardened? [18] Having eyes, see ye not? And having ears, hear ye not? And do ye not remember?

[19] When I broke the five loaves among the five thousand, how many baskets full of broken pieces took ye up? They say unto him, Twelve.

[20] And when the seven among the four thousand, how many basketfuls of broken pieces took ye up? And they say unto him, Seven.

[21] And he said unto them, Do ye not yet understand?

[§ 84]—K. The Healing of the Blind Man

Mark 8:22-26

[22] And they come unto Beit Tzaida. And they bring to him a blind man, and beseech him to touch him. [23] And he took hold of the blind man by the hand, and brought him out of the village; and when he had spit on his eyes, and laid his hands upon him, he asked him, Do you see anything? [24] And he looked up, and said, I see men; for I behold <them> as trees, walking. [25] Then again he laid his hands upon his eyes; and he looked steadfastly, and was restored, and saw all things clearly. [26] And he sent him away to his home, saying, Do not even enter into the village.

[§ 85]—L. The Confession of Peter

Matthew 16:13-20	Mark 8:27-30	Luke 9:18-21
[13] Now when Yeshua came into the parts of Caesarea Philippi, he asked his disciples, saying, Who do men say that the Son of man is?	[27] And Yeshua went forth, and his disciples, into the villages of Caesarea Philippi: and on the way he asked his disciples, saying unto them, Who do men say that I am?	[18] And it came to pass, as he was praying apart, the disciples were with him: and he asked them, saying, Who do the multitudes say that I am?
[14] And they said, Some <say> Yochanan the Baptizer; some, Eliyahu; and others, Yirmeyahu, or one of the prophets. [15] He said unto them, But who say ye that I am? [16] And Shimon Peter answered and said,	[28] And they told him, saying, Yochanan the Baptizer; and others, Eliyahu; but others, One of the prophets. [29] And he asked them, But who say ye that I am? Peter answered and said unto him, You are the Messiah.	[19] And they answering said, Yochanan the Baptizer; but others <say>, Eliyahu; and others, that one of the old prophets is risen again. [20] And he said unto them, But who say ye that I am? And Peter answering said,

You are the Messiah, the Son of the living God.

The Messiah of God.

¹⁷ And Yeshua answered and said unto him, Blessed are you, Shimon Bar-Yonah: for flesh and blood has not revealed it unto you, but my Father who is in heaven. ¹⁸ And I also say unto you, that you are Peter, and upon this rock I will build my church; and the gates of Hades shall not prevail against it. ¹⁹ I will give unto you the keys of the kingdom of heaven: and whatsoever you shall bind on earth shall be bound in heaven; and whatsoever you shall loose on earth shall be loosed in heaven.

²⁰ Then charged he the disciples that they should tell no man that he was the Messiah.

³⁰ And he charged them that they should tell no man of him.

²¹ But he charged them, and commanded <them> to tell this to no man;

[§ 86]—

M. Instruction Concerning the Death of the King

Matthew 16:21-26	Mark 8:31-37	Luke 9:22-25
[21] From that time began Yeshua to show unto his disciples, that he must go unto Yerushalayim, and suffer many things of the elders and chief priests and scribes, and be killed, and the third day be raised up.	[31] And he began to teach them, that the Son of man must suffer many things, and be rejected by the elders, and the chief priests, and the scribes, and be killed, and after three days rise again. [32] And he spoke the saying openly.	[22] saying, The Son of man must suffer many things, and be rejected of the elders and chief priests and scribes, and be killed, and the third day be raised up.
[22] And Peter took him, and began to rebuke him, saying, Be it far from you, Lord: this shall never be unto you.	And Peter took him, and began to rebuke him.	
[23] But he turned, and said unto Peter, Get you behind me, Satan: you are a stumbling-block unto me: for you mind not the things of God, but the things of men.	[33] But he turning about, and seeing his disciples, rebuked Peter, and said, Get you behind me, Satan; for you mind not the things of God, but the things of men.	
[24] Then said Yeshua unto his disciples,	[34] And he called unto him the multitude with his disciples, and said unto them,	[23] And he said unto all,
If any man would come after me, let him deny	If any man would come after me, let him deny	If any man would come after me, let him deny

127

himself, and take up his cross, and follow me.	himself, and take up his cross, and follow me.	himself, and take up his cross daily, and follow me.
[25] For whosoever would save his life shall lose it: and whosoever shall lose his life for my sake shall find it.	[35] For whosoever would save his life shall lose it; and whosoever shall lose his life for my sake and the gospel's shall save it.	[24] For whosoever would save his life shall lose it; but whosoever shall lose his life for my sake, the same shall save it.
[26] For what shall a man be profited, if he shall gain the whole world, and forfeit his life? Or what shall a man give in exchange for his life?	[36] For what does it profit a man, to gain the whole world, and forfeit his life? [37] For what should a man give in exchange for his life?	[25] For what is a man profited, if he gain the whole world, and lose or forfeit his own self?

[§§ 87–88]—

N. Instruction Concerning the Kingdom

[§ 87]—1. The Promise of Revelation

Matthew 16:27-28	Mark 8:38-9:1	Luke 9:26-27
	[38] For whosoever shall be ashamed of me and of my words in this adulterous and sinful generation, the Son of man also shall be ashamed of him,	[26] For whosoever shall be ashamed of me and of my words, of him shall the Son of man be ashamed,
[27] For the Son of man shall come in the glory of his Father with his angels; and then shall	when he comes in the glory of his Father with the holy angels.	when he comes in his own glory, and <the glory> of the Father, and of the holy angels.

128

he render unto every man according to his deeds.		

he render unto every man according to his deeds.

^{9:1} And he said unto them,

²⁸ Verily I say unto you, there are some of them that stand here, who shall in no wise taste of death, till they see the Son of man coming in his kingdom.

Verily I say unto you, There are some here of them that stand <by>, who shall in no wise taste of death, till they see the kingdom of God come with power.

²⁷ But I tell you of a truth, There are some of them that stand here, who shall in no wise taste of death, till they see the kingdom of God.

[§ 88]—2. The Transfiguration: The Revelation of the Kingdom

Matthew 17:1-8	**Mark 9:2-8**	**Luke 9:28-36a**
¹ And after six days Yeshua takes with him Peter, and Yaakov, and Yochanan his brother, and brings them up into a high mountain apart:	² And after six days Yeshua takes with him Peter, and Yaakov, and Yochanan, and brings them up into a high mountain apart by themselves:	²⁸ And it came to pass about eight days after these sayings, that he took with him Peter and Yochanan and Yaakov, and went up into the mountain to pray.
² and he was transfigured before them; and his face did shine as the sun, and his garments became white as the light.	and he was transfigured before them; ³ and his garments became glistering, exceeding white, so as no fuller on earth can whiten them.	²⁹ And as he was praying, the fashion of his countenance was altered, and his raiment <became> white <and> dazzling.

129

3 And behold, there appeared unto them Mosheh and Eliyahu talking with him.

4 And Peter answered, and said unto Yeshua, Lord, it is good for us to be here: if you will, I will make here three tabernacles; one for you, and one for Mosheh, and one for Eliyahu.

5 While he was yet speaking, behold, a bright cloud overshadowed them: and behold, a voice out of the cloud, saying,

4 And there appeared unto them Eliyahu with Mosheh: and they were talking with Yeshua.

5 And Peter answered and said to Yeshua, Rabbi, it is good for us to be here: and let us make three tabernacles; one for you, and one for Mosheh, and one for Eliyahu.

6 For he knew not what to answer; for they became sore afraid.

7 And there came a cloud overshadowing them: and there came a voice out of the cloud,

30 And behold, there talked with him two men, who were Mosheh and Eliyahu; 31 who appeared in glory, and spoke of his decease which he was about to accomplish at Yerushalayim. 32 Now Peter and they that were with him were heavy with sleep: but when they were fully awake, they saw his glory, and the two men that stood with him. 33 And it came to pass, as they were parting from him, Peter said unto Yeshua, Master, it is good for us to be here: and let us make three tabernacles; one for you, and one for Mosheh, and one for Eliyahu:

not knowing what he said.

34 And while he said these things, there came a cloud, and overshadowed them: and they feared as they entered into the cloud. 35 And a voice came

| | | out of the cloud, saying, |
| This is my beloved Son, in whom I am well pleased; hear ye him. [6] And when the disciples heard it, they fell on their face, and were sore afraid. [7] And Yeshua came and touched them and said, Arise, and be not afraid. [8] And lifting up their eyes, they saw no one, save Yeshua only. | This is my beloved Son: hear ye him.

[8] And suddenly looking round about, they saw no one any more, save Yeshua only with themselves. | This is my Son, my chosen: hear ye him.

[36a] And when the voice came, Yeshua was found alone. |

[§ 89]—O. Instruction Concerning Eliyahu

Matthew 17:9-13	Mark 9:9-13	Luke 9:36b
[9] And as they were coming down from the mountain, Yeshua commanded them, saying, Tell the vision to no man, until the Son of man be risen from the dead.	[9] And as they were coming down from the mountain, he charged them that they should tell no man what things they had seen, save when the Son of man should have risen again from the dead. [10] And they kept the saying, questioning among themselves what the rising again from the dead should mean.	[36b] And they held their peace, and told no man in those days any of the things which they had seen.

[10] And his disciples asked him, saying, Why then say the scribes that Eliyahu must first come? [11] And he answered and said, Eliyahu indeed comes, and shall restore all things:

[12] but I say into you, that Eliyahu is come already, and they knew him not, but did unto him whatsoever they would. Even so shall the Son of man also suffer of them. [13] Then understood the disciples that he spoke unto them of Yochanan the Baptizer.

[11] And they asked him, saying, <How is it> that the scribes say that Eliyahu must first come?

[12] And he said unto them, Eliyahu indeed comes first, and restores all things: and how is it written of the Son of man, that he should suffer many things and be set at nought? [13] But I say unto you, that Eliyahu is come, and they have also done unto him whatsoever they would, even as it is written of him.

[§ 90]—P. Instruction Concerning Faith

Matthew 17:14-20	Mark 9:14-29	Luke 9:37-42
[14] And when they were come to the multitude, there came to him a man, kneeling to him, saying,	[14] And when they came to the disciples, they saw a great multitude about them, and scribes questioning with them. [15] And	[37] And it came to pass, on the next day, when they were come down from the mountain, a great multitude met him.

straightway all the multitude, when they saw him, were greatly amazed, and running to him saluted him. ¹⁶ And he asked them, What question ye with them? ¹⁷ And one of the multitude answered him, Teacher,

¹⁵ Lord, have mercy on my son: for he is epileptic, and suffers grievously; for ofttimes he falls into the fire, and oft-times into the water.

I brought unto you my son, who has a dumb spirit; ¹⁸ and wheresoever it takes him, it dashes him down: and he foams, and grinds his teeth, and pines away:

³⁸ And behold, a man from the multitude cried, saying, Teacher, I beseech you to look upon my son; for he is mine only child: ³⁹ and behold, a spirit takes him, and he suddenly cries out; and it tears him that he foams, and it hardly departs from him, bruising him sorely.

¹⁶ And I brought him to your disciples, and they could not cure him.

and I spoke to your disciples that they should cast it out; and they were not able.

⁴⁰ And I besought your disciples to cast it out; and they could not.

¹⁷ And Yeshua answered and said, O faithless and perverse generation, how long shall I be with you? How long shall I bear with you? Bring him here to me.

¹⁹ And he answered them and said, O faithless generation, how long shall I be with you? how long shall I bear with you? Bring him unto me. ²⁰ And they brought him unto him: and when he saw him, straightway the spirit tare him grievously; and he fell on the ground, and wal-

⁴¹ And Yeshua answered and said, O faithless and perverse generation, how long shall I be with you, and bear with you? Bring here your son. ⁴² And as he was yet a coming, the demon dashed him down, and tare <him> grievously.

lowed foaming. [21] And he asked his father, How long time is it since this has come unto him? And he said, From a child. [22] And oft-times it has cast him both into the fire and into the waters, to destroy him: but if you can do anything, have compassion on us, and help us. [23] And Yeshua said unto him, If you can! All things are possible to him that believes. [24] Straightway the father of the child cried out, and said, I believe; help you mine unbelief. [25] And when Yeshua saw that a multitude came running together,

[18] And Yeshua rebuked him; and the demon went out of him: and the boy was cured from that hour.

he rebuked the unclean spirit, saying unto him, You dumb and deaf spirit, I command you, come out of him, and enter no more into him. [26] And having cried out, and torn him much, he came out: and <the boy> became as one dead; insomuch that the more part said, He is dead. [27] But

But Yeshua rebuked the unclean spirit, and healed the boy, and gave him back to his father.

Yeshua took him by the hand, and raised him up; and he arose.

[19] Then came the disciples to Yeshua apart, and said, Why could not we cast it out? [20] And he said unto them, Because of your little faith: for verily I say unto you, If ye have faith as a grain of mustard seed, ye shall say unto this mountain, Remove hence to yonder place; and it shall remove; and nothing shall be impossible unto you.[3]

[28] And when he was come into the house, his disciples asked him privately, <How is it> that we could not cast it out? [29] And he said unto them, This kind can come out by nothing, save by prayer.

[§ 91]—

Q. Instruction Concerning the Death of the King

Matthew 17:22-23	Mark 9:30-32	Luke 9:43-45
[22] And while they abode in Galil, Yeshua said unto them,	[30] And they went forth from thence, and passed through Galil; and he would not that any man should know it. [31] For he taught his	[43] And they were all astonished at the majesty of God. But while all were marveling at all the things which he did, he said unto his

---

[3] Many authorities, some ancient, insert verse 21: "But this kind goes not out save by prayer and fasting."

disciples, and said unto them,

disciples, [44] Let these words sink into your ears:

The Son of man shall be delivered up into the hands of men; [23] and they shall kill him, and the third day he shall be raised up. And they were exceeding sorry.

The Son of man is delivered up into the hands of men, and they shall kill him; and when he is killed, after three days he shall rise again. [32] But they understood not the saying, and were afraid to ask him.

for the Son of man shall be delivered up into the hands of men.

[45] But they understood not this saying, and it was concealed from them, that they should not perceive it; and they were afraid to ask him about this saying.

[§ 92]—R. Instruction Concerning Sonship

Matthew 17:24-27

[24] And when they were come to Kfar Nachum, they that received the half-shekel came to Peter, and said, Does not your teacher pay the half-shekel? [25] He said, Yea. And when he came into the house, Yeshua spoke first to him, saying, What do you think, Shimon? The kings of the earth, from whom do they receive toll or tribute? From their sons, or from strangers? [26] And when he said, From strangers, Yeshua said unto him, Therefore the sons are free. [27] But, lest we cause them to stumble, go you to the sea, and cast a hook, and take up the fish that first comes up; and when you have opened his mouth, you shall find a shekel: that take, and give unto them for me and you.

[§ 93]—S. Instruction Concerning Humility

Matthew 18:1-5	Mark 9:33-37	Luke 9:46-48
[1] In that hour came the disciples unto Yeshua, saying,	[33] And they came to Kfar Nachum: and when he was in the house he asked them, What were ye reasoning on the way? [34] But they held their peace: for they had disputed one with another on the way, who <was> the greatest.	[46] And there arose a reasoning among them,
Who then is greatest in the kingdom of heaven?		which of them was the greatest.
	[35] And he sat down, and called the twelve; and he said unto them, If any man would be first, he shall be last of all, and servant of all.	[47] But when Yeshua saw the reasoning of their heart,
[2] And he called to him a little child, and set him in the midst of them, [3] and said,	[36] And he took a little child, and set him in the midst of them: and taking him in his arms, he said unto them,	he took a little child, and set him by his side, [48] and said unto them,
Verily I say unto you, Except ye turn, and become as little children, ye shall in no wise enter into the kingdom of heaven. [4] Whosoever therefore shall humble himself as this little child, the	[37] Whosoever shall receive one of such little children in my name, receives me: and whosoever receives me, receives not me, but him that sent me.	Whosoever shall receive this little child in my name receives me: and whosoever shall receive me receives him that sent me: for he that is least among you all, the same is great.

same is the greatest in the kingdom of heaven.

[5] And whoso shall receive one such little child in my name receives me:

[§ 94]—T. Instruction Concerning Exclusiveness and Pride

Matthew 18:6-14	Mark 9:38-50	Luke 9:49-50
[6] But whoso shall cause one of these little ones that believe on me to stumble, it is profitable for him that a great millstone should be hanged about his neck, and \<that\> he should be sunk in the depth of the sea. [7] Woe unto the world because of occasions of stumbling!	[38] Yochanan said unto him, Teacher, we saw one casting out demons in your name; and we forbade him, because he followed not us. [39] But Yeshua said, Forbid him not: for there is no man who shall do a mighty work in my name, and be able quickly to speak evil of me.	[49] And Yochanan answered and said, Master, we saw one casting out demons in your name; and we forbade him, because he followed not with us. [50] But Yeshua said unto him, Forbid \<him\> not: for he that is not against you is for you.

Mt. cont.: For it must needs be that the occasions come; but woe to that man through whom the occasion comes! [8] And if your hand or your foot causes you to stumble, cut it off, and cast it from you: it is good

Mk. cont.: [40] For he that is not against us is for us. [41] For whosoever shall give you a cup of water to drink, because ye are Messiah's, verily I say unto you, he shall in no wise lose his reward.

for you to enter into life maimed or lame, rather than having two hands or two feet to be cast into the eternal fire. [9] And if yours eye causes you to stumble, pluck it out, and cast it from you: it is good for you to enter into life with one eye, rather than having two eyes to be cast into the hell[4] of fire. [10] See that ye despise not one of these little ones; for I say unto you, that in heaven their angels do always behold the face of my Father who is in heaven. [11] ...[5] [12] How think ye? If any man have a hundred sheep, and one of them be gone astray, does he not leave the ninety and nine, and go unto the mountains, and seek that which goes astray? [13] And if so be that he find it, verily I say unto you, he rejoices over it more than over the ninety and nine which have not gone astray. [14] Even so it is not the will of your Father who is in heaven, that one of these little ones should perish.

[42] And whosoever shall cause one of these little ones that believe on me to stumble, it were better for him if a great millstone were hanged about his neck, and he were cast into the sea. [43] And if your hand cause you to stumble, cut it off: it is good for you to enter into life maimed, rather than having your two hands to go into hell, into the unquenchable fire. [44] ... [45] And if your foot cause you to stumble, cut it off: it is good for you to enter into life lame, rather than having your two feet to be cast into hell. [46] ... [47] And if yours eye cause you to stumble, cast it out: it is good for you to enter into the kingdom of God with one eye, rather than having two eyes to be cast into hell; [48] where their worm dies not, and the fire is not quenched. [49] For everyone shall be salted with fire. [50] Salt is good: but if the salt have lost its saltiness, wherewith will ye season it? Have salt in yourselves, and be at peace one with another.[6]

---

[4] Greek: *Gehenna*.

[5] Many authorities, some ancient, insert verse 11: "For the Son of man came to save that which was lost."

[6] Mark 9:44 and 46, which are identical to verse 48, are omitted by the best ancient authorities.

[§ 95]—U. Instruction Concerning Forgiveness

Matthew 18:15-35

[15] And if your brother sin against you, go, show him his fault between you and him alone: if he hear you, you have gained your brother. [16] But if he hear <you> not, take with you one or two more, that at the mouth of two witnesses or three every word may be established. [17] And if he refuse to hear them, tell it unto the church: and if he refuse to hear the church also, let him be unto you as the Gentile and the publican. [18] Verily I say unto you, what things so ever ye shall bind on earth shall be bound in heaven; and what things so ever ye shall loose on earth shall be loosed in heaven. [19] Again I say unto you, that if two of you shall agree on earth as touching anything that they shall ask, it shall be done for them of my Father who is in heaven. [20] For where two or three are gathered together in my name, there am I in the midst of them. [21] Then came Peter and said to him, Lord, how often shall my brother sin against me, and I forgive him? Until seven times? [22] Yeshua said unto him, I say not unto you, Until seven times; but, Until seventy times seven. [23] Therefore is the kingdom of heaven likened unto a certain king, who would make a reckoning with his servants. [24] And when he had begun to reckon, one was brought unto him, that owed him ten thousand talents. [25] But forasmuch as he had not <wherewith> to pay, his lord commanded him to be sold, and his wife, and children, and all that he had, and payment to be made. [26] The servant therefore fell down and worshipped him, saying, Lord, have patience with me, and I will pay you all. [27] And the lord of that servant, being moved with compassion, released him, and forgave him the debt. [28] But that servant went out, and found one of his fellow-servants, who owed him a hundred shillings: and he laid hold on him, and took <him> by the throat, saying, Pay what you owe. [29] So his fellow-servant fell down and besought him, saying, Have patience with me, and I will pay you. [30] And he would not: but went and cast him into prison, till he should pay that which was due. [31] So when his fellow-servants saw what was done, they were exceeding sorry, and came and told unto their lord all that was done. [32] Then his lord called him unto him, and said to him, You wicked servant, I forgave you all that debt, because you besought me: [33] Should you not also have had mercy on your fellow-servant, even as I had

mercy on you? [34] And his lord was angry, and delivered him to the tormentors, till he should pay all that was due. [35] So shall also my heavenly Father do unto you, if ye forgive not everyone his brother from your hearts.

[§ 96]—V. The Challenge by the Brothers

John 7:2-9

[2] Now the feast of the Jews, the feast of tabernacles, was at hand. [3] His brethren therefore said unto him, Depart hence, and go into Yehudah, that your disciples also may behold your works which you do. [4] For no man does anything in secret, and himself seeks to be known openly. If you do these things, manifest yourself to the world. [5] For even his brethren did not believe on him. [6] Yeshua therefore said unto them, My time is not yet come; but your time is always ready. [7] The world cannot hate you; but me it hates, because I testify of it, that its works are evil. [8] Go ye up unto the feast: I go not up unto this feast; because my time is not yet fulfilled. [9] And having said these things unto them, he abode <still> in Galil.

[§ 97]—W. The Journey to Yerushalayim

Luke 9:51-56

[51] And it came to pass, when the days were well-near come that he should be received up, he steadfastly set his face to go to Yerushalayim, [52] and sent messengers before his face:

and they went, and entered into a village of the Samaritans, to make ready for him. [53] And they did not receive him, because his face was <as though he were> going to Yerushalayim. [54] And when his disciples Yaakov and Yochanan saw

John 7:10

[10] But when his brethren were gone up unto the feast, then went he also up, not publicly, but as it were in secret.

<this>, they said, Lord, will you that we bid fire to come down from heaven, and consume them? [55] But he turned, and rebuked them. [56] And they went to another village.

[§ 98]—X. Instruction Concerning Discipleship

Matthew 8:19-22

[19] And there came a scribe, and said unto him, Teacher, I will follow you whithersoever you go.
[20] And Yeshua said unto him, The foxes have holes, and the birds of the heaven <have> nests; but the Son of man has not where to lay his head.
[21] And another of the disciples said unto him, Lord, suffer me first to go and bury my father. [22] But Yeshua said unto him, Follow me; and leave the dead to bury their own dead.

Luke 9:57-62

[57] And as they went on the way, a certain man said unto him, I will follow you whithersoever you go.
[58] And Yeshua said unto him, The foxes have holes, and the birds of the heaven <have> nests; but the Son of man has not where to lay his head.
[59] And he said unto another, Follow me. But he said, Lord, suffer me first to go and bury my father. [60] But he said unto him, Leave the dead to bury their own dead; but go you and publish abroad the kingdom of God.
[61] And another also said, I will follow you, Lord; but first suffer me to bid farewell to them that are at my house. [62] But Yeshua said unto him, No man, having put his hand to the plow, and looking back, is fit for the kingdom of God.

V. THE OPPOSITION
TO THE KING
— §§ 99–112 —

[§ 99]—A. The Conflict at the Feast of Tabernacles

1. Messiah's Authority Questioned

John 7:11-15

[11] The Jews therefore sought him at the feast, and said, Where is he?
[12] And there was much murmuring among the multitudes concerning him: some said, He is a good man; others said, Not so, but he leads the multitude astray. [13] Yet no man spoke openly of him for fear of the Jews. [14] But when it was now the midst of the feast Yeshua went up into the temple, and

taught. [15] The Jews therefore marveled, saying, How knows this man letters, having never learned?

2. Messiah's Answer

John 7:16-24

[16] Yeshua therefore answered them and said, My teaching is not mine, but his that sent me. [17] If any man wills to do his will, he shall know of the teaching, whether it is of God, or <whether> I speak from myself. [18] He that speaks from himself seeks his own glory: but he that seeks the glory of him that sent him, the same is true, and no unrighteousness is in him. [19] Did not Mosheh give you the law, and <yet> none of you does the law? Why seek ye to kill me? [20] The multitude answered, You have a demon: who seeks to kill you? [21] Yeshua answered and said unto them, I did one work, and ye all marvel because thereof. [22] Mosheh has given you circumcision (not that it is of Mosheh, but of the fathers); and on the Sabbath ye circumcise a man. [23] If a man receives circumcision on the Sabbath, that the law of Mosheh may not be broken; are ye angry with me, because I made a man every whit whole on the Sabbath? [24] Judge not according to appearance, but judge righteous judgment.

3. Messiah's Person Questioned

John 7:25-27

[25] Some therefore of them of Yerushalayim said, Is not this he whom they seek to kill? [26] And lo, he speaks openly, and they say nothing unto him. Can it be that the rulers indeed know that this is the Messiah? [27] Howbeit we know this man from where he is: but when the Messiah comes, no one knows from where he is.

4. Messiah's Explanation

John 7:28-30

[28] Yeshua therefore cried in the temple, teaching and saying, Ye both know me, and know from where I am; and I am not come of myself, but he that sent me is true, whom ye know not. [29] I know him; because I am from him, and he sent me. [30] They sought therefore to take him: and no man laid his hand on him, because his hour was not yet come.

5. The People's Response

John 7:31-36

[31] But of the multitude many believed on him; and they said, When the Messiah shall come, will he do more signs than those which this man has done? [32] The Pharisees heard the multitude murmuring these things concerning him; and the chief priests and the Pharisees sent officers to take him. [33] Yeshua therefore said, Yet a little while am I with you, and I go unto him that sent me. [34] Ye shall seek me, and shall not find me: and where I am, ye cannot come. [35] The Jews therefore said among themselves, Whither will this man go that we shall not find him? Will he go unto the Dispersion among the Greeks, and teach the Greeks? [36] What is this word that he said, Ye shall seek me, and shall not find me; and where I am, ye cannot come?

6. Messiah's Invitation

John 7:37-44

[37] Now on the last day, the great <day> of the feast, Yeshua stood and cried, saying, If any man thirst, let him come unto me and drink. [38] He that believes on me, as the scripture has said, from within him shall flow rivers of living water. [39] But this spoke he of the Spirit, which they that believed on him were to receive: for the Spirit was not yet <given>; because Yeshua was not yet glorified. [40] <Some> of the multitude therefore, when they heard these words, said, This is of a truth the prophet. [41] Others said, This is the Messiah. But some said, What, does the Messiah come out of Galil? [42] Have

not the scriptures said that the Messiah comes of the seed of David, and from Beit Lechem, the village where David was? [43] So there arose a division in the multitude because of him. [44] And some of them would have taken him; but no man laid hands on him.

7. The Pharisaic Response

John 7:45-52

[45] The officers therefore came to the chief priests and Pharisees; and they said unto them, Why did ye not bring him? [46] The officers answered, Never man so spoke. [47] The Pharisees therefore answered them, Are ye also led astray? [48] Has any of the rulers believed on him, or of the Pharisees? [49] But this multitude that knows not the law are accursed. [50] Nakdimon said unto them (he that came to him before, being one of them), [51] Does our law judge a man, except it first hear from himself and know what he does? [52] They answered and said unto him, Are you also of Galil? Search, and see that out of Galil arises no prophet.

[§ 100]—B. The Conflict over the Law

John 7:53–8:11[1]

[53] <And they went every man unto his own house: [8:1] but Yeshua went unto the mount of Olives. [2] And early in the morning he came again into the temple, and all the people came unto him; and he sat down, and taught them. [3] And the scribes and the Pharisees bring a woman taken in adultery; and having set her in the midst, [4] they say unto him, Teacher, this woman has been taken in adultery, in the very act. [5] Now in the law Mosheh commanded us to stone such: what then do you say of her? [6] And this they said, trying him, that they might have <whereof> to accuse him. But Yeshua stooped down, and with his finger wrote on the ground. [7] But when they

---

[1] Most of the ancient authorities omit John 7:53-8:11, and those containing it vary from each other.

continued asking him, he lifted up himself, and said unto them, He that is without sin among you, let him first cast a stone at her. [8] And again he stooped down, and with his finger wrote on the ground. [9] And they, when they heard it, went out one by one, beginning from the eldest, <even> unto the last: and Yeshua was left alone, and the woman, where she was, in the midst. [10] And Yeshua lifted up himself, and said unto her, Woman, where are they? Did no man condemn you? [11] And she said, No man, Lord. And Yeshua said, Neither do I condemn you: go your way; from henceforth sin no more.>

[§ 101]—C. The Conflict over the Light

John 8:12-20

[12] Again therefore Yeshua spoke unto them, saying, I am the light of the world: he that follows me shall not walk in the darkness, but shall have the light of life. [13] The Pharisees therefore said unto him, You bear witness of yourself; your witness is not true. [14] Yeshua answered and said unto them, Even if I bear witness of myself, my witness is true; for I know from where I came, and whither I go; but ye know not from where I come, or whither I go. [15] Ye judge after the flesh; I judge no man. [16] Yea and if I judge, my judgment is true; for I am not alone, but I and the Father that sent me. [17] Yea and in your law it is written, that the witness of two men is true. [18] I am he that bears witness of myself, and the Father that sent me bears witness of me. [19] They said therefore unto him, Where is your Father? Yeshua answered, Ye know neither me, nor my Father: if ye knew me, ye would know my Father also. [20] These words spoke he in the treasury, as he taught in the temple: and no man took him; because his hour was not yet come.

[§ 102]—D. The Conflict over His Person

1. Messiah the True Object of Faith

John 8:21-30

[21] He said therefore again unto them, I go away, and ye shall seek me, and shall die in your sin: whither I go, ye cannot come. [22] The Jews therefore said, Will he kill himself, that he says, Whither I go, ye cannot come? [23] And he said unto them, Ye are from beneath; I am from above: ye are of this world; I am not of this world. [24] I said therefore unto you, that ye shall die in your sins: for except ye believe that I am <he>, ye shall die in your sins. [25] They said therefore unto him, Who are you? Yeshua said unto them, Even that which I have also spoken unto you from the beginning. [26] I have many things to speak and to judge concerning you: howbeit he that sent me is true; and the things which I heard from him, these speak I unto the world. [27] They perceived not that he spoke to them of the Father. [28] Yeshua therefore said, When ye have lifted up the Son of man, then shall ye know that I am <he>, and <that> I do nothing of myself, but as the Father taught me, I speak these things. [29] And he that sent me is with me; he has not left me alone; for I do always the things that are pleasing to him. [30] As he spoke these things, many believed on him.

2. Messiah the True Deliverer

a. From Sin

John 8:31-40

[31] Yeshua therefore said to those Jews that had believed him, If ye abide in my word, <then> are ye truly my disciples; [32] and ye shall know the truth, and the truth shall make you free. [33] They answered unto him, We are Avraham's seed, and have never yet been in bondage to any man: how say you, Ye shall be made free? [34] Yeshua answered them, Verily, verily, I say unto you, Everyone that commits sin is the bondservant of sin. [35] And the bondservant abides not in the house forever: the son abides forever. [36] If

therefore the Son shall make you free, ye shall be free indeed. [37] I know that ye are Avraham's seed: yet ye seek to kill me, because my word has not free course in you. [38] I speak the things which I have seen with <my> Father: and ye also do the things which ye heard from <your> father. [39] They answered and said unto him, Our father is Avraham. Yeshua said unto them, If ye were Avraham's children, ye would do the works of Avraham. [40] But now ye seek to kill me, a man that has told you the truth, which I heard from God: this did not Avraham.

b. From Satan

John 8:41-50

[41] Ye do the works of your father. They said unto him, We were not born of fornication; we have one Father, <even> God. [42] Yeshua said unto them, If God were your Father, ye would love me: for I came forth and am come from God; for neither have I come of myself, but he sent me. [43] Why do ye not understand my speech? <Even> because ye cannot hear my word. [44] Ye are of <your> father the devil, and the lusts of your father it is your will to do. He was a murderer from the beginning, and stands not in the truth, because there is no truth in him. When he speaks a lie, he speaks of his own: for he is a liar, and the father thereof. [45] But because I say the truth, ye believe me not. [46] Which of you convicts me of sin? If I say truth, why do ye not believe me? [47] He that is of God hears the words of God: for this cause ye hear <them> not, because ye are not of God. [48] The Jews answered and said unto him, Say we not well that you are a Samaritan, and have a demon? [49] Yeshua answered, I have not a demon; but I honor my Father, and ye dishonor me. [50] But I seek not mine own glory: there is one that seeks and judges.

c. From Death

John 8:51-59

[51] Verily, verily, I say unto you, If a man keep my word, he shall never see death. [52] The Jews said unto him, Now we know that you have a demon. Avraham died, and the prophets; and you say, If a man keep my word, he

shall never taste of death. [53] Are you greater than our father Avraham, who died? And the prophets died: Whom make you yourself to be? [54] Yeshua answered, If I glorify myself, my glory is nothing: it is my Father that glorifies me; of whom ye say, that he is your God; [55] and ye have not known him: but I know him; and if I should say, I know him not, I shall be like unto you, a liar: but I know him, and keep his word. [56] Your father Avraham rejoiced to see my day; and he saw it, and was glad. [57] The Jews therefore said unto him, You are not yet fifty years old, and have you seen Avraham? [58] Yeshua said unto them, Verily, verily, I say unto you, Before Avraham was born, I am. [59] They took up stones therefore to cast at him: but Yeshua hid himself, and went out of the temple.

[§ 103]—E. The Conflict over Healing of the Man Born Blind

1. Physical Healing

John 9:1-12

[1] And as he passed by, he saw a man blind from his birth. [2] And his disciples asked him, saying, Rabbi, who sinned, this man, or his parents, that he should be born blind? [3] Yeshua answered, Neither did this man sin, nor his parents: but that the works of God should be made manifest in him. [4] We must work the works of him that sent me, while it is day: the night comes, when no man can work. [5] When I am in the world, I am the light of the world. [6] When he had thus spoken, he spat on the ground, and made clay of the spittle, and anointed his eyes with the clay, [7] and said unto him, Go, wash in the pool of Shiloach (which is by interpretation, Sent). He went away therefore, and washed, and came seeing. [8] The neighbors therefore, and they that saw him aforetime, that he was a beggar, said, Is not this he that sat and begged? [9] Others said, It is he: others said, No, but he is like him. He said, I am <he>. [10] They said therefore unto him, How then were yours eyes opened? [11] He answered, The man that is called Yeshua made clay, and anointed mine eyes, and said unto me, Go to Shiloach, and wash:

so I went away and washed, and I received sight. [12] And they said unto him, Where is he? He said, I know not.

2. The First Interrogation

John 9:13-17

[13] They bring to the Pharisees him that aforetime was blind. [14] Now it was the Sabbath on the day when Yeshua made the clay, and opened his eyes. [15] Again therefore the Pharisees also asked him how he received his sight. And he said unto them, He put clay upon mine eyes, and I washed, and I see. [16] Some therefore of the Pharisees said, This man is not from God, because he keeps not the Sabbath. But others said, How can a man that is a sinner do such signs? And there was division among them. [17] They say therefore unto the blind man again, What do you say of him, in that he opened yours eyes? And he said, He is a prophet.

3. The Interrogation of the Parents

John 9:18-23

[18] The Jews therefore did not believe concerning him, that he had been blind, and had received his sight, until they called the parents of him that had received his sight, [19] and asked them, saying, Is this your son, who ye say was born blind? How then does he now see? [20] His parents answered and said, We know that this is our son, and that he was born blind: [21] but how he now sees, we know not; or who opened his eyes, we know not: ask him; he is of age; he shall speak for himself. [22] These things said his parents, because they feared the Jews: for the Jews had agreed already, that if any man should confess him <to be> Messiah, he should be put out of the synagogue. [23] Therefore said his parents, He is of age; ask him.

4. The Second Interrogation

John 9:24-34

[24] So they called a second time the man that was blind, and said unto him, Give glory to God: we know that this man is a sinner. [25] He therefore answered, Whether he is a sinner, I know not: one thing I know, that, whereas I was blind, now I see. [26] They said therefore unto him, What did he to you? How opened he yours eyes? [27] He answered them, I told you even now, and ye did not hear; wherefore would ye hear it again? Would ye also become his disciples? [28] And they reviled him, and said, You are his disciple; but we are disciples of Mosheh. [29] We know that God has spoken unto Mosheh: but as for this man, we know not from where he is. [30] The man answered and said unto them, Why, herein is the marvel, that ye know not from where he is, and <yet> he opened mine eyes. [31] We know that God hears not sinners: but if any man be a worshipper of God, and do his will, him he hears. [32] Since the world began it was never heard that anyone opened the eyes of a man born blind. [33] If this man were not from God, he could do nothing. [34] They answered and said unto him, You were altogether born in sins, and do you teach us? And they cast him out.

5. Spiritual Healing

John 9:35-41

[35] Yeshua heard that they had cast him out; and finding him, he said, Do you believe on the Son of God? [36] He answered and said, And who is he, Lord, that I may believe on him? [37] Yeshua said unto him, You have both seen him, and he it is that speaks with you. [38] And he said, Lord, I believe. And he worshipped him. [39] And Yeshua said, For judgment came I into this world, that they that see not may see; and that they that see may become blind. [40] Those of the Pharisees who were with him heard these things, and said unto him, Are we also blind? [41] Yeshua said unto them, If ye were blind, ye would have no sin: but now ye say, We see: your sin remains.

[§ 104]—F. The Conflict over the Shepherd

1. Messiah the True Shepherd

John 10:1-6

[1] Verily, verily, I say unto you, He that enters not by the door into the fold of the sheep, but climbs up some other way, the same is a thief and a robber. [2] But he that enters in by the door is the shepherd of the sheep. [3] To him the porter opens; and the sheep hear his voice: and he calls his own sheep by name, and leads them out. [4] When he has put forth all his own, he goes before them, and the sheep follow him: for they know his voice. [5] And a stranger will they not follow, but will flee from him: for they know not the voice of strangers. [6] This parable spoke Yeshua unto them: but they understood not what things they were which he spoke unto them.

2. Messiah the Door

John 10:7-10

[7] Yeshua therefore said unto them again, Verily, verily, I say unto you, I am the door of the sheep. [8] All that came before me are thieves and robbers: but the sheep did not hear them. [9] I am the door; by me if any man enter in, he shall be saved, and shall go in and go out, and shall find pasture. [10] The thief comes not, but that he may steal, and kill, and destroy: I came that they may have life, and may have <it> abundantly.

3. Messiah the Good Shepherd

John 10:11-18

[11] I am the good shepherd: the good shepherd lays down his life for the sheep. [12] He that is a hireling, and not a shepherd, whose own the sheep are not, beholds the wolf coming, and leaves the sheep, and flees, and the wolf snatches them, and scatters <them>: [13] <he flees> because he is a hireling, and cares not for the sheep. [14] I am the good shepherd; and I know mine

own, and mine own know me, [15] even as the Father knows me, and I know the Father; and I lay down my life for the sheep. [16] And other sheep I have, which are not of this fold: them also I must bring, and they shall hear my voice: and they shall become one flock, one shepherd. [17] Therefore does the Father love me, because I lay down my life, that I may take it again. [18] No one takes it away from me, but I lay it down of myself. I have power to lay it down, and I have power to take it again. This commandment received I from my Father.

4. Division

John 10:19-21

[19] There arose a division again among the Jews because of these words. [20] And many of them said, He has a demon, and is mad; why hear ye him? [21] Others said, These are not the sayings of one possessed with a demon. Can a demon open the eyes of the blind?

[§ 105]—G. The Witness of the Seventy

1. The Seventy Sent

Luke 10:1-16

[1] Now after these things the Lord appointed seventy others, and sent them two and two before his face into every city and place, whither he himself was about to come. [2] And he said unto them, The harvest indeed is plenteous, but the laborers are few: pray ye therefore the Lord of the harvest, that he send forth laborers into his harvest. [3] Go your ways; behold, I send you forth as lambs in the midst of wolves. [4] Carry no purse, no wallet, no shoes; and salute no man on the way. [5] And into whatsoever house ye shall enter, first say, Peace <be> to this house. [6] And if a son of peace be there, your peace shall rest upon him: but if not, it shall turn to you again. [7] And in that same house remain, eating and drinking such things as they give: for the laborer is worthy of his hire. Go not from house to house. [8] And into whatsoever city ye enter, and they receive you, eat such things as are set

before you: [9] and heal the sick that are therein, and say unto them, The kingdom of God is come near unto you. [10] But into whatsoever city ye shall enter, and they receive you not, go out into the streets thereof and say, [11] Even the dust from your city, that cleaves to our feet, we wipe off against you: nevertheless know this, that the kingdom of God is come near. [12] I say unto you, it shall be more tolerable in that day for Sedom, than for that city. [13] Woe unto you, Korazin! woe unto you, Beit Tzaida! For if the mighty works had been done in Tzor and Tzidon, which were done in you, they would have repented long ago, sitting in sackcloth and ashes. [14] But it shall be more tolerable for Tzor and Tzidon in the judgment, than for you. [15] And you, Kfar Nachum, shall you be exalted unto heaven? You shall be brought down unto Hades. [16] He that hears you hears me; and he that rejects you rejects me; and he that rejects me rejects him that sent me.

2. The Seventy Return

Luke 10:17-20

[17] And the seventy returned with joy, saying, Lord, even the demons are subject unto us in your name. [18] And he said unto them, I beheld Satan fallen as lightning from heaven. [19] Behold, I have given you authority to tread upon serpents and scorpions, and over all the power of the enemy: and nothing shall in any wise hurt you. [20] Nevertheless in this rejoice not, that the spirits are subject unto you; but rejoice that your names are written in heaven.

3. Messiah's Prayer

Luke 10:21-24

[21] In that same hour he rejoiced in the Holy Spirit, and said, I thank you, O Father, Lord of heaven and earth, that you did hide these things from the wise and understanding, and did reveal them unto babes: yea, Father; for so it was well-pleasing in your sight. [22] All things have been delivered unto me of my Father: and no one knows who the Son is, save the Father; and who the Father is, save the Son, and he to whomsoever the Son wills to reveal <him>. [23] And turning to the disciples, he said privately, Blessed <are> the

eyes which see the things that ye see: [24] for I say unto you, that many prophets and kings desired to see the things which ye see, and saw them not; and to hear the things which ye hear, and heard them not.

[§ 106]—H. The Conflict over the Question of Eternal Life

Luke 10:25-37

[25] And behold, a certain lawyer stood up and made trial of him, saying, Teacher, what shall I do to inherit eternal life? [26] And he said unto him, What is written in the law? How read you? [27] And he answering said, You shall love the Lord your God with all your heart, and with all your soul, and with all your strength, and with all your mind; and your neighbor as yourself. [28] And he said unto him, You have answered right: this do, and you shall live. [29] But he, desiring to justify himself, said unto Yeshua, And who is my neighbor? [30] Yeshua made answer and said, A certain man was going down from Yerushalayim to Yericho; and he fell among robbers, who both stripped him and beat him, and departed, leaving him half dead. [31] And by chance a certain priest was going down that way: and when he saw him, he passed by on the other side. [32] And in like manner a Levite also, when he came to the place, and saw him, passed by on the other side. [33] But a certain Samaritan, as he journeyed, came where he was: and when he saw him, he was moved with compassion, [34] and came to him, and bound up his wounds, pouring on <them> oil and wine; and he set him on his own beast, and brought him to an inn, and took care of him. [35] And on the morrow he took out two shillings, and gave them to the host, and said, Take care of him; and whatsoever you spend more, I, when I come back again, will repay you. [36] Which of these three, do you think, proved neighbor unto him that fell among the robbers? [37] And he said, He that showed mercy on him. And Yeshua said unto him, Go, and do you likewise.

[§ 107]—I. The Example of Fellowship

Luke 10:38-42

[38] Now as they went on their way, he entered into a certain village: and a certain woman named Marta received him into her house. [39] And she had a sister called Miriam, who also sat at the Lord's feet, and heard his word. [40] But Marta was cumbered about much serving; and she came up to him, and said, Lord, do you not care that my sister did leave me to serve alone? Bid her therefore that she help me. [41] But the Lord answered and said unto her, Marta, Marta, you are anxious and troubled about many things: [42] but one thing is needful: for Miriam has chosen the good part, which shall not be taken away from her.

[§ 108]—J. Instruction in Prayer

Luke 11:1-13

[1] And it came to pass, as he was praying in a certain place, that when he ceased, one of his disciples said unto him, Lord, teach us to pray, even as Yochanan also taught his disciples. [2] And he said unto them, When ye pray, say, Father, Hallowed be your name. Your kingdom come. [3] Give us day by day our daily bread. [4] And forgive us our sins; for we ourselves also forgive everyone that is indebted to us. And bring us not into temptation. [5] And he said unto them, Which of you shall have a friend, and shall go unto him at midnight, and say to him, Friend, lend me three loaves; [6] for a friend of mine is come to me from a journey, and I have nothing to set before him; [7] and he from within shall answer and say, Trouble me not: the door is now shut, and my children are with me in bed; I cannot rise and give you? [8] I say unto you, Though he will not rise and give him because he is his friend, yet because of his importunity he will arise and give him as many as he needs. [9] And I say unto you, Ask, and it shall be given you; seek, and ye shall find; knock, and it shall be opened unto you. [10] For everyone that asks receives; and he that seeks finds; and to him that knocks it shall be opened. [11] And of which of you that is a father shall his son ask a loaf, and he will give him a stone? Or a fish, and he for a fish will give him a serpent? [12] Or <if> he shall

ask an egg, will he give him a scorpion? [13] If ye then, being evil, know how to give good gifts unto your children, how much more shall <your> heavenly Father give the Holy Spirit to them that ask him?

[§ 109]—K. Conflict over the Healing of the Dumb Man

1. The Charge

Luke 11:14-16

[14] And he was casting out a demon <that was> dumb. And it came to pass, when the demon was gone out, the dumb man spoke; and the multitudes marveled. [15] But some of them said, By Beelzebub the prince of the demons casts he out demons. [16] And others, trying <him>, sought of him a sign from heaven.

2. The Defense

Luke 11:17-23

[17] But he, knowing their thoughts, said unto them, Every kingdom divided against itself is brought to desolation; and a house <divided> against a house falls. [18] And if Satan also is divided against himself, how shall his kingdom stand? Because ye say that I cast out demons by Beelzebub. [19] And if I by Beelzebub cast out demons, by whom do your sons cast them out? Therefore shall they be your judges. [20] But if I by the finger of God cast out demons, then is the kingdom of God come upon you. [21] When the strong <man> fully armed guards his own court, his goods are in peace: [22] but when a stronger than he shall come upon him, and overcome him, he takes from him his whole armor wherein he trusted, and divides his spoils. [23] He that is not with me is against me; and he that gathers not with me scatters.

3. The Condition of the Nation

Luke 11:24-28

[24] The unclean spirit when he is gone out of the man, passes through waterless places, seeking rest, and finding none, he says, I will turn back unto my house from where I came out. [25] And when he is come, he finds it swept and garnished. [26] Then goes he, and takes <to him> seven other spirits more evil than himself; and they enter in and dwell there: and the last state of that man becomes worse than the first. [27] And it came to pass, as he said these things, a certain woman out of the multitude lifted up her voice, and said unto him, Blessed is the womb that bore you, and the breasts which you did suck. [28] But he said, Yea rather, blessed are they that hear the word of God, and keep it.

4. The Sign to that Generation

Luke 11:29-32

[29] And when the multitudes were gathering together unto him, he began to say, This generation is an evil generation: it seeks after a sign; and there shall no sign be given to it but the sign of Yonah. [30] For even as Yonah became a sign unto the Ninevites, so shall also the Son of man be to this generation. [31] The queen of the south shall rise up in the judgment with the men of this generation, and shall condemn them: for she came from the ends of the earth to hear the wisdom of Shlomoh; and behold, a greater than Shlomoh is here. [32] The men of Nineveh shall stand up in the judgment with this generation, and shall condemn it: for they repented at the preaching of Yonah; and behold, a greater than Yonah is here.

5. The Call to the Nation

Luke 11:33-36

[33] No man, when he has lighted a lamp, puts it in a cellar, neither under the bushel, but on the stand, that they which enter in may see the light. [34] The lamp of your body is your eye: when your eye is single, your whole body

also is full of light; but when it is evil, your body also is full of darkness. [35] Look therefore whether the light that is in you be not darkness. [36] If therefore your whole body be full of light, having no part dark, it shall be wholly full of light, as when the lamp with its bright shining does give you light.

[§ 110]—L. The Conflict over Pharisaic Ritualism

Luke 11:37-54

[37] Now as he spoke, a Pharisee asked him to dine with him: and he went in, and sat down to meat. [38] And when the Pharisee saw it, he marveled that he had not first bathed himself before dinner. [39] And the Lord said unto him, Now ye the Pharisees cleanse the outside of the cup and of the platter; but your inward part is full of extortion and wickedness. [40] Ye foolish ones, did not he that made the outside make the inside also? [41] But give for alms those things which are within; and behold, all things are clean unto you. [42] But woe unto you Pharisees! For ye tithe mint and rue and every herb, and pass over justice and the love of God: but these ought ye to have done, and not to leave the other undone. [43] Woe unto you Pharisees! For ye love the chief seats in the synagogues, and the salutations in the marketplaces. [44] Woe unto you! For ye are as the tombs which appear not, and the men that walk over <them> know it not. [45] And one of the lawyers answering said unto him, Teacher, in saying this you reproach us also. [46] And he said, Woe unto you lawyers also! For ye load men with burdens grievous to be borne, and ye yourselves touch not the burdens with one of your fingers. [47] Woe unto you! For ye build the tombs of the prophets, and your fathers killed them. [48] So ye are witnesses and consent unto the works of your fathers: For they killed them, and ye build <their tombs>. [49] Therefore also said the wisdom of God, I will send unto them prophets and apostles; and <some> of them they shall kill and persecute; [50] that the blood of all the prophets, which was shed from the foundation of the world, may be required of this generation; [51] from the blood of Hevel unto the blood of Zecharyah, who perished between the altar and the sanctuary: yea, I say unto you, it shall be required of this generation. [52] Woe unto you lawyers! For ye took away the key of knowledge: ye entered not in yourselves, and

them that were entering in ye hindered. [53] And when he was come out from thence, the scribes and the Pharisees began to press upon \<him\> vehemently, and to provoke him to speak of many things; [54] laying wait for him, to catch something out of his mouth.

[§ 111]—M. Instruction of the Disciples

1. Hypocrisy

Luke 12:1-12

[1] In the meantime, when the many thousands of the multitude were gathered together, insomuch that they trod one upon another, he began to say unto his disciples first of all, Beware ye of the leaven of the Pharisees, which is hypocrisy. [2] But there is nothing covered up, that shall not be revealed; and hid, that shall not be known. [3] Wherefore whatsoever ye have said in the darkness shall be heard in the light; and what ye have spoken in the ear in the inner chambers shall be proclaimed upon the housetops. [4] And I say unto you my friends, Be not afraid of them that kill the body, and after that have no more that they can do. [5] But I will warn you whom ye shall fear: Fear him, who after he has killed has power to cast into hell; yea, I say unto you, Fear him. [6] Are not five sparrows sold for two pence? And not one of them is forgotten in the sight of God. [7] But the very hairs of your head are all numbered. Fear not: ye are of more value than many sparrows. [8] And I say unto you, Everyone who shall confess me before men, him shall the Son of man also confess before the angels of God: [9] But he that denies me in the presence of men shall be denied in the presence of the angels of God. [10] And everyone who shall speak a word against the Son of man, it shall be forgiven him: but unto him that blasphemes against the Holy Spirit it shall not be forgiven. [11] And when they bring you before the synagogues, and the rulers, and the authorities, be not anxious how or what ye shall answer, or what ye shall say: [12] for the Holy Spirit shall teach you in that very hour what ye ought to say.

2. Covetousness

a. Occasion

Luke 12:13-15

[13] And one out of the multitude said unto him, Teacher, bid my brother divide the inheritance with me. [14] But he said unto him, Man, who made me a judge or a divider over you? [15] And he said unto them, Take heed, and keep yourselves from all covetousness: for a man's life consists not in the abundance of the things which he possesses.

b. Instruction

Luke 12:16-21

[16] And he spoke a parable unto them, saying, The ground of a certain rich man brought forth plentifully: [17] and he reasoned within himself, saying, What shall I do, because I have not where to bestow my fruits? [18] And he said, This will I do: I will pull down my barns, and build greater; and there will I bestow all my grain and my goods. [19] And I will say to my soul, Soul, you have much goods laid up for many years; take your ease, eat, drink, be merry. [20] But God said unto him, You foolish one, this night is your soul required of you; and the things which you have prepared, whose shall they be? [21] So is he that lays up treasure for himself, and is not rich toward God.

c. Application

Luke 12:22-34

[22] And he said unto his disciples, Therefore I say unto you, Be not anxious for <your> life, what ye shall eat; nor yet for your body, what ye shall put on. [23] For the life is more than the food, and the body than the raiment. [24] Consider the ravens, that they sow not, neither reap; which have no store-chamber nor barn; and God feeds them: of how much more value are ye than the birds! [25] And which of you by being anxious can add a cubit unto

the measure of his life? [26] If then ye are not able to do even that which is least, why are ye anxious concerning the rest? [27] Consider the lilies, how they grow: they toil not, neither do they spin; yet I say unto you, Even Shlomoh in all his glory was not arrayed like one of these. [28] But if God does so clothe the grass in the field, which today is, and tomorrow is cast into the oven; how much more <shall he clothe> you, O ye of little faith? [29] And seek not ye what ye shall eat, and what ye shall drink, neither be ye of doubtful mind. [30] For all these things do the nations of the world seek after: but your Father knows that ye have need of these things. [31] Yet seek ye his kingdom, and these things shall be added unto you. [32] Fear not, little flock; for it is your Father's good pleasure to give you the kingdom. [33] Sell that which ye have, and give alms; make for yourselves purses which wax not old, a treasure in the heavens that fails not, where no thief draws near, neither moth destroys. [34] For where your treasure is, there will your heart be also.

3. Watchfulness

Luke 12:35-40

[35] Let your loins be girded about, and your lamps burning; [36] and be ye yourselves like unto men looking for their lord, when he shall return from the marriage feast; that, when he comes and knocks, they may straightway open unto him. [37] Blessed are those servants, whom the lord when he comes shall find watching: verily I say unto you, that he shall gird himself, and make them sit down to meat, and shall come and serve them. [38] And if he shall come in the second watch, and if in the third, and find <them> so blessed are those <servants>. [39] But know this, that if the master of the house had known in what hour the thief was coming, he would have watched, and not have left his house to be broken through. [40] Be ye also ready: for in an hour that ye think not the Son of man comes.

4. Faithfulness

Luke 12:41-48

[41] And Peter said, Lord, do you speak this parable unto us, or even unto all? [42] And the Lord said, Who then is the faithful and wise steward, whom his

lord shall set over his household, to give them their portion of food in due season? [43] Blessed is that servant, whom his lord when he comes shall find so doing. [44] Of a truth I say unto you, that he will set him over all that he has. [45] But if that servant shall say in his heart, My lord delays his coming; and shall begin to beat the menservants and the maidservants, and to eat and drink, and to be drunken; [46] the lord of that servant shall come in a day when he expects not, and in an hour when he knows not, and shall cut him asunder, and appoint his portion with the unfaithful. [47] And that servant, who knew his lord's will, and made not ready, nor did according to his will, shall be beaten with many <stripes>; [48] but he that knew not, and did things worthy of stripes, shall be beaten with few <stripes>. And to whomsoever much is given, of him shall much be required: and to whom they commit much, of him will they ask the more.

5. The Effects of His Coming

Luke 12:49-53

[49] I came to cast fire upon the earth; and what do I desire, if it is already kindled? [50] But I have a baptism to be baptized with; and how am I straitened till it be accomplished! [51] Think ye that I am come to give peace in the earth? I tell you, Nay; but rather division: [52] for there shall be from henceforth five in one house divided, three against two, and two against three. [53] They shall be divided, father against son, and son against father; mother against daughter, and daughter against her mother; mother in law against her daughter in law, and daughter in law against her mother in law.

6. The Signs of the Times

Luke 12:54-59

[54] And he said to the multitudes also, When ye see a cloud rising in the west, straightway ye say, There comes a shower; and so it comes to pass. [55] And when <ye see> a south wind blowing, ye say, There will be a scorching heat; and it comes to pass. [56] Ye hypocrites, ye know how to interpret the face of the earth and the heaven; but how is it that ye know not how to interpret this time? [57] And why even of yourselves judge ye not what is

right? [58] For as you are going with your adversary before the magistrate, on the way give diligence to be quit of him; lest haply he drag you unto the judge, and the judge shall deliver you to the officer, and the officer shall cast you into prison. [59] I say unto you, You shall by no means come out thence, till you have paid the very last mite.

7. Concerning Repentance

Luke 13:1-9

[1] Now there were some present at that very season who told him of the Galileans, whose blood Pilate had mingled with their sacrifices. [2] And he answered and said unto them, Think ye that these Galileans were sinners above all the Galileans, because they have suffered these things? [3] I tell you, Nay: but, except ye repent, ye shall all in like manner perish. [4] Or those eighteen, upon whom the tower in Shiloach fell, and killed them, think ye that they were offenders above all the men that dwell in Yerushalayim? [5] I tell you, Nay: but, except ye repent, ye shall all likewise perish. [6] And he spoke this parable; A certain man had a fig tree planted in his vineyard; and he came seeking fruit thereon, and found none. [7] And he said unto the vinedresser, Behold, these three years I come seeking fruit on this fig tree, and find none: cut it down; why does it also cumber the ground? [8] And he answering said unto him, Lord, let it alone this year also, till I shall dig about it, and dung it: [9] and if it bear fruit thenceforth, <well>; but if not, you shall cut it down.

8. Concerning Yisrael's Need

Luke 13:10-17

[10] And he was teaching in one of the synagogues on the Sabbath day. [11] And behold, a woman that had a spirit of infirmity eighteen years; and she was bowed together, and could in no wise lift herself up. [12] And when Yeshua saw her, he called her, and said to her, Woman, you are loosed from your infirmity. [13] And he laid his hands upon her: and immediately she was made straight, and glorified God. [14] And the ruler of the synagogue, being moved with indignation because Yeshua had healed on the Sabbath, an-

swered and said to the multitude, There are six days in which men ought to work: in them therefore come and be healed, and not on the day of the Sabbath. [15] But the Lord answered him, and said, Ye hypocrites, does not each one of you on the Sabbath loose his ox or his ass from the stall, and lead him away to watering? [16] And ought not this woman, being a daughter of Avraham, whom Satan had bound, lo, <these> eighteen years, to have been loosed from this bond on the day of the Sabbath? [17] And as he said these things, all his adversaries were put to shame: and all the multitude rejoiced for all the glorious things that were done by him.

9. Concerning the Kingdom Program

Luke 13:18-21

[18] He said therefore, Unto what is the kingdom of God like? And whereunto shall I liken it? [19] It is like unto a grain of mustard seed, which a man took, and cast into his own garden; and it grew, and became a tree; and the birds of the heaven lodged in the branches thereof. [20] And again he said, Whereunto shall I liken the kingdom of God? [21] It is like unto leaven, which a woman took and hid in three measures of meal, till it was all leavened.

[§ 112]—N. The Conflict at the Feast of Dedication

John 10:22-39

[22] And it was the feast of the dedication at Yerushalayim: [23] it was winter; and Yeshua was walking in the temple in Shlomoh's porch. [24] The Jews therefore came round about him, and said unto him, How long do you hold us in suspense? If you are the Messiah, tell us plainly. [25] Yeshua answered them, I told you, and ye believe not: the works that I do in my Father's name, these bear witness of me. [26] But ye believe not, because ye are not of my sheep. [27] My sheep hear my voice, and I know them, and they follow me: [28] and I give unto them eternal life; and they shall never perish, and no one shall snatch them out of my hand. [29] My Father, who has given <them> unto me, is greater than all; and no one is able to snatch <them> out of the Father's hand. [30] I and the Father are one. [31] The Jews took up stones again

to stone him. [32] Yeshua answered them, Many good works have I showed you from the Father; for which of those works do ye stone me? [33] The Jews answered him, For a good work we stone you not, but for blasphemy; and because that you, being a man, make yourself God. [34] Yeshua answered them, Is it not written in your law, I said, ye are gods? [35] If he called them gods, unto whom the word of God came (and the scripture cannot be broken), [36] say ye of him, whom the Father sanctified and sent into the world, You blaspheme; because I said, I am <the> Son of God? [37] If I do not the works of my Father, believe me not. [38] But if I do them, though ye believe not me, believe the works: that ye may know and understand that the Father is in me, and I in the Father. [39] They sought again to take him: and he went forth out of their hand.

VI. THE PREPARATION OF THE DISCIPLES BY THE KING
— §§ 113–131 —

[§ 113]—A. The Withdrawal from Yehudah

John 10:40-42

[40] And he went away again beyond the Yarden into the place where Yochanan was at the first baptizing; and there be abode. [41] And many came unto him; and they said, Yochanan indeed did no sign: but all things whatsoever Yochanan spoke of this man were true. [42] And many believed on him there.

[§ 114]—B. Instruction
Concerning Entrance into the Kingdom

Luke 13:22-35

[22] And he went on his way through cities and villages, teaching, and journeying on unto Yerushalayim. [23] And one said unto him, Lord, are they few that are saved? And he said unto them, [24] Strive to enter in by the narrow door: for many, I say unto you, shall seek to enter in, and shall not be able. [25] When once the master of the house is risen up, and has shut to the door, and ye begin to stand without, and to knock at the door, saying, Lord, open to us; and he shall answer and say to you, I know you not from where ye are; [26] then shall ye begin to say, We did eat and drink in your presence, and you did teach in our streets; [27] and he shall say, I tell you, I know not from where ye are; depart from me, all ye workers of iniquity. [28] There shall be the weeping and the gnashing of teeth, when ye shall see Avraham, and Yitzchak, and Yaakov, and all the prophets, in the kingdom of God, and yourselves cast forth without. [29] And they shall come from the east and west, and from the north and south, and shall sit down in the kingdom of God. [30] And behold, there are last who shall be first, and there are first who shall be last. [31] In that very hour there came certain Pharisees, saying to him, Get you out, and go hence: for Herod would fain kill you. [32] And he said unto them, Go and say to that fox, Behold, I cast out demons and perform cures today and tomorrow, and the third <day> I am perfected. [33] Nevertheless I must go on my way today and tomorrow and the <day> following: for it cannot be that a prophet perish out of Yerushalayim. [34] O Yerushalayim, Yerushalayim, that kills the prophets, and stones them that are sent unto her! How often would I have gathered your children together, even as a hen <gathers> her own brood under her wings, and ye would not! [35] Behold, your house is left unto you <desolate>: and I say unto you, Ye shall not see me, until ye shall say, Blessed is he that comes in the name of the Lord.

[§ 115]—C. Instruction in a Pharisee's House

1. True Sabbath Rest

Luke 14:1-6

[1] And it came to pass, when he went into the house of one of the rulers of the Pharisees on a Sabbath to eat bread, that they were watching him. [2] And behold, there was before him a certain man that had the dropsy. [3] And Yeshua answering spoke unto the lawyers and Pharisees, saying, Is it lawful to heal on the Sabbath, or not? [4] But they held their peace. And he took him, and healed him, and let him go. [5] And he said unto them, Which of you shall have an ass or an ox fallen into a well, and will not straightway draw him up on a Sabbath day? [6] And they could not answer again unto these things.

2. Humility

Luke 14:7-11

[7] And he spoke a parable unto those that were bidden, when he marked how they chose out the chief seats; saying unto them, [8] When you are bidden of any man to a marriage feast, sit not down in the chief seat; lest haply a more honorable man than you be bidden of him, [9] and he that bade you and him shall come and say to you, Give this man place; and then you shall begin with shame to take the lowest place. [10] But when you are bidden, go and sit down in the lowest place; that when he that has bidden you comes, he may say to you, Friend, go up higher: then shall you have glory in the presence of all that sit at meat with you. [11] For everyone that exalts himself shall be humbled; and he that humbles himself shall be exalted.

3. Respect of Persons

Luke 14:12-14

[12] And he said to him also that had bidden him, When you make a dinner or a supper, call not your friends, nor your brethren, nor your kinsmen, nor rich neighbors; lest haply they also bid you again, and a recompense be made to you. [13] But when you make a feast, bid the poor, the maimed, the lame, the blind: [14] and you shall be blessed; because they have not <wherewith> to recompense you: for you shall be recompensed in the resurrection of the just.

4. The Rejection of the Invitation

Luke 14:15-24

[15] And when one of them that sat at meat with him heard these things, he said unto him, Blessed is he that shall eat bread in the kingdom of God. [16] But he said unto him, A certain man made a great supper; and he bade many: [17] and he sent forth his servant at supper time to say to them that were bidden, Come; for <all> things are now ready. [18] And they all with one <consent> began to make excuse. The first said unto him, I have bought a field, and I must needs go out and see it; I pray you have me excused. [19] And another said, I have bought five yoke of oxen, and I go to prove them; I pray you have me excused. [20] And another said, I have married a wife, and therefore I cannot come. [21] And the servant came, and told his lord these things. Then the master of the house being angry said to his servant, Go out quickly into the streets and lanes of the city, and bring in here the poor and maimed and blind and lame. [22] And the servant said, Lord, what you did command is done, and yet there is room. [23] And the lord said unto the servant, Go out into the highways and hedges, and constrain <them> to come in, that my house may be filled. [24] For I say unto you, that none of those men that were bidden shall taste of my supper.

[§ 116]—D. Instruction Concerning Discipleship

Luke 14:25-35

[25] Now there went with him great multitudes: and he turned, and said unto them, [26] If any man comes unto me, and hates not his own father, and mother, and wife, and children, and brethren, and sisters, yea, and his own life also, he cannot be my disciple. [27] Whosoever does not bear his own cross, and come after me, cannot be my disciple. [28] For which of you, desiring to build a tower, does not first sit down and count the cost, whether he have <wherewith> to complete it? [29] Lest haply, when he has laid a foundation, and is not able to finish, all that behold begin to mock him, [30] saying, This man began to build, and was not able to finish. [31] Or what king, as he goes to encounter another king in war, will not sit down first and take counsel whether he is able with ten thousand to meet him that comes against him with twenty thousand? [32] Or else, while the other is yet a great way off, he sends an ambassage, and asks for conditions of peace. [33] So therefore whosoever he be of you that renounces not all that he has, he cannot be my disciple. [34] Salt therefore is good: but if even the salt have lost its savor, wherewith shall it be seasoned? [35] It is fit neither for the land nor for the dunghill: <men> cast it out. He that has ears to hear, let him hear.

[§ 117]—E. Instruction Concerning God's Attitude towards Sinners

1. The Occasion

Luke 15:1-2

[1] Now all the publicans and sinners were drawing near unto him to hear him. [2] And both the Pharisees and the scribes murmured, saying, This man receives sinners, and eats with them.

2. The Three Parables

a. The Parable of the Lost Sheep

Luke 15:3-7

[3] And he spoke unto them this parable, saying, [4] What man of you, having a hundred sheep, and having lost one of them, does not leave the ninety and nine in the wilderness, and go after that which is lost, until he find it? [5] And when he has found it, he lays it on his shoulders, rejoicing. [6] And when he comes home, he calls together his friends and his neighbors, saying unto them, Rejoice with me, for I have found my sheep which was lost. [7] I say unto you, that even so there shall be joy in heaven over one sinner that repents, <more> than over ninety and nine righteous persons, who need no repentance.

b. The Parable of the Lost Coin

Luke 15:8-10

[8] Or what woman having ten pieces of silver, if she lose one piece, does not light a lamp, and sweep the house, and seek diligently until she find it? [9] And when she has found it, she calls together her friends and neighbors, saying, Rejoice with me, for I have found the piece which I had lost. [10] Even so, I say unto you, there is joy in the presence of the angels of God over one sinner that repents.

c. The Parable of the Prodigal Son

Luke 15:11-32

[11] And he said, A certain man had two sons: [12] and the younger of them said to his father, Father, give me the portion of <your> substance that falls to me. And he divided unto them his living. [13] And not many days after, the younger son gathered all together and took his journey into a far country; and there he wasted his substance with riotous living. [14] And when he had spent all, there arose a mighty famine in that country; and he began to be in

want. [15] And he went and joined himself to one of the citizens of that country; and he sent him into his fields to feed swine. [16] And he would fain have filled his belly with the husks that the swine did eat: and no man gave unto him. [17] But when he came to himself he said, How many hired servants of my father's have bread enough and to spare, and I perish here with hunger! [18] I will arise and go to my father, and will say unto him, Father, I have sinned against heaven, and in your sight: [19] I am no more worthy to be called your son: make me as one of your hired servants. [20] And he arose, and came to his father. But while he was yet afar off, his father saw him, and was moved with compassion, and ran, and fell on his neck, and kissed him. [21] And the son said unto him, Father, I have sinned against heaven, and in your sight: I am no more worthy to be called your son. [22] But the father said to his servants, Bring forth quickly the best robe, and put it on him; and put a ring on his hand, and shoes on his feet: [23] and bring the fatted calf, <and> kill it, and let us eat, and make merry: [24] for this my son was dead, and is alive again; he was lost, and is found. And they began to be merry. [25] Now his elder son was in the field: and as he came and drew near to the house, he heard music and dancing. [26] And he called to him one of the servants, and inquired what these things might be. [27] And he said unto him, Your brother is come; and your father has killed the fatted calf, because he has received him safe and sound. [28] But he was angry, and would not go in: and his father came out, and entreated him. [29] But he answered and said to his father, Lo, these many years do I serve you, and I never transgressed a commandment of yours; and <yet> you never gave me a kid, that I might make merry with my friends: [30] but when this your son came, who has devoured your living with harlots, you killed for him the fatted calf. [31] And he said unto him, Son, you are ever with me, and all that is mine is yours. [32] But it was meet to make merry and be glad: for this your brother was dead, and is alive <again>; and <was> lost, and is found.

[§ 118]—F. Instruction Concerning Wealth

1. The Parable of the Unjust Steward

Luke 16:1-13

[1] And he said also unto the disciples, There was a certain rich man, who had a steward; and the same was accused unto him that he was wasting his goods. [2] And he called him, and said unto him, What is this that I hear of you? Render the account of your stewardship; for you can be no longer steward. [3] And the steward said within himself, What shall I do, seeing that my lord takes away the stewardship from me? I have not strength to dig; to beg I am ashamed. [4] I am resolved what to do, that, when I am put out of the stewardship, they may receive me into their houses. [5] And calling to him each one of his lord's debtors, he said to the first, How much do you owe unto my lord? [6] And he said, A hundred measures of oil. And he said unto him, Take your bond, and sit down quickly and write fifty. [7] Then said he to another, And how much do you owe? And he said, A hundred measures of wheat. He said unto him, Take your bond, and write eighty. [8] And his lord commended the unrighteous steward because he had done wisely: for the sons of this world are for their own generation wiser than the sons of the light. [9] And I say unto you, Make to yourselves friends by means of the mammon of unrighteousness; that, when it shall fail, they may receive you into the eternal tabernacles. [10] He that is faithful in a very little is faithful also in much: and he that is unrighteous in a very little is unrighteous also in much. [11] If therefore ye have not been faithful in the unrighteous mammon, who will commit to your trust the true <riches>? [12] And if ye have not been faithful in that which is another's, who will give you that which is your own? [13] No servant can serve two masters: for either he will hate the one, and love the other; or else he will hold to one, and despise the other. Ye cannot serve God and mammon.

2. The Conflict with the Pharisees

Luke 16:14-18

[14] And the Pharisees, who were lovers of money, heard all these things; and they scoffed at him. [15] And he said unto them, Ye are they that justify yourselves in the sight of men; but God knows your hearts: for that which is exalted among men is an abomination in the sight of God. [16] The law and the prophets <were> until Yochanan: from that time the gospel of the kingdom of God is preached, and every man enters violently into it. [17] But it is easier for heaven and earth to pass away, than for one tittle of the law to fall. [18] Everyone that puts away his wife, and marries another, commits adultery: and he that marries one that is put away from a husband commits adultery.

3. The Story of the Rich Man and Elazar

Luke 16:19-31

[19] Now there was a certain rich man, and he was clothed in purple and fine linen, faring sumptuously every day: [20] and a certain beggar named Elazar was laid at his gate, full of sores, [21] and desiring to be fed with the <crumbs> that fell from the rich man's table; yea, even the dogs come and licked his sores. [22] And it came to pass, that the beggar died, and that he was carried away by the angels into Avraham's bosom: and the rich man also died, and was buried. [23] And in Hades he lifted up his eyes, being in torments, and sees Avraham afar off, and Elazar in his bosom. [24] And he cried and said, Father Avraham, have mercy on me, and send Elazar, that he may dip the tip of his finger in water, and cool my tongue; for I am in anguish in this flame. [25] But Avraham said, Son, remember that you in your lifetime received your good things, and Elazar in like manner evil things: but now here he is comforted and you are in anguish. [26] And besides all this, between us and you there is a great gulf fixed, that they that would pass from hence to you may not be able, and that none may cross over from thence to us. [27] And he said, I pray you therefore, father, that you would send him to my father's house; [28] for I have five brethren; that he may testify unto them, lest they also come into this place of torment. [29] But Avraham said, They

have Mosheh and the prophets; let them hear them. [30] And he said, Nay, father Avraham: but if one go to them from the dead, they will repent. [31] And he said unto him, If they hear not Mosheh and the prophets, neither will they be persuaded, if one rise from the dead.

[§ 119]—G. Instruction Concerning Forgiveness

Luke 17:1-4

[1] And he said unto his disciples, It is impossible but that occasions of stumbling should come; but woe unto him, through whom they come! [2] It were well for him if a millstone were hanged about his neck, and he were thrown into the sea, rather than that he should cause one of these little ones to stumble. [3] Take heed to yourselves: if your brother sin, rebuke him; and if he repent, forgive him. [4] And if he sin against you seven times in the day, and seven times turn again to you, saying, I repent; you shall forgive him.

[§ 120]—H. Instruction Concerning Service

Luke 17:5-10

[5] And the apostles said unto the Lord, Increase our faith. [6] And the Lord said, If ye had faith as a grain of mustard seed, ye would say unto this sycamine tree, Be you rooted up, and be you planted in the sea; and it would obey you. [7] But who is there of you, having a servant plowing or keeping sheep, that will say unto him, when he is come in from the field, Come straightway and sit down to meat; [8] and will not rather say unto him, Make ready wherewith I may sup, and gird yourself, and serve me, till I have eaten and drunken; and afterward you shall eat and drink? [9] Does he thank the servant because he did the things that were commanded? [10] Even so ye also, when ye shall have done all the things that are commanded you, say, We are unprofitable servants; we have done that which it was our duty to do.

[§§ 121–123]—I. The Resurrection of Elazar: The First Sign of Yonah

[§ 121]—1. The Sign of Resurrection

a. The Death of Elazar

John 11:1-16

[1] Now a certain man was sick, Elazar of Beit Anyah, of the village of Miriam and her sister Marta. [2] And it was that Miriam who anointed the Lord with ointment, and wiped his feet with her hair, whose brother Elazar was sick. [3] The sisters therefore sent unto him, saying, Lord, behold, he whom you love is sick. [4] But when Yeshua heard it, he said, This sickness is not unto death, but for the glory of God, that the Son of God may be glorified thereby. [5] Now Yeshua loved Marta, and her sister, and Elazar. [6] When therefore he heard that he was sick, he abode at that time two days in the place where he was. [7] Then after this he said to the disciples, Let us go into Yehudah again. [8] The disciples say unto him, Rabbi, the Jews were but now seeking to stone you; and go you thither again? [9] Yeshua answered, Are there not twelve hours in the day? If a man walk in the day, he stumbles not, because he sees the light of this world. [10] But if a man walk in the night, he stumbles, because the light is not in him. [11] These things spoke he: and after this he said unto them, Our friend Elazar is fallen asleep; but I go, that I may awake him out of sleep. [12] The disciples therefore said unto him, Lord, if he is fallen asleep, he will recover. [13] Now Yeshua had spoken of his death: but they thought that he spoke of taking rest in sleep. [14] Then Yeshua therefore said unto them plainly, Elazar is dead. [15] And I am glad for your sakes that I was not there, to the intent ye may believe; nevertheless let us go unto him. [16] Toma therefore, who is called Didymos, said unto his fellow-disciples, Let us also go, that we may die with him.

b. Yeshua and Marta

John 11:17-27

[17] So when Yeshua came, he found that he had been in the tomb four days already. [18] Now Beit Anyah was near unto Yerushalayim, about fifteen furlongs off; [19] and many of the Jews had come to Marta and Miriam, to console them concerning their brother. [20] Marta therefore, when she heard that Yeshua was coming, went and met him: but Miriam still sat in the house. [21] Marta therefore said unto Yeshua, Lord, if you had been here, my brother had not died. [22] And even now I know that, whatsoever you shall ask of God, God will give you. [23] Yeshua said unto her, Your brother shall rise again. [24] Marta said unto him, I know that he shall rise again in the resurrection at the last day. [25] Yeshua said unto her, I am the resurrection, and the life: he that believes on me, though he die, yet shall he live; [26] and whosoever lives and believes on me shall never die. Do you believe this? [27] She said unto him, Yea, Lord: I have believed that you are the Messiah, the Son of God, <even> he that comes into the world.

c. Yeshua and Miriam

John 11:28-32

[28] And when she had said this, she went away, and called Miriam her sister secretly, saying, The Teacher is here, and calls you. [29] And she, when she heard it, arose quickly, and went unto him. [30] (Now Yeshua was not yet come into the village, but was still in the place where Marta met him.) [31] The Jews then who were with her in the house, and were consoling her, when they saw Miriam, that she rose up quickly and went out, followed her, supposing that she was going unto the tomb to weep[1] there. [32] Miriam therefore, when she came where Yeshua was, and saw him, fell down at his feet, saying unto him, Lord, if you had been here, my brother had not died.

---

[1] Greek: *wail.*

d. Yeshua and Elazar

John 11:33-44

[33] When Yeshua therefore saw her weeping, and the Jews <also> weeping[2] who came with her, he groaned in the spirit[3], and was troubled, [34] and said, Where have ye laid him? They say unto him, Lord, come and see. [35] Yeshua wept. [36] The Jews therefore said, Behold how he loved him! [37] But some of them said, Could not this man, who opened the eyes of him that was blind, have caused that this man also should not die? [38] Yeshua therefore again groaning in himself[4] comes to the tomb. Now it was a cave, and a stone lay against it. [39] Yeshua said, Take ye away the stone. Marta, the sister of him that was dead, said unto him, Lord, by this time the body stinks; for he has been <dead> four days. [40] Yeshua said unto her, Said I not unto you, that, if you believe, you should see the glory of God? [41] So they took away the stone. And Yeshua lifted up his eyes, and said, Father, I thank you that you heard me. [42] And I knew that you hear me always: but because of the multitude that stands around I said it, that they may believe that you did send me. [43] And when he had thus spoken, he cried with a loud voice, Elazar, come forth. [44] He that was dead came forth, bound hand and foot with grave-clothes[5]; and his face was bound about with a napkin. Yeshua said unto them, Loose him, and let him go.

[§ 122]—2. The Rejection of the First Sign of Yonah

John 11:45-54

[45] Many therefore of the Jews, who came to Miriam and beheld that which he did, believed on him. [46] But some of them went away to the Pharisees, and told them the things which Yeshua had done. [47] The chief priests therefore and the Pharisees gathered a council, and said, What do we? For

---

[2] Greek: *wailing.*

[3] Or, *was moved with indignation in the spirit.*

[4] Or, *being moved with indignation in himself.*

[5] Or, *grave-bands.*

this man does many signs. [48] If we let him thus alone, all men will believe on him: and the Romans will come and take away both our place and our nation. [49] But a certain one of them, Kayapha, being high priest that year, said unto them, Ye know nothing at all, [50] nor do ye take account that it is expedient for you that one man should die for the people, and that the whole nation perish not. [51] Now this he said not of himself: but, being high priest that year, he prophesied that Yeshua should die for the nation; [52] and not for the nation only, but that he might also gather together into one the children of God that are scattered abroad. [53] So from that day forth they took counsel that they might put him to death.

[54] Yeshua therefore walked no more openly among the Jews, but departed thence into the country near to the wilderness, into a city called Ephraim; and there he tarried with the disciples.

[§ 123]—3. Instruction in Light of Rejection

a. The Personal Witness to Kayapha

Luke 17:11-19

[11] And it came to pass, as they were on their way to Yerushalayim, that he was passing along the borders of Shomron and Galil. [12] And as he entered into a certain village, there met him ten men that were lepers, who stood afar off: [13] and they lifted up their voices, saying, Yeshua, Master, have mercy on us. [14] And when he saw them, he said unto them, Go and show yourselves unto the priests. And it came to pass, as they went, they were cleansed. [15] And one of them, when he saw that he was healed, turned back, with a loud voice glorifying God; [16] and he fell upon his face at his feet, giving him thanks: and he was a Samaritan. [17] And Yeshua answering said, Were not the ten cleansed? But where are the nine? [18] Were there none found that returned to give glory to God, save this stranger? [19] And he said unto him, Arise, and go your way: your faith has made you whole.

b. The New Form of the Kingdom Program

Luke 17:20-21

[20] And being asked by the Pharisees, when the kingdom of God comes, he answered them and said, The kingdom of God comes not with observation: [21] neither shall they say, Lo, here! Or, There! For lo, the kingdom of God is within you.

c. Instruction Concerning the Second Coming

Luke 17:22-37

[22] And he said unto the disciples, The days will come, when ye shall desire to see one of the days of the Son of man, and ye shall not see it. [23] And they shall say to you, Lo, there! Lo, here! Go not away, nor follow after <them>: [24] for as the lightning, when it lightens out of the one part under the heaven, shines unto the other part under heaven; so shall the Son of man be in his day. [25] But first must he suffer many things and be rejected of this generation. [26] And as it came to pass in the days of Noach, even so shall it be also in the days of the Son of man. [27] They ate, they drank, they married, they were given in marriage, until the day that Noach entered into the ark, and the flood came, and destroyed them all. [28] Likewise even as it came to pass in the days of Lot; they ate, they drank, they bought, they sold, they planted, they built; [29] but in the day that Lot went out from Sedom it rained fire and brimstone from heaven, and destroyed them all: [30] after the same manner shall it be in the day that the Son of man is revealed. [31] In that day, he that shall be on the housetop, and his goods in the house, let him not go down to take them away: and let him that is in the field likewise not return back. [32] Remember Lot's wife. [33] Whosoever shall seek to gain his life shall lose it: but whosoever shall lose <his life> shall preserve it. [34] I say unto you, In that night there shall be two men on one bed; the one shall be taken, and the other shall be left. [35] There shall be two women grinding together; the one shall be taken, and the other shall be left.[6] [37] And they answering say

---

[6] Some ancient authorities add verse 36: "There shall be two men in the field; the one shall be taken, and the other shall be left."

unto him, Where, Lord? And he said unto them, Where the body <is>, thither will the eagles also be gathered together.

[§ 124]—J. Instruction in Prayer

Luke 18:1-14

[1] And he spoke a parable unto them to the end that they ought always to pray, and not to faint; [2] saying, There was in a city a judge, who feared not God, and regarded not man: [3] and there was a widow in that city; and she came often unto him, saying, Avenge me of mine adversary. [4] And he would not for a while: but afterward he said within himself, Though I fear not God, nor regard man; [5] yet because this widow troubles me, I will avenge her, lest she wear me out by her continual coming. [6] And the Lord said, Hear what the unrighteous judge said. [7] And shall not God avenge his elect, that cry to him day and night, and <yet> he is longsuffering over them? [8] I say unto you, that he will avenge them speedily. Nevertheless, when the Son of man comes, shall he find faith on the earth?

[9] And he spoke also this parable unto certain who trusted in themselves that they were righteous, and set all others at nought: [10] Two men went up into the temple to pray; the one a Pharisee, and the other a publican. [11] The Pharisee stood and prayed thus with himself, God, I thank you, that I am not as the rest of men, extortioners, unjust, adulterers, or even as this publican. [12] I fast twice in the week; I give tithes of all that I get. [13] But the publican, standing afar off, would not lift up so much as his eyes unto heaven, but smote his breast, saying, God, be merciful[7] to me a sinner. [14] I say unto you, This man went down to his house justified rather than the other: for every-one that exalts himself shall be humbled; but he that humbles himself shall be exalted.

---

[7] Or, *be propitious.*

[§ 125]—K. Instruction on Divorce

Matthew 19:1-12

1 And it came to pass when Yeshua had finished these words, he departed from Galil, and came into the borders of Yehudah beyond the Yarden; 2 and great multitudes followed him; and he healed them there.

3 And there came unto him Pharisees, trying him, and saying, Is it lawful <for a man> to put away his wife for every cause? 4 And he answered and said, Have ye not read,

that he who made <them> from the beginning made them male and female, 5 and said, For this cause shall a man leave his father and mother, and shall cleave to his wife; and the two shall become one flesh? 6 So that they are no more two, but one flesh. What therefore God has joined together, let not man put asunder.

7 They say unto him, Why then did Mosheh command to give a bill of divorcement, and to put <her>

Mark 10:1-12

1 And he arose from thence and came into the borders of Yehudah and beyond the Yarden: and multitudes come together unto him again; and, as he was wont, he taught them again.

2 And there came unto him Pharisees, and asked him, Is it lawful for a man to put away <his> wife? Trying him.

3 And he answered and said unto them, What did Mosheh command you? 4 And they said, Mosheh suffered to write a bill of divorcement, and to put her away. 5 But Yeshua said unto them, For your hardness of heart he wrote you this commandment.

6 But from the beginning of the creation, Male and female made he them. 7 For this cause shall a man leave his father and mother, and shall cleave to his wife; 8 and the two shall become one flesh: so that they are no more two, but one flesh. 9 What therefore God has joined together, let not man put asunder.

away? [8] He said unto them, Mosheh for your hardness of heart suffered you to put away your wives: but from the beginning it has not been so.

[9] And I say unto you,

Whosoever shall put away his wife, except for fornication, and shall marry another, commits adultery: and he that marries her when she is put away commits adultery.

[10] The disciples say unto him, If the case of the man is so with his wife, it is not expedient to marry. [11] But he said unto them, Not all men can receive this saying, but they to whom it is given. [12] For there are eunuchs, that were so born from their mother's womb: and there are eunuchs, that were made eunuchs by men: and there are eunuchs, that made themselves eunuchs for the kingdom of heaven's sake. He that is able to receive it, let him receive it.

[10] And in the house the disciples asked him again of this matter.

[11] And he said unto them,

Whosoever shall put away his wife, and marry another, commits adultery against her: [12] and if she herself shall put away her husband, and marry another, she commits adultery.

[§ 126]—

L. Instruction on Entrance into the Kingdom

Matthew 19:13-15	Mark 10:13-16	Luke 18:15-17
[13] Then were there brought unto him little children, that he should lay his hands on them, and pray: and	[13] And they were bringing unto him little children, that he should touch them: and the disciples re-	[15] And they were bringing unto him also their babes, that he should touch them: but when the disciples saw

the disciples rebuked them. [14] But Yeshua said,

buked them. [14] But when Yeshua saw it, he was moved with indignation, and said unto them,

it, they rebuked them. [16] But Yeshua called them unto him, saying,

Suffer the little children, and forbid them not, to come unto me: for to such belongs the kingdom of heaven.

Suffer the little children to come unto me; forbid them not: for to such belongs the kingdom of God. [15] Verily I say unto you, Whosoever shall not receive the kingdom of God as a little child, he shall in no wise enter therein.

Suffer the little children to come unto me, and forbid them not: for to such belongs the kingdom of God. [17] Verily I say unto you, Whosoever shall not receive the kingdom of God as a little child, he shall in no wise enter therein.

[15] And he laid his hands on them, and departed thence.

[16] And he took them in his arms, and blessed them, laying his hands upon them.

[§ 127]—M. Instruction on Eternal Life

Mt. 19:16-20:16	Mark 10:17-31	Luke 18:18-30
[16] And behold, one came to him and said,	[17] And as he was going forth into the way, there ran one to him, and kneeled to him, and asked him,	[18] And a certain ruler asked him, saying,
Teacher, what good thing shall I do, that I may have eternal life? [17] And he said unto him, Why do you ask me concerning that	Good Teacher, what shall I do that I may inherit eternal life? [18] And Yeshua said unto him, Why do you call me good? None is	Good Teacher, what shall I do to inherit eternal life? [19] And Yeshua said unto him, Why do you call me good? None is

which is good? One there is who is good: but if you would enter into life, keep the commandments. [18] He said unto him, Which? And Yeshua said, You shall not kill, You shall not commit adultery, You shall not steal, You shall not bear false witness, [19] Honor your father and mother; and, You shall love your neighbor as yourself.

[20] The young man said unto him, All these things have I observed: what lack I yet?

[21] Yeshua said unto him,

If you would be perfect, go, sell that which you have, and give to the poor, and you shall have treasure in heaven: and come, follow me.

[22] But when the young man heard the saying, he went away sorrowful; for he was one that had great possessions. [23] And Yeshua said unto his disciples,

good save one, <even> God.

[19] You know the commandments, Do not kill, Do not commit adultery, Do not steal, Do not bear false witness, Do not defraud, Honor your father and mother.

[20] And he said unto him, Teacher, all these things have I observed from my youth.

And Yeshua looking upon him loved him, and said unto him,

One thing you lack: go, sell whatsoever you have, and give to the poor, and you shall have treasure in heaven: and come, follow me.

[22] But his countenance fell at the saying, and he went away sorrowful: for he was one that had great possessions. [23] And Yeshua looked round about,

good, save one, <even> God.

[20] You know the commandments, Do not commit adultery, Do not kill, Do not steal, Do not bear false witness, Honor your father and mother.

[21] And he said, All these things have I observed from my youth up.

[22] And when Yeshua heard it, he said unto him,

One thing you lack yet: sell all that you have, and distribute unto the poor, and you shall have treasure in heaven: and come, follow me.

[23] But when he heard these things, he became exceeding sorrowful; for he was very rich.

[24] And Yeshua seeing him said, How hardly

Verily I say unto you, It is hard for a rich man to enter into the kingdom of heaven.

[24] And again I say unto you, It is easier for a camel to go through a needle's eye, than for a rich man to enter into the kingdom of God. [25] And when the disciples heard it, they were astonished exceedingly, saying, Who then can be saved? [26] And Yeshua looking upon <them> said to them, With men this is impossible; but with God all things are possible. [27] Then answered Peter and said unto him, Lo, we have left all, and followed you; what then shall we have? [28] And Yeshua said unto them, Verily I say

and said unto his disciples, How hardly shall they that have riches enter into the kingdom of God! [24] And the disciples were amazed at his words. But Yeshua answered again, and said unto them, Children, how hard is it for them that trust in riches to enter into the kingdom of God! [25] It is easier for a camel to go through a needle's eye, than for a rich man to enter into the kingdom of God. [26] And they were astonished exceedingly, saying unto him, Then who can be saved? [27] Yeshua looking upon them said, With men it is impossible, but not with God: for all things are possible with God. [28] Peter began to say unto him, Lo, we have left all, and have followed you. [29] Yeshua said, Verily I say unto you, There is

shall they that have riches enter into the kingdom of God!

[25] For it is easier for a camel to enter in through a needle's eye, than for a rich man to enter into the kingdom of God. [26] And they that heard it said, Then who can be saved? [27] But he said, The things which are impossible with men are possible with God. [28] And Peter said, Lo, we have left our own, and followed you.

[9] And he said unto them, Verily I say unto

unto you, that ye who have followed me, in the regeneration when the Son of man shall sit on the throne of his glory, ye also shall sit upon twelve thrones, judging the twelve tribes of Yisrael. [29] And everyone that has left houses, or brethren, or sisters, or father, or mother, or children, or lands, for my name's sake, shall receive a hundredfold, and shall inherit eternal life. [30] But many shall be last <that are> first; and first <that are> last.

no man that has left house, or brethren, or sisters, or mother, or father, or children, or lands, for my sake, and for the gospel's sake, [30] but he shall receive a hundredfold now in this time, houses, and brethren, and sisters, and mothers, and children, and lands, with persecutions; and in the world to come eternal life. [31] But many <that are> first shall be last; and the last first.

you, There is no man that has left house, or wife, or brethren, or parents, or children, for the kingdom of God's sake, [30] who shall not receive manifold more in this time, and in the world to come eternal life.

Mt. cont.: [20:1] For the kingdom of heaven is like unto a man that was a householder, who went out early in the morning to hire laborers into his vineyard. [2] And when he had agreed with the laborers for a shilling a day, he sent them into his vineyard. [3] And he went out about the third hour, and saw others standing in the marketplace idle; [4] and to them he said, Go ye also into the vineyard, and whatsoever is right I will give you. And they went their way. [5] Again he went out about the sixth and the ninth hour, and did likewise. [6] And about the eleventh <hour> he went out, and found others standing; and he said unto them, Why stand ye here all the day idle? [7] They say unto him, Because no man has hired us. He said unto them, Go ye also into the vineyard. [8] And when even was come, the lord of the vineyard said unto his steward, Call the laborers, and pay them their hire, beginning from the last unto the first. [9] And when they came that <were hired> about the eleventh hour, they received every man a shilling. [10] And when the first came, they supposed that they would receive more; and they likewise received every man a shilling. [11] And when they received it, they murmured against the householder, [12] saying, These last have spent <but> one hour, and you have made them equal unto us, who have borne the burden of the day and the scorching heat. [13] But he answered and said to one of them, Friend, I do you no wrong: did you not agree with me for a shilling? [14] Take up that which is yours, and go your way; it is my will to give unto this last, even as unto you. [15] Is it not lawful for me to do what I will with mine own? Or is your eye evil, because I am good? [16] So the last shall be first, and the first last.

[§ 128]—N. Instruction Concerning His Death

Matthew 20:17-28	Mark 10:32-45	Luke 18:31-34
[17] And as Yeshua was going up to Yerushalayim,	[32] And they were on the way, going up to Yerushalayim; and Yeshua was going before them: and they were amazed; and they that followed were afraid.	
he took the twelve disciples apart, and on the way he said unto them,	And he took again the twelve, and began to tell them the things that were to happen unto him, [33] <saying>,	[31] And he took unto him the twelve, and said unto them,
[18] Behold, we go up to Yerushalayim; and the Son of man shall be delivered unto the chief priests and scribes; and they shall condemn him to death, [19] and shall deliver him	Behold, we go up to Yerushalayim; and the Son of man shall be delivered unto the chief priests and scribes; and they shall condemn him to death, and shall deliver him	Behold, we go up to Yerushalayim, and all the things that are written through the prophets shall be accomplished unto the Son of man. [32] For he shall be delivered up

unto the Gentiles to mock, and to scourge, and to crucify: and the third day he shall be raised up.	unto the Gentiles: [34] and they shall mock him, and shall spit upon him, and shall scourge him, and shall kill him; and after three days he shall rise again.	unto the Gentiles, and shall be mocked, and shamefully treated, and spit upon: [33] and they shall scourge and kill him: and the third day he shall rise again. [34] And they understood none of these things; and this saying was hid from them, and they perceived not the things that were said.

Mt. cont.: [20] Then came to him the mother of the sons of Zavdi with her sons, worshipping \<him>, and asking a certain thing of him.	**Mk. cont.:** [35] And there come near unto him Yaakov and Yochanan, the sons of Zavdi, saying unto him, Teacher, we would that you should do for us whatsoever we shall ask of you.
[21] And he said unto her, What would you? She said unto him, Command that these my two sons may sit, one on your right hand, and one on your left hand, in your kingdom. [22] But Yeshua answered and said, Ye know not what ye ask. Are ye able to drink the cup that I am about to drink?	[36] And he said unto them, What would ye that I should do for you? [37] And they said unto him, Grant unto us that we may sit, one on your right hand, and one on \<your> left hand, in your glory. [38] But Yeshua said unto them, Ye know not what ye ask. Are ye able to drink the cup that I drink? Or to be baptized with the baptism that I am baptized with?
They say unto him, We are able. [23] He said unto them, My cup indeed ye shall drink:	[39] And they said unto him, We are able. And Yeshua said unto them, The cup that I drink ye shall drink; and with the baptism that I am baptized withal shall ye be baptized:

but to sit on my right hand, and on <my> left hand, is not mine to give; but <it is for them> for whom it has been prepared of my Father. [24] And when the ten heard it, they were moved with indignation concerning the two brethren. [25] But Yeshua called them unto him, and said, Ye know that the rulers of the Gentiles lord it over them, and their great ones exercise authority over them. [26] Not so shall it be among you: but whosoever would become great among you shall be your minister; [27] and whosoever would be first among you shall be your servant: [28] even as the Son of man came not to be ministered unto, but to minister, and to give his life a ransom for many.

[40] but to sit on my right hand or on <my> left hand is not mine to give; but <it is for them> for whom it has been prepared. [41] And when the ten heard it, they began to be moved with indignation concerning Yaakov and Yochanan. [42] And Yeshua called them to him, and said unto them, Ye know that they who are accounted to rule over the Gentiles lord it over them; and their great ones exercise authority over them. [43] But it is not so among you: but whosoever would become great among you, shall be your minister; [44] and whosoever would be first among you, shall be servant of all. [45] For the Son of man also came not to be ministered unto, but to minister, and to give his life a ransom for many.

[§ 129]—O. The Healing of the Blind Men

Matthew 20:29-34	Mark 10:46-52	Luke 18:35-43
[29] And as they went out from Yericho, a great multitude followed him. [30] And behold, two blind men sitting by the way side,	[46] And they come to Yericho: and as he went out from Yericho, with his disciples and a great multitude, the son of Timai, Bartimai, a blind beggar, was sitting by the way side.	[35] And it came to pass, as he drew near unto Yericho, a certain blind man sat by the way side begging: [36] and hearing a multitude going by, he inquired what this meant.
when they heard that Yeshua was passing by,	[47] And when he heard that it was Yeshua the	[37] And they told him that Yeshua of Natze-

cried out, saying, Lord, have mercy on us, you son of David.

31 And the multitude rebuked them, that they should hold their peace: but they cried out the more, saying, Lord, have mercy on us, you son of David. 32 And Yeshua stood still, and called them,

and said,

What will ye that I should do unto you? 33 They say unto him, Lord, that our eyes may be opened.

34 And Yeshua, being moved with compassion, touched their eyes; and straightway they received their sight, and followed him.

Nazarene, he began to cry out, and say, Yeshua, you son of David, have mercy on me. 48 And many rebuked him, that he should hold his peace: but he cried out the more a great deal, You son of David, have mercy on me. 49 And Yeshua stood still, and said, Call ye him. And they call the blind man, saying unto him, Be of good cheer: rise, he calls you. 50 And he, casting away his garment, sprang up, and came to Yeshua. 51 And Yeshua answered him, and said, What will you that I should do unto you? And the blind man said unto him, Rabboni, that I may receive my sight. 52 And Yeshua said unto him, Go your way; your faith has made you whole. And straightway he received his sight, and followed him in the way.

ret passes by. 38 And he cried, saying, Yeshua, you son of David, have mercy on me. 39 And they that went before rebuked him, that he should hold his peace: but he cried out the more a great deal, You son of David, have mercy on me. 40 And Yeshua stood, and commanded him to be brought unto him: and when he was come near,

he asked him,

41 What will you that I should do unto you? And he said, Lord, that I may receive my sight.

42 And Yeshua said unto him, Receive your sight; your faith has made you whole. 43 And immediately he received his sight, and followed him, glorifying God: and all the people, when they saw

it, gave praise unto God.

[§§ 130-131]—
P. Instruction Concerning the Kingdom Program

[§ 130]—1. Personal Faith

Luke 19:1-10

[1] And he entered and was passing through Yericho. [2] And behold, a man called by name Zakkai; and he was a chief publican, and he was rich. [3] And he sought to see Yeshua who he was; and could not for the crowd, because he was little of stature. [4] And he ran on before, and climbed up into a sycamore tree to see him: for he was to pass that way. [5] And when Yeshua came to the place, he looked up, and said unto him, Zakkai, make haste, and come down; for today I must abide at your house. [6] And he made haste, and came down, and received him joyfully. [7] And when they saw it, they all murmured, saying, He is gone in to lodge with a man that is a sinner. [8] And Zakkai stood, and said unto the Lord, Behold, Lord, the half of my goods I give to the poor; and if I have wrongfully exacted anything of any man, I restore fourfold. [9] And Yeshua said unto him, Today is salvation come to this house, forasmuch as he also is a son of Avraham. [10] For the Son of man came to seek and to save that which was lost.

[§ 131]—2. Postponed Kingdom

Luke 19:11-28

[11] And as they heard these things, he added and spoke a parable, because he was near to Yerushalayim, and <because> they supposed that the kingdom of God was immediately to appear. [12] He said therefore, A certain nobleman went into a far country, to receive for himself a kingdom, and to

return. [13] And he called ten servants of his, and gave them ten pounds[8], and said unto them, Trade ye <herewith> till I come. [14] But his citizens hated him, and sent an ambassage after him, saying, We will not that this man reign over us. [15] And it came to pass, when he was come back again, having received the kingdom, that he commanded these servants, unto whom he had given the money, to be called to him, that he might know what they had gained by trading. [16] And the first came before him, saying, Lord, your pound has made ten pounds more. [17] And he said unto him, Well done, you good servant: because you were found faithful in a very little, you have authority over ten cities. [18] And the second came, saying, Your pound, Lord, has made five pounds. [19] And he said unto him also, Be you also over five cities. [20] And another came, saying, Lord, behold, <here is> your pound, which I kept laid up in a napkin: [21] for I feared you, because you are an austere man: you take up that which you laid not down, and reap that which you did not sow. [22] He said unto him, Out of your own mouth will I judge you, you wicked servant. You knew that I am an austere man, taking up that which I laid not down, and reaping that which I did not sow; [23] then wherefore gave you not my money into the bank, and I at my coming should have required it with interest? [24] And he said unto them that stood by, Take away from him the pound, and give it unto him that has the ten pounds. [25] And they said unto him, Lord, he has ten pounds. [26] I say unto you, that unto everyone that has shall be given; but from him that has not, even that which he has shall be taken away from him. [27] But these mine enemies, that would not that I should reign over them, bring here, and slay them before me.

[28] And when he had thus spoken, he went on before, going up to Yerushalayim.

---

[8] *Mina*, here translated as *pound*, is equal to one hundred drachmas.

VII. THE OFFICIAL PRESENTATION OF THE KING
— §§ 132–144 —

[§ 132]—A. The Arrival in Beit Anyah

John 11:55–12:1, 9-11

[55] Now the Passover of the Jews was at hand: and many went up to Yerushalayim out of the country before the Passover, to purify themselves. [56] They sought therefore for Yeshua, and spoke one with another, as they stood in the temple, What think ye? That he will not come to the feast? [57] Now the chief priests and the Pharisees had given commandment, that, if any man knew where he was, he should show it, that they might take him. [12:1] Yeshua therefore six days before the Passover came to Beit Anyah, where Elazar was, whom Yeshua raised from the dead. . . . [9] The common

people therefore of the Jews learned that he was there: and they came, not for Yeshua's sake only, but that they might see Elazar also, whom he had raised from the dead. [10] But the chief priests took counsel that they might put Elazar also to death; [11] because that by reason of him many of the Jews went away, and believed on Yeshua.

[§ 133]—B. The Triumphal Entry:
The Setting Aside of the Passover Lamb

Mt. 21:1-11, 14-17	Mark 11:1-11	Luke 19:29-44
[1] And when they drew near unto Yerushalayim, and came unto Beit Pagei, unto the mount of Olives, then Yeshua sent two disciples,	[1] And when they draw near unto Yerushalayim, unto Beit Pagei and Beit Anyah, at the mount of Olives, he sent two of his disciples,	[29] And it came to pass, when he drew near unto Beit Pagei and Beit Anyah, at the mount that is called Olivet, he sent two of the disciples,
[2] saying unto them, Go into the village that is over against you,	[2] and said unto them, Go your way into the village that is over against you:	[30] saying, Go your way into the village over against <you>;
and straightway ye shall find an ass tied, and a colt with her:	and straightway as ye enter into it, ye shall find a colt tied, whereon no man ever yet sat;	in which as ye enter ye shall find a colt tied, whereon no man ever yet sat:
loose <them>, and bring <them> unto me. [3] And if anyone says anything unto you, ye shall say, The Lord has need of them; and straightway he will send them.	loose him, and bring him. [3] And if anyone says unto you, Why do ye this? Say ye, The Lord has need of him; and straightway he will send him back here.	loose him, and bring him. [31] And if anyone asks you, Why do ye loose him? Thus shall ye say, The Lord has need of him.

6 And the disciples went, and did even as Yeshua appointed them,

7 and brought the ass, and the colt, and put on them their garments; and he sat thereon.
4 Now this is come to pass, that it might be fulfilled which was spoken through the prophet, saying, 5 Tell ye the daughter of Tzion, Behold, your King comes unto you, Meek, and riding upon an ass, And upon a colt the foal of an ass.

4 And they went away, and found a colt tied at the door without in the open street; and they loosed him. 5 And certain of them that stood there said unto them, What do ye, loosing the colt?
6 And they said unto them even as Yeshua had said: and they let them go.
7 And they bring the colt unto Yeshua, and cast on him their garments; and he sat upon him.

32 And they that were sent went away, and found even as he had said unto them. 33 And as they were loosing the colt, the owners thereof said unto them, Why loose ye the colt?
34 And they said, The Lord has need of him.

35 And they brought him to Yeshua: and they threw their garments upon the colt, and set Yeshua thereon.

Mt. cont.	**Mark cont.**	**Luke cont.**	**John 12:12-19**
8 And the most part of the multitude spread their garments in the way; and	8 And many spread their garments upon the way; and others branches,	36 And as he went, they spread their garments in the way.	12 On the morrow a great multitude that had come to the feast, when they

others cut branches from the trees, and spread them in the way.	which they had cut from the fields.		heard that Yeshua was coming to Yerushalayim, [13] took the branches of the palm trees, and went forth to meet him, and cried out,
[9] And the multitudes that went before him, and that followed, cried, saying,	[9] And they that went before, and they that followed, cried,	[37] And as he was now drawing near, <even> at the descent of the mount of Olives, the whole multitude of the disciples began to rejoice and praise God with a loud voice for all the mighty works which they had seen; [38] saying,	
Hoshannah[1] to the son of David: Blessed <is> he that comes in the name of the Lord; Hoshannah in the highest.	Hoshannah; Blessed <is> he that comes in the name of the Lord: [10] Blessed <is> the kingdom that comes, <the kingdom> of our father Da-	Blessed <is> the King that comes in the name of the Lord: peace in heaven, and glory in the highest.	Hoshannah: Blessed <is> he that comes in the name of the Lord, even the King of Yisrael.

---

[1] The Hebrew prayer: *Hoshanah Rabbah*.

10 And when he was come into Yerushalayim, all the city was stirred, saying, Who is this?

11 And the multitudes said, This is the prophet, Yeshua, from Natzeret of Galil.

14 And the blind and the lame came to him in the temple; and he healed them.

15 But when the chief priests and the scribes saw the wonderful things that he did, and the children that were crying in the temple and saying, Hoshannah to the son of David; they were moved with indignation, 16 and said unto him, Hear you what these are saying?

vid: Hoshannah in the highest.

11 And he entered into Yerushalayim, into the temple;

39 And some of the Pharisees from the multitude said unto him, Teacher,

14 And Yeshua, having found a young ass, sat thereon; as it is written,

15 Fear not, daughter of Tzion: behold, your King comes, sitting on an ass's colt.

16 These things understood not his disciples at the first: but when Yeshua was glorified, then remembered they that these things were written of him, and that they had done these things unto him.

17 The multitude therefore that was with him when he called Elazar out of the tomb, and raised him from the dead, bore witness. 18 For

And Yeshua said unto them, Yea: did ye never read, Out of the mouth of babes and sucklings you has perfected praise?

rebuke your disciples. [40] And he answered and said, I tell you that, if these shall hold their peace, the stones will cry out. [41] And when he drew near, he saw the city and wept over it, [42] saying, If you had known in this day, even you, the things which belong unto peace! But now they are hid from your eyes. [43] For the days shall come upon you, when your enemies shall cast up a bank about you, and compass you round, and keep you in on every side, [44] and shall dash you to the ground, and your children within you; and they shall not

this cause also the multitude went and met him, for that they heard that he had done this sign. [19] The Pharisees therefore said among themselves, Behold how ye prevail nothing: lo, the world is gone after him.

		leave in you one stone upon another; because you knew not the time of your visitation.
17 And he left them, and went forth out of the city to Beit Anyah, and lodged there.	and when he had looked round about upon all things, it being now eventide, he went out unto Beit Anyah with the twelve.	

[§§ 134–135]—C. The Authority of the King

[§ 134]—1. The Cursing of the Fig Tree

Matthew 21:18-19a	Mark 11:12-14
18 Now in the morning as he returned to the city, he hungered. 19a And seeing a fig tree by the way side, he came to it, and found nothing thereon, but leaves only;	12 And on the morrow, when they were come out from Beit Anyah, he hungered. 13 And seeing a fig tree afar off having leaves, he came, if haply he might find anything thereon: and when he came to it, he found nothing but leaves; for it was not the season of figs.
and he said unto it, Let there be no fruit from you henceforward forever.	14 And he answered and said unto it, No man eat fruit from you henceforward forever. And his disciples heard it.

[§ 135]—2. The Second Possession of the Temple

Matthew 21:12-13	Mark 11:15-18	Luke 19:45-48
[12] And Yeshua entered into the temple of God, and cast out all them that sold and bought in the temple, and overthrew the tables of the moneychangers, and the seats of them that sold the doves;	[15] And they come to Yerushalayim: and he entered into the temple, and began to cast out them that sold and them that bought in the temple, and overthrew the tables of the moneychangers, and the seats of them that sold the doves; [16] and he would not suffer that any man should carry a vessel through the temple. [17] And he taught, and said unto them, Is it not written,	[45] And he entered into the temple, and began to cast out them that sold,
[13] and he said unto them, It is written,		[46] saying unto them, It is written,
My house shall be called a house of prayer: but ye make it a den of robbers.	My house shall be called a house of prayer for all the nations? But ye have made it a den of robbers. [18] And the chief priests and the scribes heard it, and sought how they might destroy him: for they feared him, for all the multitude was astonished at his teaching.	And my house shall be a house of prayer: but ye have made it a den of robbers. [47] And he was teaching daily in the temple. But the chief priests and the scribes and the principal men of the people sought to destroy him: [48] and they could not find what they might do; for the people all hung upon him, listening.

[§ 136]—D. The Invitations by the King

1. The Two Invitations

John 12:20-36

20 Now there were certain Greeks among those that went up to worship at the feast: 21 these therefore came to Philip, who was of Beit Tzaida of Galil, and asked him, saying, Sir, we would see Yeshua. 22 Philip comes and tells Andrei: Andrei comes, and Philip, and they tell Yeshua. 23 And Yeshua answered them, saying, The hour is come, that the Son of man should be glorified. 24 Verily, verily, I say unto you, Except a grain of wheat fall into the earth and die, it abides by itself alone; but if it die, it bears much fruit. 25 He that loves his life loses it; and he that hates his life in this world shall keep it unto life eternal. 26 If any man serve me, let him follow me; and where I am, there shall also my servant be: if any man serve me, him will the Father honor. 27 Now is my soul troubled; and what shall I say? Father, save me from this hour. But for this cause came I unto this hour. 28 Father, glorify your name. There came therefore a voice out of heaven, <saying>, I have both glorified it, and will glorify it again. 29 The multitude therefore, that stood by, and heard it, said that it had thundered: others said, An angel has spoken to him. 30 Yeshua answered and said, This voice has not come for my sake, but for your sakes. 31 Now is the judgment of this world: now shall the prince of this world be cast out. 32 And I, if I be lifted up from the earth, will draw all men unto myself. 33 But this he said, signifying by what manner of death he should die. 34 The multitude therefore answered him, We have heard out of the law that the Messiah abides forever: and how say you, The Son of man must be lifted up? Who is this Son of man? 35 Yeshua therefore said unto them, Yet a little while is the light among you. Walk while ye have the light, that darkness overtake you not: and he that walks in the darkness knows not whither he goes. 36 While ye have the light, believe on the light, that ye may become sons of light. These things spoke Yeshua, and he departed and hid himself from them.

2. Yochanan's Summary of Messiah's Ministry

a. Summary of Yisrael

John 12:37-43

[37] But though he had done so many signs before them, yet they believed not on him: [38] that the word of Yeshayahu the prophet might be fulfilled, which he spoke, Lord, who has believed our report? And to whom has the arm of the Lord been revealed? [39] For this cause they could not believe, for that Yeshayahu said again, [40] He has blinded their eyes, and he hardened their heart; Lest they should see with their eyes, and perceive with their heart, And should turn, And I should heal them. [41] These things said Yeshayahu, because he saw his glory; and he spoke of him. [42] Nevertheless even of the rulers many believed on him; but because of the Pharisees they did not confess <it>, lest they should be put out of the synagogue: [43] for they loved the glory <that is> of men more than the glory <that is> of God.

b. Summary of Yeshua

John 12:44-50

[44] And Yeshua cried and said, He that believes on me, believes not on me, but on him that sent me. [45] And he that beholds me beholds him that sent me. [46] I am come a light into the world, that whosoever believes on me may not abide in the darkness. [47] And if any man hear my sayings, and keep them not, I judge him not: for I came not to judge the world, but to save the world. [48] He that rejects me, and receives not my sayings, has one that judges him: the word that I spoke, the same shall judge him in the last day. [49] For I spoke not from myself; but the Father that sent me, he had given me a commandment, what I should say, and what I should speak. [50] And I know that his commandment is life eternal: the things therefore which I speak, even as the Father has said unto me, so I speak.

[§ 137]—E. The Proof of Authority

Matthew 21:19b-22	Mark 11:19-26[2]
	[19] And every evening he went forth out of the city. [20] And as they passed by in the morning,
[19b] And immediately the fig tree withered away.	they saw the fig tree withered away from the roots.
[20] And when the disciples saw it, they marveled, saying, How did the fig tree immediately wither away?	[21] And Peter calling to remembrance said unto him, Rabbi, behold, the fig tree which you cursed is withered away.
[21] And Yeshua answered and said unto them,	[22] And Yeshua answering said unto them, Have faith in God.
Verily I say unto you, If ye have faith, and doubt not, ye shall not only do what is done to the fig tree, but even if ye shall say unto this mountain, Be you taken up and cast into the sea, it shall be done.	[23] Verily I say unto you, Whosoever shall say unto this mountain, Be you taken up and cast into the sea; and shall not doubt in his heart, but shall believe that what he said comes to pass; he shall have it.
	[24] Therefore I say unto you,
[22] And all things, whatsoever ye shall ask in prayer, believing, ye shall receive.	All things whatsoever ye pray and ask for, believe that ye receive them, and ye shall have them.
	[25] And whensoever ye stand praying, forgive, if ye have anything against anyone; that your Father also who is in heaven may forgive you your trespasses.[3]

---

[2] Luke 21:37-38 is to be found at the end of § 145.

[3] Many ancient authorities add verse 26: "But if ye do not forgive, neither will your Father who is in heaven forgive your trespasses."

[§§ 138–141]—
F. The Authority of the King Challenged:
The Testing of the Lamb

[§ 138]—1. By Priests and Elders

a. The Attack

Matthew 21:23	Mark 11:27-28	Luke 20:1-2
[23] And when he was come into the temple, the chief priests and the elders of the people came unto him as he was teaching, and said,	[27] And they come again to Yerushalayim: and as he was walking in the temple, there come to him the chief priests, and the scribes, and the elders; [28] and they said unto him,	[1] And it came to pass, on one of the days, as he was teaching the people in the temple, and preaching the gospel, there came upon him the chief priests and the scribes with the elders; [2] and they spoke, saying unto him, Tell us:
By what authority do you these things? And who gave you this authority?	By what authority do you these things? Or who gave you this authority to do these things?	By what authority do you these things? Or who is he that gave you this authority?

b. The Answer

Matthew 21:24-27	Mark 11:29-33	Luke 20:3-8

[24] And Yeshua answered and said unto them, I also will ask you one question, which if ye tell me, I likewise will tell you by what authority I do these things.

[25] The baptism of Yochanan, from where was it? From heaven or from men?

And they reasoned with themselves, saying, If we shall say, From heaven; he will say unto us, Why then did ye not believe him?

[26] But if we shall say, From men; we fear the multitude; for all hold Yochanan as a prophet.

[27] And they answered Yeshua, and said, We know not. He also said unto them, Neither tell I you by what authority I do these things.

---

[29] And Yeshua said unto them, I will ask of you one question, and answer me, and I will tell you by what authority I do these things.

[30] The baptism of Yochanan, was it from heaven, or from men? Answer me.

[31] And they reasoned with themselves, saying, If we shall say, From heaven; He will say, Why then did ye not believe him?

[32] But should we say, From men – they feared the people: for all verily held Yochanan to be a prophet.

[33] And they answered Yeshua and said, We know not. And Yeshua said unto them, Neither tell I you by what authority I do these things.

---

[3] And he answered and said unto them, I also will ask you a question; and tell me:

[4] The baptism of Yochanan, was it from heaven, or from men?

[5] And they reasoned with themselves, saying, If we shall say, From heaven; he will say, Why did ye not believe him?

[6] But if we shall say, From men; all the people will stone us: for they are persuaded that Yochanan was a prophet.

[7] And they answered, that they knew not from where <it was>.

[8] And Yeshua said unto them, Neither tell I you by what authority I do these things.

(1) The Parable of the Two Sons

Matthew 21:28-32

[28] But what think ye? A man had two sons; and he came to the first, and said, Son, go work today in the vineyard. [29] And he answered and said, I will not: but afterward he repented himself, and went. [30] And he came to the second, and said likewise. And he answered and said, I <go>, sir: and went not. [31] Which of the two did the will of his father? They say, The first. Yeshua said unto them, Verily I say unto you, that the publicans and the harlots go into the kingdom of God before you. [32] For Yochanan came unto you in the way of righteousness, and ye believed him not; but the publicans and the harlots believed him: and ye, when ye saw it, did not even repent yourselves afterward, that ye might believe him.

(2) The Parable of the Householder

Matthew 21:33-46	Mark 12:1-12	Luke 20:9-19
[33] Hear another parable: There was a man that was a householder, who planted a vineyard, and set a hedge about it, and digged a winepress in it, and built a tower, and let it out to husbandmen, and went into another country.	[1] And he began to speak unto them in parables. A man planted a vineyard, and set a hedge about it, and digged a pit for the winepress, and built a tower, and let it out to husbandmen, and went into another country.	[9] And he began to speak unto the people this parable: A man planted a vineyard, and let it out to husbandmen, and went into another country for a long time.
[34] And when the season of the fruits drew near, he sent his servants to the husbandmen, to receive his fruits. [35] And the husbandmen took his	[2] And at the season he sent to the husbandmen a servant, that he might receive from the husbandmen of the fruits of the vineyard. [3] And they took him,	[10] And at the season he sent unto the husbandmen a servant, that they should give him of the fruit of the vineyard: but the husbandmen beat him,

servants, and beat one, and killed another, and stoned another.

36 Again, he sent other servants more than the first: and they did unto them in like manner.

37 But afterward he sent unto them his son, saying, They will reverence my son.

38 But the husbandmen, when they saw the son, said among themselves,

This is the heir; come, let us kill him, and take his inheritance.

39 And they took him, and cast him forth out of the vineyard, and killed him.

40 When therefore the lord of the vineyard shall come, what will he do unto those husbandmen?

and beat him, and sent him away empty.

4 And again he sent unto them another servant; and him they wounded in the head, and handled shamefully.

5 And he sent another; and him they killed: and many others; beating some, and killing some.

6 He had yet one, a beloved son: he sent him last unto them, saying, They will reverence my son.

7 But those husbandmen said among themselves,

This is the heir; come, let us kill him, and the inheritance shall be ours.

8 And they took him, and killed him, and cast him forth out of the vineyard.

9 What therefore will the lord of the vineyard do?

and sent him away empty.

11 And he sent yet another servant: and him also they beat, and handled him shamefully, and sent him away empty.

12 And he sent yet a third: and him also they wounded, and cast him forth.

13 And the lord of the vineyard said, What shall I do? I will send my beloved son; it may be they will reverence him.

14 But when the husbandmen saw him, they reasoned one with another, saying,

This is the heir; let us kill him, that the inheritance may be ours.

15 And they cast him forth out of the vineyard, and killed him.

What therefore will the lord of the vineyard do unto them?

41 They say unto him, He will miserably destroy those miserable men, and will let out the vineyard unto other husbandmen, who shall render him the fruits in their seasons. 42 Yeshua said unto them, Did ye never read in the scriptures,

The stone which the builders rejected, The same was made the head of the corner; This was from the Lord, And it is marvelous in our eyes? 43 Therefore say I unto you, The kingdom of God shall be taken away from you, and shall be given to a nation bringing forth the fruits thereof. 44 And he that falls on this stone shall be broken to pieces: but on whomsoever it shall fall, it will scatter him as dust. 45 And when the chief priests and the Pharisees heard his parables, they perceived that he spoke of

He will come and destroy the husbandmen, and will give the vineyard unto others.

10 Have ye not read even this scripture:

The stone which the builders rejected, The same was made the head of the corner; 11 This was from the Lord, And it is marvelous in our eyes?

16 He will come and destroy these husbandmen, and will give the vineyard unto others. And when they heard it, they said, God forbid.

17 But he looked upon them, and said, What then is this that is written,

The stone which the builders rejected, The same was made the head of the corner?

18 Everyone that falls on that stone shall be broken to pieces; but on whomsoever it shall fall, it will scatter him as dust. 19 And the scribes and the chief priests

them. [46] And when they sought to lay hold on him, they feared the multitudes, because they took him for a prophet.

[12] And they sought to lay hold on him; and they feared the multitude; for they perceived that he spoke the parable against them: and they left him, and went away.

sought to lay hands on him in that very hour; and they feared the people: for they perceived that he spoke this parable against them.

(3) The Parable of the Wedding

Matthew 22:1-14

[1] And Yeshua answered and spoke again in parables unto them, saying, [2] The kingdom of heaven is likened unto a certain king, who made a marriage feast for his son, [3] and sent forth his servants to call them that were bidden to the marriage feast: and they would not come. [4] Again he sent forth other servants, saying, Tell them that are bidden, Behold, I have made ready my dinner; my oxen and my fatlings are killed, and all things are ready: come to the marriage feast. [5] But they made light of it, and went their ways, one to his own farm, another to his merchandise; [6] and the rest laid hold on his servants, and treated them shamefully, and killed them. [7] But the king was angry; and he sent his armies, and destroyed those murderers, and burned their city. [8] Then said he to his servants, The wedding is ready, but they that were bidden were not worthy. [9] Go ye therefore unto the partings of the highways, and as many as ye shall find, bid to the marriage feast. [10] And those servants went out into the highways, and gathered together all as many as they found, both bad and good: and the wedding was filled with guests. [11] But when the king came in to behold the guests, he saw there a man who had not on a wedding-garment: [12] and he said unto him, Friend, how came you in here not having a wedding-garment? And he was speechless. [13] Then the king said to the servants, Bind him hand and foot, and cast him out into the outer darkness; there shall be the weeping and the gnashing of teeth. [14] For many are called, but few chosen.

[§ 139]—2. By Pharisees and Herodians

a. The Attack

Matthew 22:15-17	Mark 12:13-15a	Luke 20:20-22
[15] Then went the Pharisees, and took counsel how they might ensnare him in <his> talk. [16] And they send to him their disciples, with the Herodians, saying,	[13] And they send unto him certain of the Pharisees and of the Herodians, that they might catch him in talk. [14] And when they were come, they say unto him,	[20] And they watched him, and sent forth spies, who feigned themselves to be righteous, that they might take hold of his speech, so as to deliver him up to the rule and to the authority of the governor. [21] And they asked him, saying,
Teacher, we know that you are true, and teach the way of God in truth, and care not for anyone: for you regard not the person of men. [17] Tell us therefore, What do you think? Is it lawful to give tribute unto Caesar, or not?	Teacher, we know that you are true, and care not for anyone; for you regard not the person of men, but of a truth teach the way of God: Is it lawful to give tribute unto Caesar, or not? [15a] Shall we give, or shall we not give?	Teacher, we know that you say and teach rightly, and accept not the person <of any>, but of a truth teach the way of God: [22] Is it lawful for us to give tribute unto Caesar, or not?

b. The Answer

Matthew 22:18-22	Mark 12:15b-17	Luke 20:23-26
[18] But Yeshua perceived their wickedness, and said, Why make ye trial of me, ye	[15b] But he, knowing their hypocrisy, said unto them, Why make ye trial of me?	[23] But he perceived their craftiness, and said unto them,

hypocrites? [19] Show me the tribute money. And they brought unto him a denarius.	Bring me a denarius, that I may see it. [16] And they brought it.	[24] Show me a denarius.
[20] And he said unto them,	And he said unto them,	
Whose is this image and superscription? [21] They say unto him,	Whose is this image and superscription? And they said unto him,	Whose image and superscription has it? And they said,
Caesar's.	Caesar's.	Caesar's.
Then said he unto them,	[17] And Yeshua said unto them,	[25] And he said unto them,
Render therefore unto Caesar the things that are Caesar's; and unto God the things that are God's.	Render unto Caesar the things that are Caesar's, and unto God the things that are God's.	Then render unto Caesar the things that are Caesar's, and unto God the things that are God's.
[22] And when they heard it, they marveled, and left him, and went away.	And they marveled greatly at him.	[26] And they were not able to take hold of the saying before the people: and they marveled at his answer, and held their peace.

[§ 140]—3. By Sadducees

a. The Attack

Matthew 22:23-28	Mark 12:18-23	Luke 20:27-33
[23] On that day there came to him Sadducees, they that say that there is no resurrection: and they asked	[18] And there come unto him Sadducees, who say that there is no resurrection; and they asked him, saying,	[27] And there came to him certain of the Sadducees, they that say that there is no resurrection; [28] and

him, [24] saying, Teacher, Mosheh said, If a man die, having no children, his brother shall marry his wife, and raise up seed unto his brother.

[25] Now there were with us seven brethren: and the first married and deceased, and having no seed left his wife unto his brother; [26] in like manner the second also, and the third, unto the seventh. [27] And after them all, the woman died. [28] In the resurrection therefore whose wife shall she be of the seven? For they all had her.

[19] Teacher, Mosheh wrote unto us, If a man's brother die, and leave a wife behind him, and leave no child, that his brother should take his wife, and raise up seed unto his brother. [20] There were seven brethren: and the first took a wife, and dying left no seed; [21] and the second took her, and died, leaving no seed behind him; and the third likewise: [22] and the seven left no seed. Last of all the woman also died. [23] In the resurrection whose wife shall she be of them? For the seven had her to wife.

they asked him, saying, Teacher, Mosheh wrote unto us, that if a man's brother die, having a wife, and he be childless, his brother should take the wife, and raise up seed unto his brother. [29] There were therefore seven brethren: and the first took a wife, and died childless; [30] and the second: [31] and the third took her; and likewise the seven also left no children, and died. [32] Afterward the woman also died. [33] In the resurrection therefore whose wife of them shall she be? For the seven had her to wife.

b. The Answer

Matthew 22:29-33	Mark 12:24-27	Luke 20:34-40
[29] But Yeshua answered and said unto them, Ye do err, not knowing the scriptures, nor the power of God. [30] For in	[24] Yeshua said unto them, Is it not for this cause that ye err, that ye know not the scrip-	[34] And Yeshua said unto them, The sons of this world marry, and are given in marriage: [35] but they

the resurrection they neither marry, nor are given in marriage, but are as angels in heaven.

[31] But as touching the resurrection of the dead, have ye not read that which was spoken unto you by God, saying, [32] I am the God of Avraham, and the God of Yitzchak, and the God of Yaakov? God is not <the God> of the dead, but of the living.

[33] And when the multitudes heard it, they were astonished at his teaching.

tures, nor the power of God? [25] For when they shall rise from the dead, they neither marry, nor are given in marriage; but are as angels in heaven.

[26] But as touching the dead, that they are raised; have ye not read in the book of Mosheh, in <the place concerning> the Bush, how God spoke unto him, saying, I <am> the God of Avraham, and the God of Yitzchak, and the God of Yaakov? [27] He is not the God of the dead, but of the living: ye do greatly err.

that are accounted worthy to attain to that world, and the resurrection from the dead, neither marry, nor are given in marriage: [36] for neither can they die any more: for they are equal unto the angels; and are sons of God, being sons of the resurrection.

[37] But that the dead are raised, even Mosheh showed, in <the place concerning> the Bush, when he calls the Lord the God of Avraham, and the God of Yitzchak, and the God of Yaakov. [38] Now he is not the God of the dead, but of the living: for all live unto him.

[39] And certain of the scribes answering said, Teacher, you have well said. [40] For they dared not any more ask him any question.

[§ 141]—3. By Pharisees

a. The Attack

Matthew 22:34-36	Mark 12:28
[34] But the Pharisees, when they heard that he had put the Sadducees to silence, gathered themselves together. [35] And one of them, a lawyer, asked him a question, trying him: [36] Teacher, which is the great commandment in the law?	[28] And one of the scribes came, and heard them questioning together, and knowing that he had answered them well, asked him, What commandment is the first of all?

b. The Answer

Matthew 22:37-40	Mark 12:29-34
[37] And he said unto him, You shall love the Lord your God with all your heart, and with all your soul, and with all your mind. [38] This is the great and first commandment.	[29] Yeshua answered, The first is, Hear, O Yisrael; The Lord our God, the Lord is one: [30] and you shall love the Lord your God with all your heart, and with all your soul, and with all your mind, and with all your strength.
[39] And a second like <unto it> is this, You shall love your neighbor as yourself. [40] On these two commandments the whole law hangs, and the prophets.	[31] The second is this, You shall love your neighbor as yourself. There is none other commandment greater than these. [32] And the scribe said unto him, Of a truth, Teacher, you have well said that he is one; and there is none other but he: [33] and to love him with all the heart, and with all the understanding, and with all the strength,

and to love his neighbor as himself, is much more than all whole burnt-offerings and sacrifices. [34] And when Yeshua saw that he answered discreetly, he said unto him, You are not far from the kingdom of God. And no man after that dared ask him any question.

[§ 142]—G. The Challenge by the King

Matthew 22:41-46	Mark 12:35-37	Luke 20:41-44
[41] Now while the Pharisees were gathered together, Yeshua asked them a question, [42] saying, What think ye of the Messiah? Whose son is he? They say unto him, <The son> of David. [43] He said unto them, How then did David in the Spirit call him Lord, saying, [44] The Lord said unto my Lord, Sit you on my right hand, Till I put your enemies underneath your feet? [45] If David then called him Lord, how is he his son? [46] And no one was able to answer him a word, neither dared any man from that day	[35] And Yeshua answered and said, as he taught in the temple, How say the scribes that the Messiah is the son of David? [36] David himself said in the Holy Spirit, The Lord said unto my Lord, Sit you on my right hand, Till I make your enemies the footstool of your feet. [37] David himself calls him Lord; and from where is he his son? And the common people heard him gladly.	[41] And he said unto them, How say they that the Messiah is David's son? [42] For David himself said in the book of Psalms, The Lord said unto my Lord, Sit you on my right hand, [43] Till I make your enemies the footstool of your feet. [44] David therefore calls him Lord, and how is he his son?

forth ask him any more questions.

[§ 143]—H. The Judgment by the King

1. To the Disciples and Multitudes

Matthew 23:1-12	Mark 12:38-40	Luke 20:45-47
[1] Then spoke Yeshua to the multitudes and to his disciples, [2] saying, The scribes and the Pharisees sit on Mosheh's seat: [3] all things therefore whatsoever they bid you, <these> do and observe: but do not ye after their works; for they say, and do not. [4] Yea, they bind heavy burdens and grievous to be borne, and lay them on men's shoulders; but they themselves will not move them with their finger. [5] But all their works they do to be seen of men: for they make broad their phylacteries, and enlarge the borders <of their garments>, [6] and love the	[38] And in his teaching he said, Beware of the scribes, who desire to walk in long robes, and <to have> salutations in the marketplaces, [39] and chief seats in the	[45] And in the hearing of all the people he said unto his disciples, [46] Beware of the scribes, who desire to walk in long robes, and love salutations in the marketplaces, and chief seats in the syna-

chief place at feasts, and the chief seats in the synagogues, [7] and the salutations in the marketplaces, and to be called of men, Rabbi.

[8] But be not ye called Rabbi: for one is your teacher, and all ye are brethren. [9] And call no man your father on the earth: for one is your Father, <even> he who is in heaven. [10] Neither be ye called masters: for one is your master, <even> the Messiah. [11] But he that is greatest among you shall be your servant. [12] And whosoever shall exalt himself shall be humbled; and whosoever shall humble himself shall be exalted.

synagogues, and chief places at feasts: [40] they that devour widows' houses, and for a pretense make long prayers; these shall receive greater condemnation.

gogues, and chief places at feasts; [47] who devour widows' houses, and for a pretense make long prayers: these shall receive greater condemnation.

2. To the Pharisees

Matthew 23:13-36

[13] But woe unto you, scribes and Pharisees, hypocrites! Because ye shut the kingdom of heaven against men: for ye enter not in yourselves, neither suffer ye them that are entering in to enter.[4]

[15] Woe unto you, scribes and Pharisees, hypocrites! For ye compass sea and land to make one proselyte; and when he is become so, ye make him two-fold more a son of hell than yourselves.

[16] Woe unto you, ye blind guides, that say, Whosoever shall swear by the temple, it is nothing; but whosoever shall swear by the gold of the temple, he is a debtor. [17] Ye fools and blind: for which is greater, the gold, or the temple that has sanctified the gold? [18] And, Whosoever shall swear by the altar, it is nothing; but whosoever shall swear by the gift that is upon it, he is a debtor. [19] Ye blind: for which is greater, the gift, or the altar that sanctifies the gift? [20] He therefore that swears by the altar, swears by it, and by all things thereon. [21] And he that swears by the temple, swears by it, and by him that dwells therein. [22] And he that swears by the heaven, swears by the throne of God, and by him that sits thereon.

[23] Woe unto you, scribes and Pharisees, hypocrites! For ye tithe mint and anise and cumin, and have left undone the weightier matters of the law, justice, and mercy, and faith: but these ye ought to have done, and not to have left the other undone. [24] Ye blind guides, that strain out the gnat, and swallow the camel!

[25] Woe unto you, scribes and Pharisees, hypocrites! For ye cleanse the out-side of the cup and of the platter, but within they are full from extortion and excess. [26] You blind Pharisee, cleanse first the inside of the cup and of the platter, that the outside thereof may become clean also.

---

[4] Some ancient authorities insert here, or after verse 12, verse 14: "Woe unto you, scribes and Pharisees, hypocrites! For ye devour widows' houses, even while for a pretense ye make long prayers: therefore ye shall receive greater condemnation."

[27] Woe unto you, scribes and Pharisees, hypocrites! For ye are like unto whited sepulchers, which outwardly appear beautiful, but inwardly are full of dead men's bones, and of all uncleanness. [28] Even so ye also outwardly appear righteous unto men, but inwardly ye are full of hypocrisy and iniquity.

[29] Woe unto you, scribes and Pharisees, hypocrites! For ye build the sepulchers of the prophets, and garnish the tombs of the righteous, [30] and say, If we had been in the days of our fathers, we should not have been partakers with them in the blood of the prophets. [31] Wherefore ye witness to yourselves, that ye are sons of them that slew the prophets. [32] Fill ye up then the measure of your fathers. [33] Ye serpents, ye offspring of vipers, how shall ye escape the judgment of hell[5]? [34] Therefore, behold, I send unto you prophets, and wise men, and scribes: some of them shall ye kill and crucify; and some of them shall ye scourge in your synagogues, and persecute from city to city: [35] that upon you may come all the righteous blood shed on the earth, from the blood of Hevel the righteous unto the blood of Zecharyah son of Berechyah, whom ye slew between the sanctuary and the altar. [36] Verily I say unto you, All these things shall come upon this generation.

3. The Lament

Matthew 23:37-39

[37] O Yerushalayim, Yerushalayim, that kills the prophets, and stones them that are sent unto her! How often would I have gathered your children together, even as a hen gathers her chickens under her wings, and ye would not! [38] Behold, your house is left unto you desolate. [39] For I say unto you, Ye shall not see me henceforth, till ye shall say, Blessed <is> he that comes in the name of the Lord.

---

[5] Greek: *Gehenna*.

[§ 144]—I. Instruction at the Treasury

Mark 12:41-44	Luke 21:1-4
[41] And he sat down over against the treasury, and beheld how the multitude cast money into the treasury: and many that were rich cast in much.	[1] And he looked up, and saw the rich men that were casting their gifts into the treasury.
[42] And there came a poor widow, and she cast in two mites, which make a farthing.	[2] And he saw a certain poor widow casting in thither two mites.
[43] And he called unto him his disciples, and said unto them,	[3] And he said,
Verily I say unto you, This poor widow cast in more than all they that are casting into the treasury:	Of a truth I say unto you, This poor widow cast in more than they all:
[44] for they all did cast in of their superfluity; but she of her want did cast in all that she had, <even> all her living.	[4] for all these did of their superfluity cast in unto the gifts; but she of her want did cast in all the living that she had.

VIII. The Preparation for the Death of the King
— §§ 145–164 —

[§ 145]—A. The Olivet Discourse:
The Prophecies of the King

1. The Historical Setting

Matthew 24:1-2	Mark 13:1-2	Luke 21:5-6
[1] And Yeshua went out from the temple, and was going on his way; and his disciples came	[1] And as he went forth out of the temple, one of his disciples said unto him, Teacher,	[5] And as some spoke of the temple, how it was adorned with goodly stones and offerings,

to him to show him the buildings of the temple.	behold, what manner of stones and what manner of buildings!	
[2] But he answered and said unto them, See ye not all these things? Verily I say unto you, There shall not be left here one stone upon another, that shall not be thrown down.	[2] And Yeshua said unto him, See you these great buildings? There shall not be left here one stone upon another, which shall not be thrown down.	he said, [6] As for these things which ye behold, the days will come, in which there shall not be left here one stone upon another, that shall not be thrown down.

2. The Three Questions

Matthew 24:3	Mark 13:3-4	Luke 21:7
[3] And as he sat on the mount of Olives, the disciples came unto him privately, saying,	[3] And as he sat on the mount of Olives over against the temple, Peter and Yaakov and Yochanan and Andrei asked him privately,	[7] And they asked him, saying,
Tell us, when shall these things be? And what <shall be> the sign of your coming, and of the end of the world[1]?	[4] Tell us, when shall these things be? And what <shall be> the sign when these things are all about to be accomplished?	Teacher, when therefore shall these things be? And what <shall be> the sign when these things are about to come to pass?

---

[1] Or, *the consummation of the world.*

3. The General Characteristics of the Age
Between the Two Comings

Matthew 24:4-6	Mark 13:5-7	Luke 21:8-9
[4] And Yeshua answered and said unto them, Take heed that no man lead you astray. [5] For many shall come in my name, saying, I am the Messiah; and shall lead many astray. [6] And ye shall hear of wars and rumors of wars; see that ye be not troubled: for \<these things\> must needs come to pass; but the end is not yet.	[5] And Yeshua began to say unto them, Take heed that no man lead you astray. [6] Many shall come in my name, saying, I am \<he\>; and shall lead many astray. [7] And when ye shall hear of wars and rumors of wars, be not troubled: \<these things\> must needs come to pass; but the end is not yet.	[8] And he said, Take heed that ye be not led astray: for many shall come in my name, saying, I am \<he\>; and, The time is at hand: go ye not after them. [9] And when ye shall hear of wars and tumults, be not terrified: for these things must needs come to pass first; but the end is not immediately.

4. The Sign of the End of the Age

Matthew 24:7-8	Mark 13:8	Luke 21:10-11
[7] For nation shall rise against nation, and kingdom against kingdom; and there shall be famines and earthquakes in divers places. [8] But all these things	[8] For nation shall rise against nation, and kingdom against kingdom; there shall be earthquakes in divers places; there shall be famines: these things	[10] Then said he unto them, Nation shall rise against nation, and kingdom against kingdom; [11] and there shall be great earthquakes, and in divers places famines and pesti-

are the beginning of travail.	are the beginning of travail.	lences; and there shall be terrors and great signs from heaven.

5. The Personal Experiences of the Apostles

Mark 13:9-13	Luke 21:12-19
[9] But take ye heed to yourselves: for they shall deliver you up to councils; and in synagogues shall ye be beaten; and before governors and kings shall ye stand for my sake, for a testimony unto them.	[12] But before all these things, they shall lay their hands on you, and shall persecute you, delivering you up to the synagogues and prisons, bringing you before kings and governors for my name's sake. [13] It shall turn out unto you for a testimony.
[10] And the gospel must first be preached unto all the nations. [11] And when they lead you <to judgment>, and deliver you up, be not anxious beforehand what ye shall speak: but whatsoever shall be given you in that hour, that speak ye; for it is not ye that speak, but the Holy Spirit. [12] And brother shall deliver up brother to death, and the father his child; and children shall rise up against parents, and cause them to be put to death.	[14] Settle it therefore in your hearts, not to meditate beforehand how to answer: [15] for I will give you a mouth and wisdom, which all your adversaries shall not be able to withstand or to gainsay.
	[16] But ye shall be delivered up even by parents, and brethren, and kinsfolk, and friends; and <some> of you shall they cause to be put to death.
[13] And ye shall be hated of all men for my name's sake: but he that endures to the end, the same shall be saved.	[17] And ye shall be hated of all men for my name's sake. [18] And not a hair of your head shall perish. [19] In your patience ye shall win your souls.

6. The Sign of the Fall of Yerushalayim

Luke 21:20-24

[20] But when ye see Yerushalayim compassed with armies, then know that her desolation is at hand. [21] Then let them that are in Yehudah flee unto the mountains; and let them that are in the midst of her depart out; and let not them that are in the country enter therein. [22] For these are days of vengeance, that all things which are written may be fulfilled. [23] Woe unto them that are with child and to them that give suck in those days! For there shall be great distress upon the land, and wrath unto this people. [24] And they shall fall by the edge of the sword, and shall be led captive into all the nations: and Yerushalayim shall be trodden down of the Gentiles, until the times of the Gentiles be fulfilled.

7. The Great Tribulation

a. The First Half

Matthew 24:9-14

[9] Then shall they deliver you up unto tribulation, and shall kill you: and ye shall be hated of all the nations for my name's sake. [10] And then shall many stumble, and shall deliver up one another, and shall hate one another. [11] And many false prophets shall arise, and shall lead many astray. [12] And because iniquity shall be multiplied, the love of the many shall wax cold. [13] But he that endures to the end, the same shall be saved. [14] And this gospel of the kingdom shall be preached in the whole world for a testimony unto all the nations; and then shall the end come.

b. The Second Half

Matthew 24:15-28	Mark 13:14-23

[15] When therefore ye see the abomination of desolation, which was spoken of through Daniel the prophet, standing in the holy place (let him that reads understand), [16] then let them that are in Yehudah flee unto the mountains: [17] let him that is on the housetop not go down to take out things that are in his house: [18] and let him that is in the field not return back to take his cloak.

[19] But woe unto them that are with child and to them that give suck in those days! [20] And pray ye that your flight be not in the winter, neither on a Sabbath: [21] for then shall be great tribulation, such as has not been from the beginning of the world until now, no, nor ever shall be.

[22] And except those days had been shortened, no flesh would have been saved: but for the elect's sake those days shall be shortened.

[23] Then if any man shall say unto you, Lo, here is the messiah, or, Here; believe <it> not. [24] For there shall arise false messiahs, and false prophets, and shall show great signs and wonders; so as to lead astray, if possible, even the elect.

[14] But when ye see the abomination of desolation standing where he ought not (let him that reads understand),

then let them that are in Yehudah flee unto the mountains: [15] and let him that is on the housetop not go down, nor enter in, to take anything out his house: [16] and let him that is in the field not return back to take his cloak.

[17] But woe unto them that are with child and to them that give suck in those days! [18] And pray ye that it be not in the winter. [19] For those days shall be tribulation, such as there has not been the like from the beginning of the creation which God created until now, and never shall be.

[20] And except the Lord had shortened the days, no flesh would have been saved; but for the elect's sake, whom he chose, he shortened the days.

[21] And then if any man shall say unto you, Lo, here is the messiah; or, Lo, there; believe <it> not: [22] for there shall arise false messiahs and false prophets, and shall show signs and wonders, that they may lead astray, if possible, the elect.

25 Behold, I have told you before-hand.

26 If therefore they shall say unto you, Behold, he is in the wilderness; go not forth: Behold, he is in the inner chambers; believe <it> not.

27 For as the lightning comes forth from the east, and is seen even unto the west; so shall be the coming of the Son of man. 28 Wheresoever the carcase is, there will the eagles[2] be gathered together.

23 But take ye heed: behold, I have told you all things beforehand.

8. The Second Coming

Matthew 24:29-30	Mark 13:24-26	Luke 21:25-27
29 But immediately after the tribulation of those days the sun shall be darkened, and the moon shall not give her light, and the stars shall fall from heaven,	24 But in those days, after that tribulation, the sun shall be dark-ened, and the moon shall not give her light, 25 and the stars shall be falling from heaven,	25 And there shall be signs in sun and moon and stars; and upon the earth distress of nations, in perplexity for the roaring of the sea and the billows; 26 men fainting for fear, and for expectation of the things which are coming on the world:
and the powers of the heavens shall be shaken: 30 and then shall appear the sign of the	and the powers that are in the heavens shall be shaken.	for the powers of the heavens shall be shaken.

[2] Or, *vultures*.

Son of man in heaven: and then shall all the tribes of the earth mourn,		
and they shall see the Son of man coming on the clouds of heaven with power and great glory.	[26] And then shall they see the Son of man coming in clouds with great power and glory.	[27] And then shall they see the Son of man coming in a cloud with power and great glory.

9. The Regathering of Yisrael

Matthew 24:31	Mark 13:27
[31] And he shall send forth his angels with a great sound of a trumpet, and they shall gather together his elect from the four winds, from one end of heaven to the other.	[27] And then shall he send forth the angels, and shall gather together his elect from the four winds, from the uttermost part of the earth to the uttermost part of heaven.

10. The Exhortation

Luke 21:28

[28] But when these things begin to come to pass, look up, and lift up your heads; because your redemption draws near.

11. The Parable of the Fig Tree

Matthew 24:32-35	Mark 13:28-32	Luke 21:29-33
[32] Now from the fig tree learn her parable: when her branch is now become tender, and puts forth its	[28] Now from the fig tree learn her parable: when her branch is now become tender, and puts forth its	[29] And he spoke to them a parable: Behold the fig tree, and all the trees: [30] when they now shoot forth, ye

leaves, ye know that the summer is near;

³³ even so ye also, when ye see all these things, know ye that he is near, <even> at the doors. ³⁴ Verily I say unto you, This generation shall not pass away, till all these things be accomplished.

³⁵ Heaven and earth shall pass away, but my words shall not pass away.

leaves, ye know that the summer is near;

²⁹ even so ye also, when ye see these things coming to pass, know ye that he is near, <even> at the doors. ³⁰ Verily I say unto you, This generation shall not pass away, until all these things be accomplished.

³¹ Heaven and earth shall pass away: but my words shall not pass away. ³² But of that day or that hour knows no one, not even the angels in heaven, neither the Son, but the Father.

see it and know of your own selves that the summer is now near.

³¹ Even so ye also, when ye see these things coming to pass, know ye that the kingdom of God is near. ³² Verily I say unto you, This generation shall not pass away, till all things be accomplished.

³³ Heaven and earth shall pass away: but my words shall not pass away.

12. The Rapture

Matthew 24:36-42

³⁶ But of that day and hour knows no one, not even the angels of heaven, neither the Son, but the Father only. ³⁷ And as <were> the days of Noach, so shall be the coming of the Son of man. ³⁸ For as in those days which were before the flood they were eating and drinking,

Luke 21:34-36

³⁴ But take heed to yourselves, lest haply your hearts be overcharged with surfeiting, and drunkenness, and cares of this life, and that day come on you suddenly as a snare: ³⁵ for <so> shall it come upon all them that dwell on the face of all the earth. ³⁶ But watch ye at every

marrying and giving in marriage, until the day that Noach entered into the ark, [39] and they knew not until the flood came, and took them all away; so shall be the coming of the Son of man. [40] Then shall two men be in the field; one is taken, and one is left: [41] two women <shall be> grinding at the mill; one is taken, and one is left. [42] Watch therefore: for ye know not on what day your Lord comes.

season, making supplication, that ye may prevail to escape all these things that shall come to pass, and to stand before the Son of man.

13. Parables Urging Watchfulness, Readiness, and Labor

a. The Parable of the Porter

Mark 13:33-37

[33] Take ye heed, watch and pray: for ye know not when the time is. [34] <It is> as <when> a man, sojourning in another country, having left his house, and given authority to his servants, to each one his work, commanded also the porter to watch. [35] Watch therefore: for ye know not when the lord of the house comes, whether at even, or at midnight, or at cockcrowing, or in the morning; [36] lest coming suddenly he find you sleeping. [37] And what I say unto you I say unto all, Watch.

b. The Parable of the Master of the House

Matthew 24:43-44

[43] But know this, that if the master of the house had known in what watch the thief was coming, he would have watched, and would not have suffered his house to be broken through. [44] Therefore be ye also ready; for in an hour that ye think not the Son of man comes.

c. The Parable of the Faithful Servant and the Evil Servant

Matthew 24:45-51

[45] Who then is the faithful and wise servant, whom his lord has set over his household, to give them their food in due season? [46] Blessed is that servant, whom his lord when he comes shall find so doing. [47] Verily I say unto you, that he will set him over all that he has. [48] But if that evil servant shall say in his heart, My lord tarries; [49] and shall begin to beat his fellow-servants, and shall eat and drink with the drunken; [50] the lord of that servant shall come in a day when he expects not, and in an hour when he knows not, [51] and shall cut him asunder, and appoint his portion with the hypocrites: there shall be the weeping and the gnashing of teeth.

d. The Parable of the Ten Virgins

Matthew 25:1-13

[1] Then shall the kingdom of heaven be likened unto ten virgins, who took their lamps, and went forth to meet the bridegroom. [2] And five of them were foolish, and five were wise. [3] For the foolish, when they took their lamps, took no oil with them: [4] but the wise took oil in their vessels with their lamps. [5] Now while the bridegroom tarried, they all slumbered and slept. [6] But at midnight there is a cry, Behold, the bridegroom! Come ye forth to meet him. [7] Then all those virgins arose, and trimmed their lamps. [8] And the foolish said unto the wise, Give us of your oil; for our lamps are going out. [9] But the wise answered, saying, Peradventure there will not be enough for us and you: go ye rather to them that sell, and buy for yourselves. [10] And while they went away to buy, the bridegroom came; and they that were ready went in with him to the marriage feast: and the door was shut. [11] Afterward came also the other virgins, saying, Lord, Lord, open to us. [12] But he answered and said, Verily I say unto you, I know you not. [13] Watch therefore, for ye know not the day nor the hour.

e. The Parable of the Talents

Matthew 25:14-30

[14] For <it is> as <when> a man, going into another country, called his own servants, and delivered unto them his goods. [15] And unto one he gave five talents, to another two, to another one; to each according to his several ability; and he went on his journey. [16] Straightway he that received the five talents went and traded with them, and made other five talents. [17] In like manner he also that <received> the two gained other two. [18] But he that received the one went away and digged in the earth, and hid his lord's money. [19] Now after a long time the lord of those servants comes, and makes a reckoning with them. [20] And he that received the five talents came and brought other five talents, saying, Lord, you delivered unto me five talents: lo, I have gained other five talents. [21] His lord said unto him, Well done, good and faithful servant: you have been faithful over a few things, I will set you over many things; enter you into the joy of your lord. [22] And he also that <received> the two talents came and said, Lord, you delivered unto me two talents: lo, I have gained other two talents. [23] His lord said unto him, Well done, good and faithful servant: you have been faithful over a few things, I will set you over many things; enter you into the joy of your lord. [24] And he also that had received the one talent came and said, Lord, I knew you that you are a hard man, reaping where you did not sow, and gathering where you did not scatter; [25] and I was afraid, and went away and hid your talent in the earth: lo, you have your own. [26] But his lord answered and said unto him, You wicked and slothful servant, you knew that I reap where I sowed not, and gather where I did not scatter; [27] you ought there-fore to have put my money to the bankers, and at my coming I should have received back mine own with interest. [28] Take ye away therefore the talent from him, and give it unto him that has the ten talents. [29] For unto everyone that has shall be given, and he shall have abundance: but from him that has not, even that which he has shall be taken away. [30] And cast ye out the unprofitable servant into the outer darkness: there shall be the weeping and the gnashing of teeth.

14. The Judgment of the Gentiles

Matthew 25:31-46

[31] But when the Son of man shall come in his glory, and all the angels with him, then shall he sit on the throne of his glory: [32] and before him shall be gathered all the nations: and he shall separate them one from another, as the shepherd separates the sheep from the goats; [33] and he shall set the sheep on his right hand, but the goats on the left. [34] Then shall the King say unto them on his right hand, Come, ye blessed of my Father, inherit the kingdom prepared for you from the foundation of the world: [35] for I was hungry, and ye gave me to eat; I was thirsty, and ye gave me drink; I was a stranger, and ye took me in; [36] naked, and ye clothed me; I was sick, and ye visited me; I was in prison, and ye came unto me. [37] Then shall the righteous answer him, saying, Lord, when saw we you hungry, and fed you? Or athirst, and gave you drink? [38] And when saw we you a stranger, and took you in? Or naked, and clothed you? [39] And when saw we you sick, or in prison, and came unto you? [40] And the King shall answer and say unto them, Verily I say unto you, Inasmuch as ye did it unto one of these my brethren, <even> these least, ye did it unto me. [41] Then shall he say also unto them on the left hand, Depart from me, ye cursed, into the eternal fire which is prepared for the devil and his angels: [42] for I was hungry, and ye did not give me to eat; I was thirsty, and ye gave me no drink; [43] I was a stranger, and ye took me not in; naked, and ye clothed me not; sick, and in prison, and ye visited me not. [44] Then shall they also answer, saying, Lord, when saw we you hungry, or athirst, or a stranger, or naked, or sick, or in prison, and did not minister unto you? [45] Then shall he answer them, saying, Verily I say unto you, Inasmuch as ye did it not unto one of these least, ye did it not unto me. [46] And these shall go away into eternal punishment: but the righteous into eternal life.

15. Luke's Summary

Luke 21:37-38

[37] And every day he was teaching in the temple; and every night he went out, and lodged in the mount that is called Olivet. [38] And all the people came early in the morning to him in the temple, to hear him.

[§§ 146–160]—
B. The Preparation for Messiah's Death

[§ 146]—1. The Prediction of His Death

Matthew 26:1-2

[1] And it came to pass, when Yeshua had finished all these words, he said unto his disciples, [2] Ye know that after two days the Passover comes, and the Son of man is delivered up to be crucified.

[§ 147]—2. The Conspiracy of the Rulers

Matthew 26:3-5	Mark 14:1-2	Luke 22:1-2
	[1] Now after two days was <the feast of> the Passover and the unleavened bread:	[1] Now the feast of unleavened bread drew near, which is called the Passover.
[3] Then were gathered together the chief priests, and the elders of the people, unto the court of the high priest, who was called Kayapha; [4] and they	and the chief priests and the scribes sought how they might take him with subtlety, and kill him: [2] for they said, Not during the feast, lest haply there shall	[2] And the chief priests and the scribes sought how they might put him to death; for they feared the people.

took counsel together that they might take Yeshua by subtlety, and kill him. ⁵ But they said, Not during the feast, lest a tumult arise among people.	be a tumult of the people.

[§ 148]—3. The Pouring of Ointment

Matthew 26:6-13	**Mark 14:3-9**	**John 12:2-8**
⁶ Now when Yeshua was in Beit Anyah, in the house of Shimon the leper,	³ And while he was in Beit Anyah in the house of Shimon the leper, as he sat at meat,	² So they made him a supper there: and Marta served; but Elazar was one of them that sat at meat with him.
⁷ there came unto him a woman having an alabaster cruse of exceeding precious ointment, and she poured it upon his head, as he sat at meat.	there came a woman having an alabaster cruse of ointment of pure nard very costly; <and> she broke the cruse, and poured it over his head.	³ Miriam therefore took a pound of ointment of pure nard, very precious, and anointed the feet of Yeshua, and wiped his feet with her hair: and the house was filled with the odor of the ointment.
⁸ But when the disciples saw it, they had indignation, saying, To what purpose is this waste?	⁴ But there were some that had indignation among themselves, <saying>, To what purpose has this waste of the ointment been made? ⁵ For this ointment might have been	⁴ But Yehudah Ish Kriyot, one of his disciples, that should betray him, said,
⁹ For this <ointment> might have been sold		⁵ Why was not this ointment sold for three

for much, and given to the poor.

10 But Yeshua perceiving it said unto them, Why trouble ye the woman? For she has wrought a good work upon me.
11 For ye have the poor always with you; but me ye have not always.

12 For in that she poured this ointment upon my body, she did it to prepare me for burial.
13 Verily I say unto you, Wheresoever this gospel shall be preached in the whole world, that also which this woman has done shall be spoken of for a memorial of her.

sold for above three hundred shillings, and given to the poor.
And they murmured against her.

6 But Yeshua said, Let her alone; why trouble ye her? She has wrought a good work on me.

7 For ye have the poor always with you, and whensoever ye will ye can do them good: but me ye have not always.
8 She has done what she could; she has anointed my body beforehand for the burying.
9 And verily I say unto you, Wheresoever the gospel shall be preached throughout the whole world, that also which this woman has done shall be spoken of for a memorial of her.

hundred shillings, and given to the poor?
6 Now this he said, not because he cared for the poor; but because he was a thief, and having the bag took away what was put therein.
7 Yeshua therefore said, Suffer her to keep it against the day of my burying.

8 For the poor ye have always with you; but me ye have not always.

[§ 149]—4. The Promise to Betray

Matthew 26:14-16	Mark 14:10-11	Luke 22:3-6
[14] Then one of the twelve, who was called Yehudah Ish Kriyot, went unto the chief priests,	[10] And Yehudah Ish Kriyot, he that was one of the twelve, went away unto the chief priests,	[3] And Satan entered into Yehudah who was called Ish Kriyot, being of the number of the twelve. [4] And he went away, and communed with the chief priests and captains,
[15] and said, What are ye willing to give me, and I will deliver him unto you? And they weighed unto him thirty pieces of silver.	that he might deliver him unto them. [11] And they, when they heard it, were glad, and promised to give him money.	how he might deliver him unto them. [5] And they were glad, and covenanted to give him money.
[16] And from that time he sought opportunity to deliver him <unto them.>	And he sought how he might conveniently deliver him <unto them>.	[6] And he consented, and sought opportunity to deliver him unto them in the absence of the multitude.

[§§ 150–160]—
5. The Last Passover and the First Lord's Supper

[§ 150]—a. The Preparation for the Seder[3]

Matthew 26:17-19	Mark 14:12-16	Luke 22:7-13
[17] Now on the first <day> of unleavened bread the disciples came to Yeshua, saying, Where will you that we make ready for you to eat the Passover?	[12] And on the first day of unleavened bread, when they sacrificed the Passover, his disciples say unto him, Where will you that we go and make ready that you may eat the Passover?	[7] And the day of unleavened bread came, on which the Passover must be sacrificed. [8] And he sent Peter and Yochanan, saying, Go and make ready for us the Passover, that we may eat. [9] And they said unto him, Where will you that we make ready?
[18] And he said, Go into the city to such a man, and say unto him,	[13] And he sent two of his disciples, and said unto them, Go into the city, and there shall meet you a man bearing a pitcher of water: follow him; [14] and wheresoever he shall enter in, say to the master of the house,	[10] And he said unto them, Behold, when ye are entered into the city, there shall meet you a man bearing a pitcher of water; follow him into the house whereinto he goes. [11] And ye shall say unto the master of the house,
The Teacher said, My time is at hand; I keep	The Teacher said, Where is my guest-	The Teacher said unto you, Where is the

---

[3] The seder, a meal whose Hebrew name means "order," marks the beginning of the Feast of Passover.

the Passover at your house with my disciples.	chamber, where I shall eat the Passover with my disciples? [15] And he will himself show you a large upper room furnished <and> ready: and there make ready for us.	guestchamber, where I shall eat the Passover with my disciples? [12] And he will show you a large upper room furnished: there make ready.
[19] And the disciples did as Yeshua appointed them; and they made ready the Passover.	[16] And the disciples went forth, and came into the city, and found as he had said unto them: and they made ready the Passover.	[13] And they went, and found as he had said unto them: and they made ready the Passover.

[§ 151]—b. The Start of the Passover Observance

Matthew 26:20	Mark 14:17	Luke 22:14-16
[20] Now when even was come, he was sitting at meat with the twelve disciples;	[17] And when it was evening he comes with the twelve.	[14] And when the hour was come, he sat down, and the apostles with him. [15] And he said unto them, With desire I have desired to eat this Passover with you before I suffer: [16] for I say unto you, I shall not eat it, until it be fulfilled in the kingdom of God.

[§ 152]—c. The First Cup

Luke 22:17-18

[17] And he received a cup, and when he had given thanks, he said, Take this, and divide it among yourselves: [18] for I say unto you, I shall not drink from henceforth of the fruit of the vine, until the kingdom of God shall come.

[§ 153]—d. The Washing of the Feet and the First Prediction of the Betrayal by Yehudah

John 13:1-20

[1] Now before the feast of the Passover, Yeshua knowing that his hour was come that he should depart out of this world unto his Father, having loved his own that were in the world, he loved them unto the end. [2] And during supper, the devil having already put into the heart of Yehudah Ish Kriyot, Shimon's <son>, to betray him, [3] <Yeshua>, knowing that the Father had given all the things into his hands, and that he came forth from God, and goes unto God, [4] rose from supper, and laid aside his garments; and he took a towel, and girded himself. [5] Then he poured water into the basin, and began to wash the disciples' feet, and to wipe them with the towel wherewith he was girded. [6] So he came to Shimon Peter. He said unto him, Lord, do you wash my feet? [7] Yeshua answered and said unto him, What I do you know not now; but you shall understand hereafter. [8] Peter said unto him, You shall never wash my feet. Yeshua answered him, If I wash you not, you have no part with me. [9] Shimon Peter said unto him, Lord, not my feet only, but also my hands and my head. [10] Yeshua said to him, He that is bathed needs not save to wash his feet, but is clean every whit: and ye are clean, but not all. [11] For he knew him that should betray him; therefore said he, Ye are not all clean.

[12] So when he had washed their feet, and taken his garments, and sat[4] down again, he said unto them, Know ye what I have done to you? [13] Ye call me, Teacher, and, Lord: and ye say well; for so I am. [14] If I then, the Lord and

---

[4] Greek: reclined.

the Teacher, have washed your feet, ye also ought to wash one another's feet. [15] For I have given you an example, that ye also should do as I have done to you. [16] Verily, verily, I say unto you, a servant is not greater than his lord; neither one that is sent greater than he that sent him. [17] If ye know these things, blessed are ye if ye do them. [18] I speak not of you all: I know whom I have chosen: but that the scripture may be fulfilled: He that eats my bread lifted up his heel against me. [19] From henceforth I tell you before it come to pass, that, when it is come to pass, ye may believe that I am <he>. [20] Verily, verily, I say unto you, he that receives whomsoever I send receives me; and he that receives me receives him that sent me.

[§ 154]—e. Karpas:[5]
The Second Prediction of the Betrayal by Yehudah

Matthew 26:21-25	Mark 14:18-21	Luke 22:21-23
[21] and as they were eating, he said, Verily I say unto you, that one of you shall betray me.	[18] And as they sat and were eating, Yeshua said, Verily I say unto you, One of you shall betray me, <even> he that eats with me.	
[22] And they were exceeding sorrowful, and began to say unto him everyone, Is it I, Lord?	[19] They began to be sorrowful, and to say unto him one by one, Is it I?	
[23] And he answered and said, He that	[20] And he said unto them, <It is> one of the	[21] But behold, the hand of him that betrays me

---

[5] Karpas is one of the traditional ceremonies of the Passover Seder. It follows the washing of hands. This Hebrew term comes from the Greek *karpos*, which refers to a fresh, raw vegetable. The ceremony consists of everyone dipping a piece of green vegetable (usually parsley or celery) into salt water and then eating it. Green is a symbol of spring, the symbol of youth. It reminds the Jewish people that when Yisrael was young, in the springtime of her nationhood, God saved her by means of salt water. It is a reminder that God divided the Red Sea and allowed the Jews to cross on dry land, but the Egyptian army was drowned.

dipped his hand with me in the dish, the same shall betray me. [24] The Son of man goes, even as it is written of him: but woe unto that man through whom the Son of man is betrayed! Good were it for that man if he had not been born. [25] And Yehudah, who betrayed him, answered and said, Is it I, Rabbi? He said unto him, You have said.	twelve, he that dips with me in the dish. [21] For the Son of man goes, even as it is written of him: but woe unto that man through whom the Son of man is betrayed! Good were it for that man if he had not been born.	is with me on the table. [22] For the Son of man indeed goes, as it has been determined: but woe unto that man through whom he is betrayed! [23] And they began to question among themselves, which of them it was that should do this thing.

[§ 155]—f. The Breaking of the Middle Matzah

Mt. 26:26	Mark 14:22	Luke 22:19	I Cor. 11:23-24
[26] And as they were eating, Yeshua took bread, and blessed, and broke it; and he gave to the disciples, and said,	[22] And as they were eating, he took bread, and when he had blessed, he broke it, and gave to them, and said,	[19] And he took bread, and when he had given thanks, he broke it, and gave to them, saying,	[23] For I received of the Lord that which also I delivered unto you, that the Lord Yeshua in the night in which he was betrayed took bread; [24] and when he had given

			thanks, he broke it, and said,
Take, eat; this is my body.	Take ye: this is my body.	This is my body which is given for you: this do in remembrance of me.	This is my body, which is for you: this do in re-membrance of me.

[§ 156]—g. The Sop:[6]
The Third Prediction of the Betrayal by Yehudah

John 13:21-30

[21] When Yeshua had thus said, he was troubled in the spirit, and testified, and said, Verily, verily, I say unto you, that one of you shall betray me. [22] The disciples looked one on another, doubting of whom he spoke. [23] There was at the table reclining in Yeshua' bosom one of his disciples, whom Yeshua loved. [24] Shimon Peter therefore beckons to him, and said unto him, Tell <us> who it is of whom he speaks. [25] He leaning back, as he was, on Yeshua' breast said unto him, Lord, who is it? [26] Yeshua therefore answered, He it is, for whom I shall dip the sop, and give it him. So when he had dipped the sop, he took and gave it to Yehudah, <the son> of Shimon Ish Kriyot. [27] And after the sop, then entered Satan into him. Yeshua therefore said unto him, What you do, do quickly. [28] Now no man at the table knew for what intent he spoke this unto him. [29] For some thought, because Yehudah had the bag, that Yeshua said unto him, Buy what things we have

---

[6] One of the ceremonial items prepared for the Passover is called *charoset*, a mixture of apples, nuts, honey, cinnamon, lemon juice, and wine. It is prepared the day before Passover so that by Passover night, it has become a deep brown color. It symbolizes brick mortar and is a reminder of the fact that when the Jews were slaves in Egypt, they had to make mortar and bricks to build the cities of Pharaoh. The officiator of the seder dips a piece of unleavened bread first into the charoset and then into bitter herbs, such as horseradish. He then passes the sop to one of the guests and repeats this procedure until all participants and he himself receive their portion.

need of for the feast; or, that he should give something to the poor. [30] He then having received the sop went out straightway: and it was night.

[§ 157]—h. The Third Cup

Mt. 26:27-29	Mark 14:23-25	Luke 22:20	I Cor. 11:25-26
[27] And he took a cup, and gave thanks, and gave to them, saying, Drink ye all of it; [28] for this is my blood of the covenant, which is poured out for many unto remission of sins. [29] But I say unto you, I shall not drink henceforth of this fruit of the vine, until that day when I drink it new with you in my Father's kingdom.	[23] And he took a cup, and when he had given thanks, he gave to them: and they all drank of it. [24] And he said unto them, This is my blood of the covenant, which is poured out for many. [25] Verily I say unto you, I shall no more drink of the fruit of the vine, until that day when I drink it new in the kingdom of God.	[20] And the cup in like manner after supper, saying, This cup is the new covenant in my blood, <even> that which is poured out for you.	[25] In like manner also the cup, after supper, saying, This cup is the new covenant in my blood: this do, as often as ye drink <it>, in remembrance of me. [26] For as often as ye eat this bread, and drink the cup, ye proclaim the Lord's death till he come.

[§ 158]—i. A Lesson in Greatness

Luke 22:24-30

[24] And there arose also a contention among them, which of them was accounted to be greatest. [25] And he said unto them, The kings of the Gentiles have lordship over them; and they that have authority over them are called

Benefactors. [26] But ye <shall> not <be> so: but he that is the greater among you, let him become as the younger; and he that is chief, as he that does serve. [27] For which is greater, he that sits at meat, or he that serves? Is not he that sits at meat? But I am in the midst of you as he that serves. [28] But ye are they that have continued with me in my temptations; [29] and I appoint unto you a kingdom, even as my Father appointed unto me, [30] that ye may eat and drink at my table in my kingdom; and ye shall sit on thrones judging the twelve tribes of Yisrael.

[§ 159]—j. The Prediction of Peter's Denial

John 13:31-38

[31] When therefore he was gone out, Yeshua said, Now is the Son of man glorified, and God is glorified in him; [32] and God shall glorify him in himself, and straightway shall he glorify him. [33] Little children, yet a little while I am with you. Ye shall seek me: and as I said unto the Jews, Whither I go, ye cannot come; so now I say unto you. [34] A new commandment I give unto you, that ye love one another; even as I have loved you, that ye also love one another. [35] By this shall all men know that ye are my disciples, if ye have love one to another. [36] Shimon Peter said unto him, Lord, whither go you? Yeshua answered, Whither I go, you cannot follow now; but you shall follow afterwards.

Mt. 26:31-35	Mark 14:27-31	Luke 22:31-38	John cont.
[31] Then said Yeshua unto them, All ye shall be offended in me this night: for it is written, I will smite the shepherd, and the sheep of the	[27] And Yeshua said unto them, All ye shall be offended: for it is written, I will smite the shepherd, and the sheep shall be scattered abroad.	[31] Shimon, Shimon, behold, Satan asked to have you, that he might sift you as wheat: [32] but I made supplication for you, that your faith fail not; and do	

flock shall be scattered abroad.

[32] But after I am raised up, I will go before you into Galil.
[33] But Peter answered and said unto him, If all shall be offended in you, I will never be offended.
[34] Yeshua said unto him, Verily I say unto you, that this night, before the cock crow, you shall deny me thrice.

[35] Peter said unto him, Even if I must die with you, <yet> will I not deny you. Likewise also said all the disciples.

[28] Howbeit, after I am raised up, I will go before you into Galil.
[29] But Peter said unto him, Although all shall be offended, yet will not I.

[30] And Yeshua said unto him, Verily I say unto you, that you today, <even> this night, before the cock crow twice, shall deny me thrice.

[31] But he spoke exceedingly vehemently, If I must die with you, I will not deny you. And in like manner also said they all.

you, when once you have turned again, establish your brethren.

[33] And he said unto him, Lord, with you I am ready to go both to prison and to death.

[34] And he said, I tell you, Peter, the cock shall not crow this day, until you shall thrice deny that you know me.

[37] Peter said unto him, Lord, why cannot I follow you even now? I will lay down my life for you.
[38] Yeshua answered, Will you lay down your life for me? Verily, verily, I say unto you, The cock shall not crow, till you have denied me thrice.

Lk. cont.: [35] And he said unto them, When I sent you forth without purse, and wallet, and shoes, lacked ye anything? And they said, Nothing. [36] And

he said unto them, But now, he that has a purse, let him take it, and likewise a wallet; and he that has none, let him sell his cloak, and buy a sword.
[37] For I say unto you, that this which is written must be fulfilled in me, And he was reckoned with transgressors: for that which concerns me has fulfillment. [38] And they said, Lord, behold, here are two swords. And he said unto them, It is enough.

[§ 160]—k. The Hallel[7]

Matthew 26:30	**Mark 14:26**
[30] And when they had sung a hymn, they went out unto the mount of Olives.	[26] And when they had sung a hymn, they went out unto the mount of Olives.

[§§ 161–162]—
C. The Promises and Admonitions by the King

[§ 161]—1. In the Upper Room

John 14

[1] Let not your heart be troubled: believe in God, believe also in me. [2] In my Father's house are many mansions; if it were not so, I would have told you; for I go to prepare a place for you. [3] And if I go and prepare a place for you, I come again, and will receive you unto myself; that where I am, <there> ye may be also. [4] And whither I go, ye know the way. [5] Toma said unto him, Lord, we know not whither you go; how know we the way? [6] Yeshua said unto him, I am the way, and the truth, and the life: no one comes unto the

---

[7] To bring the Passover observance to a close, the seder guests sing Psalms 113 – 118, especially focusing on Psalms 117 and 118. While singing, they drink the fourth cup of wine, called *Hallel*, or the cup of praise, which gives this last part of the Passover observance its name.

Father, but by me. [7] If ye had known me, ye would have known my Father also: from henceforth ye know him, and have seen him. [8] Philip said unto him, Lord, show us the Father, and it suffices us. [9] Yeshua said unto him, Have I been so long time with you, and do you not know me, Philip? He that has seen me has seen the Father; how say you, Show us the Father? [10] Believe you not that I am in the Father, and the Father in me? The words that I say unto you I speak not from myself: but the Father abiding in me does his works. [11] Believe me that I am in the Father, and the Father in me: or else believe me for the very works' sake. [12] Verily, verily, I say unto you, he that believes on me, the works that I do shall he do also; and greater <works> than these shall he do; because I go unto the Father. [13] And whatsoever ye shall ask in my name, that will I do, that the Father may be glorified in the Son. [14] If ye shall ask anything in my name, that will I do. [15] If ye love me, ye will keep my commandments. [16] And I will pray the Father, and he shall give you another Comforter, that he may be with you forever, [17] <even> the Spirit of truth: whom the world cannot receive; for it beholds him not, neither knows him: ye know him; for he abides with you, and shall be in you. [18] I will not leave you desolate: I come unto you. [19] Yet a little while, and the world beholds me no more; but ye behold me: because I live, ye shall live also. [20] In that day ye shall know that I am in my Father, and ye in me, and I in you. [21] He that has my commandments, and keeps them, he it is that loves me: and he that loves me shall be loved of my Father, and I will love him, and will manifest myself unto him. [22] Yehudah (not Ish Kriyot) said unto him, Lord, what is come to pass that you will manifest yourself unto us, and not unto the world? [23] Yeshua answered and said unto him, If a man love me, he will keep my word: and my Father will love him, and we will come unto him, and make our abode with him. [24] He that loves me not keeps not my words: and the word which ye hear is not mine, but the Father's who sent me.

[25] These things have I spoken unto you, while <yet> abiding with you. [26] But the Comforter, <even> the Holy Spirit, whom the Father will send in my name, he shall teach you all things, and bring to your remembrance all that I said unto you. [27] Peace I leave with you; my peace I give unto you: not as the world gives, give I unto you. Let not your heart be troubled, neither let it be fearful. [28] Ye heard how I said to you, I go away, and I come unto you. If ye loved me, ye would have rejoiced, because I go unto the Father: for the

Father is greater than I. [29] And now I have told you before it come to pass, that, when it is come to pass, ye may believe. [30] I will no more speak much with you, for the prince of the world comes: and he has nothing in me; [31] but that the world may know that I love the Father, and as the Father gave me commandment, even so I do. Arise, let us go hence.

[§ 162]—2. On the Way to Gethsemane

John 15 & 16

[1] I am the true vine, and my Father is the husbandman. [2] Every branch in me that bears not fruit, he takes it away: and every <branch> that bears fruit, he cleanses it, that it may bear more fruit. [3] Already ye are clean because of the word which I have spoken unto you. [4] Abide in me, and I in you. As the branch cannot bear fruit of itself, except it abide in the vine; so neither can ye, except ye abide in me. [5] I am the vine, ye are the branches: He that abides in me, and I in him, the same bears much fruit: for apart from me ye can do nothing. [6] If a man abide not in me, he is cast forth as a branch, and is withered; and they gather them, and cast them into the fire, and they are burned. [7] If ye abide in me, and my words abide in you, ask whatsoever ye will, and it shall be done unto you. [8] Herein is my Father glorified, that ye bear much fruit; and <so> shall ye be my disciples. [9] Even as the Father has loved me, I also have loved you: abide ye in my love. [10] If ye keep my commandments, ye shall abide in my love; even as I have kept my Father's commandments, and abide in his love. [11] These things have I spoken unto you, that my joy may be in you, and <that> your joy may be made full. [12] This is my commandment, that ye love one another, even as I have loved you. [13] Greater love has no man than this, that a man lay down his life for his friends. [14] Ye are my friends, if ye do the things which I command you. [15] No longer do I call you servants; for the servant knows not what his lord does: but I have called you friends; for all things that I heard from my Father, I have made known unto you. [16] Ye did not choose me, but I chose you, and appointed you, that ye should go and bear fruit, and <that> your fruit should abide: that whatsoever ye shall ask of the Father in my name, he may give it you. [17] These things I command you, that ye may love one another. [18] If the world hates you, ye know that it has hated me before <it hated> you. [19] If ye were of the world, the world would love its own: but

because ye are not of the world, but I chose you out of the world, therefore the world hates you. [20] Remember the word that I said unto you, A servant is not greater than his lord. If they persecuted me, they will also persecute you; if they kept my word, they will keep yours also. [21] But all these things will they do unto you for my name's sake, because they know not him that sent me. [22] If I had not come and spoken unto them, they had not had sin: but now they have no excuse for their sin. [23] He that hates me hates my Father also. [24] If I had not done among them the works which none other did, they had not had sin: but now have they both seen and hated both me and my Father. [25] But <this comes to pass>, that the word may be fulfilled that is written in their law, They hated me without a cause. [26] But when the Comforter is come, whom I will send unto you from the Father, <even> the Spirit of truth, which proceeds from the Father, he shall bear witness of me: [27] and ye also bear witness, because ye have been with me from the beginning.

[16:1] These things have I spoken unto you, that ye should not be caused to stumble. [2] They shall put you out of the synagogues: yea, the hour comes, that whosoever kills you shall think that he offers service unto God. [3] And these things will they do, because they have not known the Father, nor me. [4] But these things have I spoken unto you, that when their hour is come, ye may remember them, how that I told you. And these things I said not unto you from the beginning, because I was with you. [5] But now I go unto him that sent me; and none of you asks me, Whither go you? [6] But because I have spoken these things unto you, sorrow has filled your heart. [7] Nevertheless I tell you the truth: It is expedient for you that I go away; for if I go not away, the Comforter will not come unto you; but if I go, I will send him unto you. [8] And he, when he is come, will convict the world in respect of sin, and of righteousness, and of judgment: [9] of sin, because they believe not on me; [10] of righteousness, because I go to the Father, and ye behold me no more; [11] of judgment, because the prince of this world has been judged. [12] I have yet many things to say unto you, but ye cannot bear them now. [13] Howbeit when he, the Spirit of truth, is come, he shall guide you into all the truth: for he shall not speak from himself; but what things soever he shall hear, <these> shall he speak: and he shall declare unto you the things that are to come. [14] He shall glorify me: for he shall take of mine, and shall declare <it> unto you. [15] All things whatsoever the Father has are mine:

therefore said I, that he takes of mine, and shall declare \<it\> unto you. [16] A little while, and ye behold me no more; and again a little while, and ye shall see me. [17] \<Some\> of his disciples therefore said one to another, What is this that he said unto us, A little while, and ye behold me not; and again a little while, and ye shall see me: and, Because I go to the Father? [18] They said therefore, What is this that he said, A little while? We know not what he said. [19] Yeshua perceived that they were desirous to ask him, and he said unto them, Do ye inquire among yourselves concerning this, that I said, A little while, and ye behold me not, and again a little while, and ye shall see me? [20] Verily, verily, I say unto you, that ye shall weep and lament, but the world shall rejoice: ye shall be sorrowful, but your sorrow shall be turned into joy. [21] A woman when she is in travail has sorrow, because her hour is come: but when she is delivered of the child, she remembers no more the anguish, for the joy that a man is born into the world. [22] And ye therefore now have sorrow: but I will see you again, and your heart shall rejoice, and your joy no one takes away from you. [23] And in that day ye shall ask me no question. Verily, verily, I say unto you, if ye shall ask anything of the Father, he will give it you in my name. [24] Hitherto have ye asked nothing in my name: ask, and ye shall receive, that your joy may be made full.

[25] These things have I spoken unto you in dark sayings: the hour comes, when I shall no more speak unto you in dark sayings, but shall tell you plainly of the Father. [26] In that day ye shall ask in my name: and I say not unto you, that I will pray the Father for you; [27] for the Father himself loves you, because ye have loved me, and have believed that I came forth from the Father. [28] I came out from the Father, and am come into the world: again, I leave the world, and go unto the Father. [29] His disciples say, Lo, now you speak plainly, and speak no dark saying. [30] Now know we that you know all things, and need not that any man should ask you: by this we believe that you came forth from God. [31] Yeshua answered them, Do ye now believe? [32] Behold, the hour comes, yea, is come, that ye shall be scattered, every man to his own, and shall leave me alone: and \<yet\> I am not alone, because the Father is with me. [33] These things have I spoken unto you, that in me ye may have peace. In the world ye have tribulation: but be of good cheer; I have overcome the world.

[§ 163]—D. The High Priestly Prayer

1. Concerning Himself

John 17:1-8

[1] These things spoke Yeshua; and lifting up his eyes to heaven, he said, Father, the hour is come; glorify your Son, that the son may glorify you: [2] even as you gave him authority over all flesh, that to all whom you have given him, he should give eternal life. [3] And this is life eternal, that they should know you the only true God, and him whom you did send, <even> Yeshua Messiah. [4] I glorified you on the earth, having accomplished the work which you have given me to do. [5] And now, Father, glorify you me with your own self with the glory which I had with you before the world was. [6] I manifested your name unto the men whom you gave me out of the world: yours they were, and you gave them to me; and they have kept your word. [7] Now they know that all things whatsoever you have given me are from you: [8] for the words which you gave me I have given unto them; and they received <them>, and knew of a truth that I came forth from you, and they believed that you did send me.

2. Concerning the Apostles

a. Preservation

John 17:9-14

[9] I pray for them: I pray not for the world, but for those whom you have given me; for they are yours: [10] and all things that are mine are yours, and yours are mine: and I am glorified in them. [11] And I am no more in the world, and these are in the world, and I come to you. Holy Father, keep them in your name which you have given me, that they may be one, even as we <are>. [12] While I was with them, I kept them in your name which you have given me: and I guarded them, and not one of them perished, but the son of perdition; that the scripture might be fulfilled. [13] But now I come to you; and these things I speak in the world, that they may have my joy made

full in themselves. [14] I have given them your word; and the world hated them, because they are not of the world, even as I am not of the world.

b. Protection

John 17:15-16

[15] I pray not that you should take them from the world, but that you should keep them from the evil <one>. [16] They are not of the world even as I am not of the world.

c. Sanctification

John 17:17-19

[17] Sanctify them in the truth: your word is truth. [18] As you did send me into the world, even so sent I them into the world. [19] And for their sakes I sanctify myself, that they themselves also may be sanctified in truth.

3. Concerning All Believers

a. Unity

John 17:20-23

[20] Neither for these only do I pray, but for them also that believe on me through their word; [21] that they may all be one; even as you, Father, <are> in me, and I in you, that they also may be in us: that the world may believe that you did send me. [22] And the glory which you have given me I have given unto them; that they may be one, even as we <are> one; [23] I in them, and you in me, that they may be perfected into one; that the world may know that you did send me, and loved them, even as you loved me.

b. Glorification

John 17:24-26

[24] Father, I desire that they also whom you have given me be with me where I am, that they may behold my glory, which you have given me: for you loved me before the foundation of the world. [25] O righteous Father, the world knew you not, but I knew you; and these knew that you did send me; [26] and I made known unto them your name, and will make it known; that the love wherewith you loved me may be in them, and I in them.

[§ 164]—E. The Agony of Gat Shemen

Mt. 26:36-46	Mark 14:32-42	Luke 22:39-46	John 18:1
[36] Then came Yeshua with them unto a place called Gat Shemen, and said unto his disciples, Sit ye here, while I go yonder and pray.	[32] And they come unto a place which was named Gat She-men: and he said unto his disciples, Sit ye here, while I pray.	[39] And he came out, and went, as his custom was, unto the mount of Olives; and the disciples also followed him.	[1] When Yeshua had spoken these words, he went forth with his disciples over the brook Ki-dron, where was a garden, into which he en-tered, himself and his disciples.

Matthew cont.	Mark cont.	Luke cont.
[37] And he took with him Peter and the two sons of Zavdi, and began to be sorrowful and sore troubled.	[33] And he takes with him Peter and Yaakov and Yochanan, and began to be greatly amazed, and sore trou-bled.	

[38] Then said he unto them, My soul is exceeding sorrowful, even unto death: abide ye here, and watch with me.
[39] And he went forward a little, and fell on his face, and prayed, saying,

My Father, if it be possible, let this cup pass away from me: nevertheless, not as I will, but as you will.

[34] And he said unto them, My soul is exceeding sorrowful even unto death: abide ye here, and watch.
[35] And he went forward a little, and fell on the ground, and prayed that, if it were possible, the hour might pass away from him.
[36] And he said, Abba, Father, all things are possible unto you; remove this cup from me: howbeit not what I will, but what you will.

[40] And when he was at the place, he said unto them, Pray that ye enter not into temptation.
[41] And he was parted from them about a stone's cast; and he kneeled down and prayed,

[42] saying, Father, if you be willing, remove this cup from me: nevertheless not my will, but yours, be done.

[43] And there appeared unto him an angel from heaven, strengthening him.
[44] And being in an agony he prayed more earnestly; and his sweat became as it were great drops of blood falling down upon the ground.
[45] And when he rose up from his prayer, he came unto the disciples, and found them sleeping for sorrow,
[46] and said unto them, Why sleep ye? Rise and

[40] And he comes unto the disciples, and finds them sleeping, and said unto Peter, What, could ye not watch with me one hour?
[41] Watch and pray, that

[37] And he comes, and finds them sleeping, and says unto Peter, Shimon, are you sleeping? Could you not watch one hour?
[38] Watch and pray, that

ye enter not into temptation: the spirit indeed is willing, but the flesh is weak.

⁴² Again a second time he went away, and prayed, saying, My Father, if this cannot pass away, except I drink it, your will be done.

⁴³ And he came again and found them sleeping, for their eyes were heavy.

⁴⁴ And he left them again, and went away, and prayed a third time, saying again the same words.

⁴⁵ Then comes he to the disciples, and said unto them,

Sleep on now, and take your rest: behold, the hour is at hand, and the Son of man is betrayed into the hands of sinners.

⁴⁶ Arise, let us be going: behold, he is at hand that betrays me.

ye enter not into temptation: the spirit indeed is willing, but the flesh is weak.

³⁹ And again he went away, and prayed, saying the same words.

⁴⁰ And again he came, and found them sleeping, for their eyes were very heavy; and they knew not what to answer him.

⁴¹ And he comes the third time, and says unto them,

Sleep on now, and take your rest: it is enough; the hour is come; behold, the Son of man is betrayed into the hands of sinners.

⁴² Arise, let us be going: behold, he that betrays me is at hand.

pray, that ye enter not into temptation.

IX. THE TRIAL OF THE KING
— §§ 165–175 —

[§ 165]—A. The Arrest

Mt. 26:47-56	Mark 14:43-52	Luke 22:47-53	John 18:2-11
			[2] Now Yehudah also, who betrayed him, knew the place: for Yeshua ofttimes resorted thither with his disciples.
[47] And while he yet spoke, lo,	[43] And straightway, while he	[47] While he yet spoke, behold, a	[3] Yehudah then, having received

Yehudah, one of the twelve, came, and with him a great multitude with swords and staves, from the chief priests and elders of the people.

yet spoke, comes Yehudah, one of the twelve, and with him a multitude with swords and staves, from the chief priests and the scribes and the elders.

multitude, and he that was called Yehudah, one of the twelve, went before them;

the band <of soldiers>, and officers from the chief priests and the Pharisees, comes thither with lanterns and torches and weapons.

[4] Yeshua therefore, knowing all the things that were coming upon him, went forth, and said unto them, Whom seek ye? [5] They answered him, Yeshua of Natzeret. Yeshua said unto them, I am <he>.

[48] Now he that betrayed him gave them a sign, saying, Whomsoever I shall kiss, that is he: take him.

[44] Now he that betrayed him had given them a token, saying, Whomsoever I shall kiss, that is he; take him, and lead him away safely.

and he drew near unto Yeshua to kiss him. [48] But Yeshua said unto him, Yehudah, do you betray the Son of man with a kiss?

And Yehudah also, who betrayed him, was standing with them.

[49] And straightway he came to Yeshua, and said, Hail, Rabbi; and kissed him.

[45] And when he was come, straightway he came to him, and said, Rabbi;

50 And Yeshua said unto him, Friend, <do> that for which you are come.	and kissed him.		6 When therefore he said unto them, I am <he>, they went backward, and fell to the ground. 7 Again therefore he asked them, Whom seek ye? And they said, Yeshua of Natzeret. 8 Yeshua answered, I told you that I am <he>; if therefore ye seek me, let these go their way: 9 that the word might be fulfilled which he spoke, Of those whom you have given me I lost not one.
Then they came and laid hands on Yeshua, and took him.	46 And they laid hands on him, and took him.	49 And when they that were about him saw what would follow, they said, Lord, shall we smite with the sword?	
51 And behold, one of them	47 But a certain one of them	50 And a certain one of them	10 Shimon Peter therefore having

that were with Yeshua stretched out his hand, and drew his sword, and smote the servant of the high priest, and struck off his ear. [52] Then said Yeshua unto him, Put up again your sword into its place: for all they that take the sword shall perish with the sword. [53] Or do you think that I cannot beseech my Father, and he shall even now send me more than twelve legions of angels? [54] How then should the scriptures be fulfilled that thus it must be?

that stood by drew his sword, and smote the servant of the high priest, and struck off his ear.

smote the servant of the high priest, and struck off his right ear.

[51] But Yeshua answered and said, Suffer ye <them> thus far. And he touched his ear, and healed him.

a sword drew it, and struck the high priest's servant, and cut off his right ear. Now the servant's name was Melech.

[11] Yeshua therefore said unto Peter, Put up the sword into the sheath: the cup which the Father has given me, shall I not drink it?

Mt. cont.

[55] In that hour said Yeshua to the multitudes,

Mk. Cont.

[48] And Yeshua answered and said unto

Lk. Cont.

[52] And Yeshua said unto the chief priests,

Are ye come out as against a robber with swords and staves to seize me? I sat daily in the temple teaching, and ye took me not. [56] But all this is come to pass, that the scriptures of the prophets might be fulfilled.

Then all the disciples left him, and fled.

them, Are ye come out, as against a robber, with swords and staves to seize me? [49] I was daily with you in the temple teaching, and ye took me not: but <this is done> that the scriptures might be fulfilled.

[50] And they all left him, and fled. [51] And a certain young man followed with him, having a linen cloth cast about him, over <his> naked <body>: and they lay hold on him; [52] but he left the linen cloth, and fled naked.

and captains of the temple, and elders, that were come against him, Are ye come out, as against a robber, with swords and staves? [53] When I was daily with you in the temple, ye stretched not forth your hands against me: but this is your hour, and the power of darkness.

[§§ 166–170]—B. The Religious Trial

[§ 166]—1. The Trial before Chanan

John 18:12-14, 19-23

[12] So the band and the chief captain, and the officers of the Jews, seized Yeshua and bound him, [13] and led him to Chanan first; for he was father in law to Kayapha, who was high priest that year. [14] Now Kayapha was he that gave counsel to the Jews, that it was expedient that one man should die for

the people. . . . [19] The high priest therefore asked Yeshua of his disciples, and of his teaching. [20] Yeshua answered him, I have spoken openly to the world; I ever taught in synagogues, and in the temple, where all the Jews come together; and in secret spoke I nothing. [21] Why do you ask me? Ask them that have heard <me>, what I spoke unto them: behold, these know the things which I said. [22] And when he had said this, one of the officers standing by struck Yeshua with his hand, saying, Do you answer the high priest so? [23] Yeshua answered him, If I have spoken evil, bear witness of the evil: but if well, why do you smite me?

[§ 167]—2. The Trial Before Kayapha

Matthew 26:57, 59-68	Mark 14:53, 55-65	Luke 22:54a	John 18:24
[57] And they that had taken Yeshua led him away to <the house of> Kayapha the high priest, where the scribes and the elders were gathered together.	[53] And they led Yeshua away to the high priest: and there come together with him all the chief priests and the elders and the scribes.	[54a] And they seized him, and led him <away>, and brought him into the high priest's house.	[24] Chanan therefore sent him bound unto Kayapha the high priest.
Mt. cont. [59] Now the chief priests and the whole council sought false witness against Yeshua, that they might put him to death; [60] and they found it not, though many false witnesses came. But afterward came two, [61] and said,	**Mk. cont.** [55] Now the chief priests and the whole council sought witness against Yeshua to put him to death; and found it not. [56] For many bore false witness against him, and their witness agreed not together. [57] And there stood up certain, and bore false witness against him, saying,		

This man said, I am able to destroy the temple of God, and to build it in three days.

[62] And the high priest stood up, and said unto him, do you answer nothing? What is it which these witness against you?
[63] But Yeshua held his peace.

And the high priest said unto him, I adjure you by the living God, that you tell us whether you are the Messiah, the Son of God.
[64] Yeshua said unto him, You have said: nevertheless I say unto you, Henceforth ye shall see the Son of man sitting at the right hand of Power, and coming on the clouds of heaven.
[65] Then the high priest rent his garments, saying, He has spoken blasphemy: what further need have we of witnesses? Behold, now ye have heard the blasphemy: [66] what think ye?
They answered and said, He is worthy of death.
[67] Then did they spit in his face and buffet him: and some smote him with the palms of their hands, [68] saying, Prophesy unto us, you Messiah: who is he that struck you?

[58] We heard him say, I will destroy this temple that is made with hands, and in three days I will build another made without hands. [59] And not even so did their witness agree together.
[60] And the high priest stood up in the midst, and asked Yeshua, saying, do you answer nothing? What is it which these witness against you?
[61] But he held his peace, and answered nothing.
Again the high priest asked him, and said unto him, Are you the Messiah, the Son of the Blessed?

[62] And Yeshua said, I am: and ye shall see the Son of man sitting at the right hand of Power, and coming with the clouds of heaven.

[63] And the high priest rent his clothes, and said, What further need have we of witnesses? [64] Ye have heard the blasphemy: what think ye?

And they all condemned him to be worthy of death.
[65] And some began to spit on him, and to cover his face, and to buffet him, and to say unto him, Prophesy: and the officers received him with blows of their hands.

[§ 168]—3. The Denial by Peter

Mt. 26:58, 69-75	Mk. 14:54, 66-72	Lk. 22:54b-62	Jn. 18:15-18, 25-27
[58] But Peter followed him afar off,	[54] And Peter had followed him afar off,	[54b] But Peter followed afar off.	[15] And Shimon Peter followed Yeshua, and <so did> another disciple. Now that disciple was known unto the high priest, and entered in with Yeshua into the court of the high priest; [16] but Peter was standing at the door without. So the other disciple, who was known unto the high priest, went out and spoke unto her that kept the door, and brought in Peter.
unto the court of the high priest, and entered in, and sat with the officers, to see the end.	even within, into the court of the high priest; and he was sitting with the officers, and warming himself in the light <of the fire>.	[55] And when they had kindled a fire in the midst of the court, and had sat down together, Peter sat in the midst of them.	

[69] Now Peter was sitting without in the court: and a maid came unto him, saying, You also were with Yeshua the Galilean.

[70] But he denied before them all, saying, I know not what you say.

[71] And when he was gone out into the porch, another <maid> saw him, and said unto them that were there, This man also was with Yeshua of Natzeret.

[72] And again he denied with an oath, I know not the man.

[66] And as Peter was beneath in the court, there comes one of the maids of the high priest; [67] and seeing Peter warming himself, she looked upon him, and said, You also were with the Nazarene, <even> Yeshua. [68] But he denied, saying, I neither know, nor understand what you say: and he went out into the porch; and the cock crew. [69] And the maid saw him, and began again to say to them that stood by, This is <one> of them.

[70] But he again denied it.

[56] And a certain maid seeing him as he sat in the light <of the fire>, and looking steadfastly upon him, said, This man also was with him.

[57] But he denied, saying, Woman, I know him not.

[58] And after a little while another saw him, and said, You also are <one> of them.

But Peter said, Man, I am not.

[17] The maid therefore that kept the door said unto Peter, Are you also <one> of this man's disciples?

He said, I am not.

[18] Now the servants and the officers were standing <there>, having made a fire of coals; for it was cold; and they were warming themselves: and Peter also was with them, standing and warming himself.

⁷³ And after a little while they that stood by came and said to Peter, Of a truth you also are <one> of them; for your speech makes you known.

And after a little while again they that stood by said to Peter, of a truth you are <one> of them; for you are a Galilean.

⁵⁹ And after the space of about one hour another confidently affirmed, saying, Of a truth this man also was with him; for he is a Galilean.

²⁵ Now Shimon Peter was standing and warming himself. They said therefore unto him, Are you also <one> of his disciples? He denied, and said, I am not.

²⁶ One of the servants of the high priest, being a kinsman of him whose ear Peter cut off, said, Did not I see you in the garden with him?

⁷⁴ Then began he to curse and to swear, I know not the man.

And straightway the cock crew.

⁷¹ But he began to curse, and to swear, I know not this man of whom ye speak.
⁷² And straightway the second time the cock crew.

⁶⁰ But Peter said, Man, I know not what you say. And immediately, while he yet spoke, the cock crew.
⁶¹ And the Lord turned, and looked upon Peter. And Peter remembered the word of the Lord, how that he said unto him, Before the cock crow this

²⁷ Peter therefore denied again:

and straightway the cock crew.

⁷⁵ And Peter remembered the word which Yeshua had said, Before the cock crow, you shall deny me thrice.

And Peter called to mind the word, how that Yeshua said unto him, Before the cock crow twice, you

	shall deny me thrice.	day you shall deny me thrice.
And he went out, and wept bitterly.	And when he thought thereon, he wept.	[62] And he went out, and wept bitterly.

[§ 169]—4. The Mockery and Beating

Luke 22:63-65

[63] And the men that held <Yeshua> mocked him, and beat him. [64] And they blindfolded him, and asked him, saying, Prophesy: who is he that struck you? [65] And many other things spoke they against him, reviling him.

[§ 170]—5. The Condemnation by the Sanhedrin

Matthew 27:1	Mark 15:1a	Luke 22:66-71
[1] Now when morning was come, all the chief priests and the elders of the people took counsel against Yeshua to put him to death:	[1a] And straightway in the morning the chief priests with the elders and scribes, and the whole council, held a consultation,[1]	[66] And as soon as it was day, the assembly of the elders of the people was gathered together, both chief priests and scribes; and they led him away into their council, saying, [67] If you are the Messiah, tell us.

LK. cont.: But he said unto them, If I tell you, ye will not believe: [68] and if I ask <you>, ye will not answer. [69] But from henceforth shall the Son of man be seated at the right hand of the power of God. [70] And they all said, Are you then the Son of God? And he said unto them, Ye say that I am. [71] And

---

[1] Continued in § 172.

they said, What further need have we of witness? For we ourselves have heard from his own mouth.

[§ 171]—C. The Death of Yehudah

Matthew 27:3-10

³ Then Yehudah, who betrayed him, when he saw that he was condemned, repented himself, and brought back the thirty pieces of silver to the chief priests and elders, ⁴ saying, I have sinned in that I betrayed innocent blood. But they said, What is that to us? See you <to it>. ⁵ And he cast down the pieces of silver into the sanctuary, and departed; and he went away and hanged himself. ⁶ And the chief priests took the pieces of silver, and said, It is not lawful to put them into the treasury, since it is the price of blood. ⁷ And they took counsel, and bought with them the potter's field, to bury strangers in. ⁸ Wherefore that field was called, the field of blood, unto this day. ⁹ Then was fulfilled that which was spoken through Yirmeyahu the prophet, saying, And they took the thirty pieces of silver, the price of him that was priced, whom <certain> of the children of Yisrael did price; ¹⁰ and they gave them for the potter's field, as the Lord appointed me.

Acts 1:18-19

¹⁸ (Now this man obtained a field with the reward of his iniquity; and falling headlong, he burst asunder in the midst, and all his bowels gushed out. ¹⁹ And it became known to all the dwellers at Yerushalayim; insomuch that in their language that field was called Chakeil D'ma [Akeldama], that is, The field of blood.)

[§§ 172–175]—D. The Civil Trial

[§ 172]—1. The First Trial Before Pilate

Mt. 27:2, 11-14	Mk. 15:1b-5	Lk. 23:1-5	Jn. 18:28-38
[2] and they bound him, and led him away, and delivered him up to Pilate the governor. [11] Now Yeshua stood before the governor:	[1b] and bound Yeshua, and carried him away, and delivered him up to Pilate.	[1] And the whole company of them rose up, and brought him before Pilate.	[28] They lead Yeshua therefore from Kayapha into the Praetorium: and it was early; and they themselves entered not into the Praetorium, that they might not be defiled, but might eat the Passover. [29] Pilate therefore went out unto them, and said, What accusation bring ye against this man?
		[2] And they began to accuse him, saying, We found this man perverting our nation, and forbidding to give tribute to Caesar, and saying that he	[30] They answered and said unto him, If this man were not an evildoer, we should not have delivered him up unto you. [31] Pilate therefore said unto

		himself is Messiah a king.	them, Take him yourselves, and judge him according to your law. The Jews said unto him, It is not lawful for us to put any man to death: [32] that the word of Yeshua might be fulfilled, which he spoke, signifying by what manner of death he should die.
And the governor asked him, saying,	[2] And Pilate asked him,	[3] And Pilate asked him, saying,	[33] Pilate therefore entered again into the Praetorium, and called Yeshua, and said unto him,
Are you the King of the Jews? And Yeshua said unto him,	Are you the King of the Jews? And he answering said unto him,	Are you the King of the Jews? And he answered him and said,	Are you the King of the Jews? [34] Yeshua answered,
You say.	You say.	You say.	Do you say this of yourself, or did others tell you it concerning me? [35] Pilate answered, Am I a Jew? Your own nation and the

chief priests delivered you unto me: what have you done? [36] Yeshua answered, My kingdom is not of this world: if my kingdom were of this world, then would my servants fight, that I should not be delivered to the Jews: but now is my kingdom not from hence. [37] Pilate therefore said unto him, Are you a king then? Yeshua answered, You say that I am a king. To this end have I been born, and to this end am I come into the world, that I should bear witness un-to the truth. Every one that is of the truth hears my voice. [38] Pilate said unto him, What is truth?

		[4] And Pilate said unto the chief priests and the multitudes,	And when he had said this, he went out again unto the Jews, and said unto them,
		I find no fault in this man.	I find no crime in him.
[12] And when he was accused by the chief priests and elders, he answered nothing.	[3] And the chief priests accused him of many things.	[5] But they were the more urgent, saying, He stirs up the people, teaching throughout all Yehudah, and beginning from Galil even unto this place.	
[13] Then said Pilate unto him, Hear you not how many things they witness against you? [14] And he gave him no answer, not even to one word: insomuch that the governor marveled greatly.	[4] And Pilate again asked him, saying, do you answer nothing? Behold how many things they accuse you of. [5] But Yeshua no more answered anything; insomuch that Pilate marveled.		

[§ 173]—2. The Trial before Herod Antipas

Luke 23:6-12

[6] But when Pilate heard it, he asked whether the man were a Galilean. [7] And when he knew that he was of Herod's jurisdiction, he sent him unto Herod, who himself also was at Yerushalayim in these days. [8] Now when Herod saw Yeshua, he was exceeding glad: for he was of a long time desirous to see

him, because he had heard concerning him; and he hoped to see some miracle done by him. [9] And he questioned him in many words; but he answered him nothing. [10] And the chief priests and the scribes stood, vehemently accusing him. [11] And Herod with his soldiers set him at nought, and mocked him, and arraying him in gorgeous apparel sent him back to Pilate. [12] And Herod and Pilate became friends with each other that very day: for before they were at enmity between themselves.

[§ 174]—3. The Second Trial before Pilate

Mt. 27:15-26	Mk. 15:6-15	Lk. 23:13-25	Jn. 18:39–19:16
[15] Now at the feast the governor was wont to release unto the multitude one prisoner, whom they would. [16] And they had then a notable prisoner, called Bar Abba.	[6] Now at the feast he used to release unto them one prisoner, whom they asked of him. [7] And there was one called Bar Abba, \<lying\> bound with them that had made insurrection, men who in the insurrection had committed murder. [8] And the multitude went up and began to ask him \<to do\> as he was wont to do unto them.	[13] And Pilate called together the chief priests	

277

and the rulers and the people, [14] and said unto them, Ye brought unto me this man, as one that perverts the people: and behold, I having examined him before you, found no fault in this man touching those things whereof ye accuse him: [15] no, nor yet Herod: for he sent him back unto us; and behold, nothing worthy of death has been done by him. [16] I will therefore chastise him, and release him. [2]

[17] When therefore they were gathered together, Pilate said unto them,

[9] And Pilate answered them, saying, Will ye that I release unto you the

[39] But ye have a custom, that I should release unto you one at the Passover:

---

[2] Many ancient authorities insert verse 17: "Now he must needs release unto them at the feast one prisoner."

Whom will ye that I release unto you? Bar Abba, or Yeshua who is called Messiah? [18] For he knew that for envy they had delivered him up. [19] And while he was sitting on the judgment-seat, his wife sent unto him, saying, Have you nothing to do with that righteous man; for I have suffered many things this day in a dream because of him. [20] Now the chief priests and the elders persuaded the multitudes that they should ask for Bar Abba, and destroy Yeshua. [21] But the governor answered and said unto them, Which of the two will ye

King of the Jews?

[10] For he perceived that for envy the chief priests had delivered him up.

[11] But the chief priests stirred up the multitude, that he should rather release Bar Abba unto them.

will ye therefore that I release unto you the King of the Jews?

that I release unto you? And they said, Bar Abba.

[18] But they cried out all together, saying, Away with this man, and release unto us Bar Abba: [19] one who for a certain insurrection made in the city, and for murder, was cast into prison.

[40] They cried out therefore again, saying, Not this man, but Bar Abba.

(Now Bar Abba was a robber <rebel>.)

[19:1] Then Pilate therefore took Yeshua, and scourged him. [2] And the soldiers platted a crown of thorns, and put it on his head, and arrayed him in a purple garment; [3] and they came unto him, and said, Hail, King of the Jews! And they struck him with their hands. [4] And Pilate went out again, and said unto them, Behold, I

			bring him out to you, that ye may know that I find no crime in him. [5] Yeshua therefore came out, wearing the crown of thorns and the purple garment.
[22] Pilate said unto them, What then shall I do unto Yeshua who is called Messiah?	[12] And Pilate again answered and said unto them, What then shall I do unto him whom ye call the King of the Jews?	[20] And Pilate spoke unto them again, desiring to release Yeshua;	And <Pilate> said unto them, Behold, the man! [6] When therefore the chief priests and the officers saw him,
They all say, Let him be crucified.	[13] And they cried out again, Crucify him.	[21] but they shouted, saying, Crucify, crucify him.	they cried out, saying, Crucify <him>, crucify <him>!
[23] And he said, Why, what evil has he done?	[14] And Pilate said unto them, Why, what evil has he done?	[22] And he said unto them the third time, Why, what evil has this man done? I have found no cause of death in him: I will therefore chastise him and release him.	Pilate said unto them, Take him yourselves, and crucify him: for I find no crime in him.
But they cried out exceedingly, saying, Let him be crucified.	But they cried out exceedingly, Crucify him.		[7] The Jews answered him, We have a law, and by that law he

281

ought to die, because he made himself the Son of God. [8] When Pilate therefore heard this saying, he was the more afraid; [9] and he entered into the Praetorium again, and said unto Yeshua, Whence are you? But Yeshua gave him no answer. [10] Pilate therefore said unto him, Speak you not unto me? Know you not that I have power to release you, and have power to crucify you? [11] Yeshua answered him, You would have no power against me, except it were given you from above: therefore he that delivered me unto you has greater sin.

24 So when Pilate saw that he prevailed nothing, but rather that a tumult was arising, he took water, and washed his hands before the multitude, saying, I am innocent of the blood of this righteous man; see ye <to it>. 25 And all the people answered and said, His blood <be> on us, and on our children. 26 Then released he unto them Bar Abba; but Yeshua he scourged and delivered to be crucified.

15 And Pilate, wishing to content the multitude, released unto them Bar Abba, and delivered Yeshua, when he had scourged him, to be crucified.

23 But they were urgent with loud voices, asking that he might be crucified. And their voices prevailed. 24 And Pilate gave sentence that what they asked for should be done. 25 And he released him that for insurrection and murder had been cast into prison, whom they asked for; but Yeshua he delivered up to their will.

12 Upon this Pilate sought to release him: but the Jews cried out, saying, If you release this man, you are not Caesar's friend: everyone that makes himself a king speaks against Caesar. 13 When Pilate therefore heard these words, he brought Yeshua out, and sat down on the judgment seat at a place called The Pavement, but in Hebrew, Gabbeta. 14 Now it was the Preparation of the Passover: it was about the sixth hour. And he said unto the Jews, Behold, your King! 15 They therefore cried out, Away with <him>, away with <him>,

crucify him! Pilate said unto them, Shall I crucify your King? The chief priests answered, We have no king but Caesar. [16] Then therefore he delivered him unto them to be crucified.

[§ 175]—4. The Mockery

Matthew 27:27-30	Mark 15:16-19
[27] Then the soldiers of the governor took Yeshua into the Praetorium, and gathered unto him the whole band.[3] [28] And they stripped him, and put on him a scarlet robe. [29] And they platted a crown of thorns and put it upon his head, and a reed in his right hand; and they kneeled down before him, and mocked him, saying, Hail, King of the Jews! [30] And they spat upon him, and took the reed and smote him on the head.	[16] And the soldiers led him away within the court, which is the Praetorium; and they call together the whole band. [17] And they clothe him with purple, and platting a crown of thorns, they put it on him; [18] and they began to salute him, Hail, King of the Jews! [19] And they smote his head with a reed, and spat upon him, and bowing their knees worshipped him.

---

[3] Or, *cohort.*

X. THE DEATH OF THE KING
— §§ 176–181 —

[§ 176]—A. The Procession to Golgota

Mt. 27:31-34	Mark 15:20-23	Luke 23:26-33a	John 19:17
[31] And when they had mocked him, they took off from him the robe, and put on him his garments, and led him away to crucify him.	[20] And when they had mocked him, they took off from him the purple, and put on him his garments. And they lead him out to crucify him.		[17] They took Yeshua therefore: and he went out, bearing the cross for himself,

[32] And as they came out, they found a man of Kirenyah, Shimon by name: him they compelled to go <with them>, that he might bear his cross.	[21] And they compel one passing by, Shimon of Kirenyah, coming from the country, the father of Alexander and Rufus, to go <with them>, that he might bear his cross.	[26] And when they led him away, they laid hold upon one Shimon of Kirenyah, coming from the country, and laid on him the cross, to bear it after Yeshua.

Lk. cont.: [27] And there followed him a great multitude of the people, and of women who bewailed and lamented him. [28] But Yeshua turning unto them said, Daughters of Yerushalayim, weep not for me, but weep for yourselves, and for your children. [29] For behold, the days are coming, in which they shall say, Blessed are the barren, and the wombs that never bore, and the breasts that never gave suck. [30] Then shall they begin to say to the mountains, Fall on us; and to the hills, Cover us. [31] For if they do these things in the green tree, what shall be done in the dry?

Mt. cont.	**Mk. cont.**	**Lk. cont.**	**Jn. cont.**
[33] And they were come unto a place called Golgota, that is to say, The place of a skull, [34] they gave him wine to drink mingled with gall: and when he had tasted it, he would not drink.	[22] And they bring him unto the place Golgota, which is, being interpreted, The place of a skull. [23] And they offered him wine mingled with myrrh: but he received it not.	[33a] And when they came unto the place which is called The skull,	[32] And there were also two others, malefactors, led with him to be put to death unto the place called The place of a skull, which is called in Hebrew, Golgota:

[§§ 177–179]—B. The Crucifixion

[§ 177]—1. The First Three Hours: The Wrath of Men

Mt. 27:35-44	Mark 15:24-32	Luke 23:33b-43	John 19:18-27
35 And when they had crucified him,	24 And they crucify him,	33b there they crucified him, and the malefactors, one on the right hand and the other on the left. 34 And Yeshua said, Father, forgive them; for they know not what they	18 where they crucified him, and with him two others, on either side one, and Yeshua in the midst.
they parted his garments among them, casting lots;	and part his garments among them, casting lots upon them, what each should take. 25 And it was the third hour, and they crucified him.	do. And parting his garments among them, they cast lots.	23 The soldiers therefore, when they had crucified Yeshua, took his garments and made four parts, to every soldier a part; and also the coat: now the coat was without seam, woven from the top throughout. 24 They said therefore one to another, Let us not tear it, but

			cast lots for it, whose it shall be: that the scripture might be fulfilled, which said, They parted my gar- ments among them, And upon my vesture did they cast lots. [25] These things therefore the soldiers did.
[36] and they sat and watched him there. [37] And they set up over his head his accusation written,	[26] And the su- perscription of his accusation was written over,	[38] And there was also a super- scription over him,	[19] And Pilate wrote a title also, and put it on the cross. And there was written,
THIS IS YESHUA THE KING OF THE JEWS.	THE KING OF THE JEWS.	THIS IS THE KING OF THE JEWS.	YESHUA OF NATZE- RET, THE KING OF THE JEWS. [20] This title therefore read many of the Jews, for the place where Yeshua was crucified was near to the city; and it was writ- ten in Hebrew, <and> in Latin, <and> in Greek. [21] The chief

priests of the Jews therefore said to Pilate, Write not, The King of the Jews; but that he said, I am King of the Jews. ²² Pilate answered, What I have written I have written.

²⁶ When Yeshua therefore saw his mother, and the disciple standing by whom he loved, he said unto his mother, Woman, behold, your son! ²⁷ Then said he to the disciple, Behold, your mother! And from that hour the disciple took her unto his own home.

Mt. cont.: ³⁸ Then are there crucified with him two robbers, one on the right hand and

Mk. cont.: ²⁷ And with him they crucify two robbers; one on his right hand, and one on

Lk. cont.:

one on the left. [39] And they that passed by railed on him, wagging their heads, [40] and saying, You that destroy the temple, and build it in three days, save yourself: if you are the Son of God, come down from the cross.

[41] In like manner also the chief priests mocking <him>, with the scribes and elders, said,

[42] He saved others; himself he cannot save. He is the King of Yisrael; let him now come down from the cross, and we will believe on him. [43] He trusts on God; let him deliver him now, if he desires him: for he said, I am the Son of God.

his left.[1] [29] And that passed by railed on him, wagging their heads, and saying, Ha! You that destroy the temple, and buildest it in three days, [30] save yourself, and come down from the cross.

[31] In like manner also the chief priests mocking <him> among themselves with the scribes said, He saved others; himself he cannot save. [32] Let the Messiah, the King of Yisrael, now come down from the cross, that we may see and believe.

[35] And the people stood beholding. And the rulers also scoffed at him, saying, He saved others; let him save himself, if this is the Messiah of God, his chosen.

[36] And the soldiers also mocked him, coming to him, offering him vinegar, [37] and saying, If you are the King of the Jews, save yourself.

---

[1] Many ancient authorities insert verse 28: "And the scripture was fulfilled, which said, And he was reckoned with transgressors."

44 And the robbers also that were crucified with him cast upon him the same reproach.	And they that were crucified with him reproached him.	39 And one of the malefactors that were hanged railed on him, saying, Are you not the Messiah? 40 But the other answered, and rebuking him said, Do you not even fear God, seeing you are in the same condemnation? 41 And we indeed justly; for we receive the due reward of our deeds: but this man has done nothing amiss. 42 And he said, Yeshua, remember me when you come in your kingdom. 43 And he said unto him, Verily I say unto thee, Today shall you be with me in Paradise.

[§ 178]—2. The Second Three Hours: The Wrath of God

Mt. 27:45-50	Mark 15:33-37	Luke 23:44-46	John 19:28-30
45 Now from the sixth hour there was darkness over all the land until the ninth hour.	33 And when the sixth hour was come, there was darkness over the whole land until the ninth hour.	44 And it was now about the sixth hour, and a darkness came over the whole land until the ninth hour, 45 the sun's light	

46 And about the ninth hour Yeshua cried with a loud voice, saying, Eli, Eli, lama sabachthani? That is, My God, my God, why have you forsaken me?

47 And some of them stood there, when they heard it, said, This man calls Eliyahu.
48 And straightway one of them ran, and took a sponge, and filled it with vinegar, and put it on a reed, and gave him to drink.
49 And the rest said, Let be; let us see whether Eliyahu comes to save him.

34 And at the ninth hour Yeshua cried with a loud voice, Eloi, Eloi, lama sabachthani? Which is, being interpreted, My God, my God, why have you forsaken me?

35 And some of them that stood by, when they heard it, said, Behold, he calls Eliyahu.
36 And one ran, and filling a sponge full of vinegar, put it on a reed, and gave him to drink,

saying, Let be; let us see whether Eliyahu comes to take him down.

failing:[2]

28 After this Yeshua, knowing that all things are now finished, that the scripture might be accomplished, said, I thirst. 29 There was set there a vessel full of vinegar: so they put a sponge full of the vinegar upon hyssop,

[2] Cont. in §179.

			and brought it to his mouth.
			30 When Yeshua therefore had received the vinegar, he said,
			he said,
50 And Yeshua cried again with a loud voice,	37 And Yeshua uttered a loud voice,	46 And Yeshua, crying with a loud voice, said, Father, into your hands I commend my spirit: and having said this,	It is finished:
			and he bowed his head, and
and yielded up his spirit.	and gave up the ghost.	he gave up the ghost.	gave up his spirit.

[§ 179]—3. The Accompanying Signs

Matthew 27:51-56	Mark 15:38-41	Luke 23:45b, 47-49
51 And behold, the veil of the temple was rent in two from the top to the bottom; and the earth did quake; and the rocks were rent; 52 and the tombs were opened; and many bodies of the saints that had fallen asleep were raised; 53 and coming forth out of the tombs after his resurrection they entered	38 And the veil of the temple was rent in two from the top to the bottom.	45b and the veil of the temple was rent in the midst.

into the holy city and appeared unto many.

[54] Now the centurion, and they that were with him watching Yeshua, when they saw the earthquake, and the things that were done, feared exceedingly, saying, Truly this was the Son of God.

[55] And many women were there beholding from afar, who had followed Yeshua from Galil, ministering unto him: [56] among whom was Miriam Magdalit, and Miriam the mother of Yaakov and Yosei, and the mother of the sons of Zavdi.

[39] And when the centurion, who stood by over against him, saw that he so gave up the ghost, he said, Truly this man was the Son of God.

[40] And there were also women beholding from afar: among whom <were> both Miriam Magdalit, and Miriam the mother of Yaakov the less and of Yosei, and Shulamit; [41] who, when he was in Galil, followed him, and ministered unto him; and many other women that came up with him unto Yerushalayim.

[47] And when the centurion saw what was done, he glorified God, saying, Certainly this was a righteous man.

[48] And all the multitudes that came together to this sight, when they beheld the things that were done, returned smiting their breasts. [49] And all his acquaintance, and the women that followed with him from Galil, stood afar off, seeing these things.

[§ 180]—C. The Burial of the Messiah

John 19:31-37

[31] The Jews therefore, because it was the Preparation, that the bodies should not remain on the cross upon the Sabbath (for the day of that Sabbath was a high <day>), asked of Pilate that their legs might be broken, and <that> they might be taken away. [32] The soldiers therefore came, and broke the legs of the first, and of the other that was crucified with him: [33] but

when they came to Yeshua, and saw that he was dead already, they broke not his legs: [34] howbeit one of the soldiers with a spear pierced his side, and straightway there came out blood and water. [35] And he that had seen has borne witness, and his witness is true: and he knows that he said true, that ye also may believe. [36] For these things came to pass, that the scripture might be fulfilled, A bone of him shall not be broken. [37] And again another scripture said, They shall look on him whom they pierced.

Mt. 27:57-60	Mark 15:42-46	Luke 23:50-54	John 19:38-42
[57] And when even was come,	[42] And when even was now come, because it was the Preparation, that is, the day before the Sabbath,		
there came a rich man from Ramatayim, named Yoseph,	[43] there came Yoseph of Ramatayim, a councillor of honorable estate,	[50] And behold, a man named Yoseph, who was a councillor, a good and righteous man [51] (he had not consented to their counsel and deed), <a man> of Ramatayim, a city of the Jews,	[38] And after these things Yoseph of Ramatayim,
who also himself was Yeshua's disciple:	who also himself was looking for the kingdom of God;	who was looking for the kingdom of God:	being a disciple of Yeshua, but secretly for fear of the Jews,
[58] this man went to Pilate, and	and he boldly went in unto	[52] this man went to Pilate, and	asked of Pilate that he might

asked for the body of Yeshua.	Pilate, and asked for the body of Yeshua. [44] And Pilate marveled if he were already dead: and calling unto him the centurion, he asked him whether he had been any while dead. [45] And when he learned it of the centurion,	asked for the body of Yeshua.	take away the body of Yeshua:
Then Pilate commanded it to be given up. [59] And Yoseph took the body,	he granted the corpse to Yoseph. [46] And he bought a linen cloth, and taking him down,	[53] And he took it down,	and Pilate gave \<him> leave. He came therefore, and took away his body. [39] And there came also Nakdimon, he who at the first came to him by night, bringing a mixture of myrrh and aloes, about a hundred pounds. [40] So they took the body of Yeshua, and bound it in linen cloths with the spices, as the
and wrapped it in a clean linen cloth,	wound him in the linen cloth,	and wrapped it in a linen cloth,	

⁶⁰ and laid it in his own new tomb, which he had hewn out in the rock: and he rolled a great stone to the door of the tomb, and departed.

and laid him in a tomb which had been hewn out of a rock; and he rolled a stone against the door of the tomb.

and laid him in a tomb that was hewn in stone, where never man had yet lain.

⁵⁴ And it was the day of the Preparation, and the Sabbath drew on.

custom of the Jews is to bury. ⁴¹ Now in the place where he was crucified there was a garden; and in the garden a new tomb wherein was never man yet laid. ⁴² There then because of the Jews' Preparation (for the tomb was near at hand) they laid Yeshua.

[§ 181]—D. The Sealing of the Tomb

Matthew 27:61-66	Mark 15:47	Luke 23:55-56
⁶¹ And Miriam Magdalit was there, and the other Miriam, sitting over against the sepulcher.	⁴⁷ And Miriam Magdalit and Miriam the \<mother\> of Yosei beheld where he was laid.	⁵⁵ And the women, who had come with him out of Galil, followed after, and beheld the tomb, and how his body was laid. ⁵⁶ And they returned, and prepared spices and ointments. And on the Sabbath they rested according to the commandment.

Mt. cont.: [62] Now on the morrow, which is <the day> after the Preparation, the chief priests and the Pharisees were gathered together unto Pilate, [63] saying, Sir, we remember that that deceiver said while he was yet alive, After three days I rise again. [64] Command therefore that the sepulcher be made sure until the third day, lest haply his disciples come and steal him away, and say unto the people, He is risen from the dead: and the last error will be worse than the first. [65] Pilate said unto them, Ye have a guard: go, make it <as> sure as ye can. [66] So they went, and made the sepulcher sure, sealing the stone, the guard being with them.

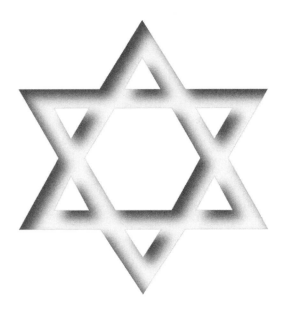

XI. THE RESURRECTION AND ASCENSION OF THE KING
— §§ 182–197 —

[§ 182]—A. The Dawning of Resurrection Day

Matthew 28:1	Mark 16:1
[1] Now late on the Sabbath day, as it began to dawn toward the first \<day\> of the week, came Miriam Magdalit and the other Miriam to see the sepulcher.	[1] And when the Sabbath was past, Miriam Magdalit, and Miriam the \<mother\> of Yaakov, and Shulamit, bought spices, that they might come and anoint him.

[§ 183]—B. The Opening of the Tomb

Matthew 28:2-4

[2] And behold, there was a great earthquake; for an angel of the Lord descended from heaven, and came and rolled away the stone, and sat upon it. [3] His appearance was as lightning, and his raiment white as snow: [4] and for fear of him the watchers did quake, and became as dead men.

[§ 184]—C. The Visit of the Women

Mt. 28:5-8	Mark 16:2-8	Luke 24:1-8	John 20:1
	[2] And very early on the first day of the week, they come to the tomb when the sun was risen. [3] And they were saying among themselves, Who shall roll us away the stone from the door of the tomb? [4] And looking up, they see that the stone is rolled back: for it was exceeding great. [5] And entering into the tomb,	[1] But on the first day of the week, at early dawn, they came unto the tomb, bringing the spices which they had prepared. [2] And they found the stone rolled away from the tomb. [3] And they entered in, and found not the body of the Lord	[1] Now on the first <day> of the week comes Miriam Magdalit early, while it was yet dark, unto the tomb, and sees the stone taken away from the tomb.

they saw a young man sitting on the right side, arrayed in a white robe; and they were amazed.

5 And the angel answered and said unto the women, Fear not ye; for I know that ye seek Yeshua, who has been crucified. 6 He is not here; for he is risen, even as he said. Come, see the place where the Lord lay.

6 And he said unto them,

Be not amazed: ye seek Yeshua, the Nazarene, who has been crucified: he is risen; he is not here: behold, the place where they laid him!

Yeshua. 4 And it came to pass, while they were perplexed thereabout, behold, two men stood by them in dazzling apparel: 5 and as they were affrighted and bowed down their faces to the earth, they said unto them,

Why seek ye the living among the dead? 6 He is not here, but is risen: remember how he spoke unto you when he was yet in Galil, 7 saying that the Son of man must be delivered up into the hands of sinful men, and be crucified, and the third day rise again. 8 And they remembered his words,

7 And go quickly, and tell his disciples, He is risen from the

7 But go, tell his disciples and Peter, He goes before you into

dead; and lo, he goes before you into Galil; there shall ye see him: lo, I have told you.
[8] And they departed quickly from the tomb with fear and great joy, and ran to bring his disciples word.

Galil: there shall ye see him, as he said unto you.

[8] And they went out, and fled from the tomb; for trembling and astonishment had come upon them: and they said nothing to anyone; for they were afraid.

[§ 185]—D. The Report to the Apostles

Luke 24:9-12

[9] and returned from the tomb, and told all these things to the eleven, and to all the rest. [10] Now they were Miriam Magdalit, and Yochanah, and Miriam the <mother> of Yaakov: and the other women with them told these things unto the apostles. [11] And these words appeared in their sight as idle talk; and they disbelieved them.
[12] But Peter arose, and ran unto the tomb;

John 20:2-10

[2] She runs therefore, and comes to Shimon Peter, and to the other disciple whom Yeshua loved, and said unto them, They have taken away the Lord out of the tomb, and we know not where they have laid him.

[3] Peter therefore went forth, and the other disciple, and they went toward the tomb. [4] And they ran both together: and the other disci-

and stooping and looking in, he sees the linen cloths by themselves;

and he departed to his home, wondering at that which was come to pass.

ple outran Peter, and came first to the tomb; [5] and stooping and looking in, he sees the linen cloths lying; yet entered he not in. [6] Shimon Peter therefore also comes, following him, and entered into the tomb; and he beholds the linen cloths lying, [7] and the napkin, that was upon his head, not lying with the linen cloths, but rolled up in a place by itself. [8] Then entered in therefore the other disciple also, who came first to the tomb, and he saw, and believed. [9] For as yet they knew not the scripture, that he must rise from the dead. [10] So the disciples went away again unto their own home.

[§ 186]—E. The First Appearance:
To Miriam Magdalit

Mark 16:9-11	John 20:11-18
	[11] But Miriam was standing without at the tomb weeping: so, as she wept, she stooped and looked into the tomb; [12] and she beholds two angels in white sitting, one at the head, and one at the feet, where the body of Yeshua had lain. [13] And they say unto her, Woman, why do you weep? She said unto them, Because they have taken away my Lord, and I know not where they have laid him.

[9] Now when he was risen early on the first day of the week, he appeared first to Miriam Magdalit, from whom he had cast out seven demons. [1]

[10] She went and told them that had been with him, as they mourned and wept.

[11] And they, when they heard that he was alive, and had been seen of her, disbelieved.

[14] When she had thus said, she turned herself back, and beholds Yeshua standing, and knew not that it was Yeshua. [15] Yeshua said unto her, Woman, why do you weep? Whom are you seeking? She, supposing him to be the gardener, said unto him, Sir, if you have borne him hence, tell me where you have laid him, and I will take him away. [16] Yeshua said unto her, Miriam. She turned herself, and said unto him in Hebrew, Rabboni; which is to say, Teacher. [17] Yeshua said to her, Touch me not; for I am not yet ascended unto the Father: but go unto my brethren, and say to them, I ascend unto my Father and your Father, and my God and your God. [18] Miriam Magdalit comes and tells the disciples, I have seen the Lord; and <that> he had said these things unto her.

---

[1] The oldest manuscripts and some other authorities omit from verse 9 to the end. Some other authorities end the Gospel of Luke differently.

[§ 187]—F. The Second Appearance: To the Women

Matthew 28:9-10

[9] And behold, Yeshua met them, saying, All hail. And they came and took hold of his feet, and worshipped him. [10] Then said Yeshua unto them, Fear not: go tell my brethren that they depart into Galil, and there shall they see me.

[§ 188]—G. The Report of the Guard: The Rejection of the Second Sign of Yonah

Matthew 28:11-15

[11] Now while they were going, behold, some of the guard came into the city, and told unto the chief priests all the things that were come to pass. [12] And when they were assembled with the elders, and had taken counsel, they gave much money unto the soldiers, [13] saying, Say ye, His disciples came by night, and stole him away while we slept. [14] And if this come to the governor's ears, we will persuade him, and rid you of care. [15] So they took the money, and did as they were taught: and this saying was spread abroad among the Jews, <and continues> until this day.

[§ 189]—H. The Third Appearance: To the Two on the Emmaus Road

Mark 16:12-13	Luke 24:13-32
[12] And after these things he was manifested in another form unto two of them, as they walked, on their way into the country. [13] And they went away and told it unto the rest: neither believed they them.	[13] And behold, two of them were going that very day to a village named Emmaus, which was threescore furlongs from Yerushalayim. [14] And they communed with each other of all these things which had

happened. [15] And it came to pass, while they communed and questioned together, that Yeshua himself drew near, and went with them. [16] But their eyes were holden that they should not know him.

Lk. cont. [17] And he said unto them, What communications are these that ye have one with another, as ye walk? And they stood still, looking sad. [18] And one of them, named Kliyopas, answering said unto him, Do you alone sojourn in Yerushalayim and not know the things which are come to pass there in these days? [19] And he said unto them, What things? And they said unto him, The things concerning Yeshua the Nazarene, who was a prophet mighty in deed and word before God and all the people: [20] and how the chief priests and our rulers delivered him up to be condemned to death, and crucified him. [21] But we hoped that it was he who should redeem Yisrael. Yea and besides all this, it is now the third day since these things came to pass. [22] Moreover certain women of our company amazed us, having been early at the tomb; [23] and when they found not his body, they came, saying, that they had also seen a vision of angels, who said that he was alive. [24] And certain of them that were with us went to the tomb, and found it even so as the women had said: but him they saw not. [25] And he said unto them, O foolish men, and slow of heart to believe in all that the prophets have spoken! [26] Behooved it not the Messiah to suffer these things, and to enter into his glory? [27] And beginning from Mosheh and from all the prophets, he interpreted to them in all the scriptures the things concerning himself. [28] And they drew near unto the village, whither they were going: and he made as though he would go further. [29] And they constrained him, saying, Abide with us; for it is toward evening, and the day is now far spent. And he went in to abide with them. [30] And it came to pass, when he had sat down with them to meat, he took the bread and blessed; and breaking <it> he gave to them. [31] And their eyes were opened, and they knew him; and he vanished out of their sight. [32] And they said one to another, Was not our heart burning within us, while he spoke to us in the way, while he opened to us the scriptures?

[§ 190]—I. The Fourth Appearance: To Peter

Luke 24:33-35

[33] And they rose up that very hour, and returned to Yerushalayim, and found the eleven gathered together, and them that were with them, [34] saying, The Lord is risen indeed, and has appeared to Shimon. [35] And they rehearsed the things <that happened> in the way, and how he was known of them in the breaking of the bread.

I Corinthians 15:5a

[5a] and that he appeared to Keipha;

[§ 191]—J. The Fifth Appearance: To the Ten

Mark 16:14

[14] And afterward he was manifested unto the eleven themselves as they sat at meat;

Luke 24:36-43

[36] And as they spoke these things,

he himself stood in the midst of them, and said unto them, Peace <be> unto you. [37] But they were terrified and affrighted, and supposed that they beheld a spirit.

John 20:19-25

[19] When therefore it was evening, on that day, the first <day> of the week, and when the doors were shut where the disciples were, for fear of the Jews,

Yeshua came and stood in the midst, and said unto them, Peace <be> unto you.

and he upbraided them with their unbelief and hardness of heart, because they believed not them that had seen him after he was risen.

[38] And he said unto them, Why are ye troubled? And wherefore do questionings arise in your heart? [39] See my hands and my feet, that it is I myself: handle me, and see; for a spirit has not flesh and bones, as ye behold me having. [40] And when he had said this, he showed them his hands and his feet. [41] And while they still disbelieved for joy, and wondered, he said unto them, Have ye here anything to eat? [42] And they gave him a piece of a broiled fish. [43] And he took it, and ate before them.

[20] And when he had said this, he showed unto them his hands and his side. The disciples therefore were glad, when they saw the Lord. [21] Yeshua therefore said to them again, Peace <be> unto you: as the Father has sent me, even so send I you. [22] And when he had said this, he breathed on them, and said unto them, Receive ye the Holy Spirit: [23] whosoever sins ye forgive, they are forgiven unto them; whosoever <sins> ye retain, they are retained.

[24] But Toma, one of the twelve, called Didymos, was not with them when Yeshua came. [25] The other disciples therefore said unto him, We have seen the Lord. But he

said unto them, Except I shall see in his hands the print of the nails, and put my hand into his side, I will not believe.

[§ 192]—K. The Sixth Appearance: To the Eleven

I Corinthians 15:5b

5b ... then to the twelve;

John 20:26-31

26 And after eight days again his disciples were within, and Toma with them. Yeshua comes, the doors being shut, and stood in the midst, and said, Peace <be> unto you. 27 Then said he to Toma, Reach here your finger, and see my hands; and reach <here> your hand, and put it into my side: and be not faithless, but believing. 28 Toma answered and said unto him, My Lord and my God. 29 Yeshua said unto him, Because you have seen me, you have believed: blessed <are> they that have not seen, and <yet> have believed. 30 Many other signs therefore did Yeshua in the presence of the disciples, which are not written in this book: 31 but these are written, that ye may believe that Yeshua is the Messiah, the Son of God; and that believing ye may have life in his name.

[§ 193]—L. The Seventh Appearance: To the Seven

John 21:1-25

1 After these things Yeshua manifested himself again to the disciples at the sea of Tverya; and he manifested <himself> on this wise. 2 There was together Shimon Peter, and Toma called Didymos, and Netanel of Kana in Galil, and the <sons> of Zavdi, and two other of his disciples. 3 Shimon Peter said unto them, I go a fishing. They say unto him, We also come with you.

They went forth, and entered into the boat; and that night they took noth-ing. [4] But when day was now breaking, Yeshua stood on the beach: yet the disciples knew not that it was Yeshua. [5] Yeshua therefore said unto them, Children, have ye anything to eat? They answered him, No. [6] And he said unto them, Cast the net on the right side of the boat, and ye shall find. They cast therefore, and now they were not able to draw it for the multitude of fishes. [7] That disciple therefore whom Yeshua loved said unto Peter, It is the Lord. So when Shimon Peter heard that it was the Lord, he girt his coat about him (for he was naked), and cast himself into the sea. [8] But the other disciples came in the little boat (for they were not far from the land, but about two hundred cubits off), dragging the net <full> of fishes. [9] So when they got out upon the land, they see a fire of coals there, and fish laid thereon, and bread. [10] Yeshua said unto them, Bring of the fish which ye have now taken. [11] Shimon Peter therefore went up, and drew the net to land, full of great fishes, a hundred and fifty and three: and for all there were so many, the net was not rent. [12] Yeshua said unto them, Come <and> break your fast. And none of the disciples dared inquire of him, Who are you? Knowing that it was the Lord. [13] Yeshua comes, and takes the bread, and gives them, and the fish likewise. [14] This is now the third time that Yeshua was manifested to the disciples, after that he was risen from the dead.

[15] So when they had broken their fast, Yeshua said to Shimon Peter, Shimon, <son> of Yochanan, do you love me more than these? He said unto him, Yea, Lord; you know that I love you. He said unto him, Feed my lambs. [16] He said to him again a second time, Shimon, <son> of Yochanan, do you love me? He said unto him, Yea, Lord; you know that I love you. He said unto him, Tend my sheep. [17] He said unto him the third time, Do you love me? And he said unto him, Lord, you know all things; you know that I love you. Yeshua said unto him, Feed my sheep. [18] Verily, verily, I say unto you, When you were young, you girded yourself, and walked whither you would: but when you shall be old, you shall stretch forth your hands, and another shall gird you, and carry you whither you would not. [19] Now this he spoke, signi-fying by what manner of death he should glorify God. And when he had spoken this, he said unto him, Follow me. [20] Peter, turning about, sees the disciple whom Yeshua loved following; who also leaned back on his breast at the supper, and said, Lord, who is he that betrays you? [21] Peter therefore

seeing him said to Yeshua, Lord, and what shall this man do? [22] Yeshua said unto him, If I will that he tarry till I come, what <is that> to you? Follow you me. [23] This saying therefore went forth among the brethren, that that disciple should not die: yet Yeshua said not unto him, that he should not die; but, If I will that he tarry till I come, what <is that> to you?

[24] This is the disciple that bears witness of these things, and wrote these things: and we know that his witness is true.

[25] And there are also many other things which Yeshua did, the which if they should be written every one, I suppose that even the world itself would not contain the books that should be written.

[§ 194]—M. The Eighth Appearance:
To the Five Hundred

Matthew 28:16-20	Mark 16:15-18	I Corinthians 15:6
[16] But the eleven disciples went into Galil, unto the mountain where Yeshua had appointed them. [17] And when they saw him, they worshipped <him>; but some doubted. [18] And Yeshua came to them and spoke unto them, saying, All authority has been given unto me in heaven and on earth. [19] Go ye therefore, and make disciples of all the nations, baptizing them into the name of	[15] And he said unto them, Go ye into all the world, and preach the gospel to the	[6] then he appeared to above five hundred brethren at once, of whom the greater part remain until now, but some are fallen asleep;

the Father and of the Son and of the Holy Spirit: [20] teaching them to observe all things whatsoever I commanded you: and lo, I am with you always, even unto the end of the world[2].

whole creation. [16] He that believes and is baptized shall be saved; but he that disbelieves shall be condemned. [17] And these signs shall accompany them that believe: in my name shall they cast out demons; they shall speak with new tongues; [18] they shall take up serpents, and if they drink any deadly thing, it shall in no wise hurt them; they shall lay hands on the sick, and they shall recover.

[§ 195]—N. The Ninth Appearance: To Yaakov

I Corinthians 15:7

[7] then he appeared to Yaakov; then to all the apostles;

[§ 196]—O. The Tenth Appearance: To the Eleven

Luke 24:44-49

[44] And he said unto them, These are my words which I spoke unto you,

Acts 1:3-8

[3] To whom he also showed himself alive after his passion by many

---

[2] Or, *the consummation of the age.*

while I was yet with you, that all things must needs be fulfilled, which are written in the law of Mosheh, and the prophets, and the psalms, concerning me. [45] Then opened he their mind, that they might understand the scriptures; [46] and he said unto them, Thus it is written, that the Messiah should suffer, and rise again from the dead the third day; [47] and that repentance and remission of sins should be preached in his name unto all the nations, beginning from Yerushalayim. [48] Ye are witnesses of these things. [49] And behold, I send forth the promise of my Father upon you: but tarry ye in the city, until ye be clothed with power from on high.

proofs, appearing unto them by the space of forty days, and speaking the things concerning the kingdom of God: [4] and, being assembled together with them, he charged them not to depart from Yerushalayim, but to wait for the promise of the Father, which, <said he>, ye heard from me: [5] For Yochanan indeed baptized with water; but ye shall be baptized in the Holy Spirit not many days hence. [6] They therefore, when they were come together, asked him, saying, Lord, do you at this time restore the kingdom to Yisrael? [7] And he said unto them, It is not for you to know times or seasons, which the Father has set within His own authority. [8] But ye shall receive power, when the Holy Spirit is come upon you: and ye shall be my witnesses both in Yerushalayim, and in all Yehudah and Shomron, and unto the uttermost part of the earth.

[§ 197]—P. The Ascension of the King

Mark 16:19-20	Luke 24:50-53	Acts 1:9-12
	[50] And he led them out until <they were> over against Beit Anyah: and he lifted up his hands, and blessed them.	

[19] So then the Lord Yeshua, after he had spoken unto them, was received up into heaven, and sat down at the right hand of God.

[20] And they went forth, and preached everywhere, the Lord working with them, and confirming the word by the signs that followed. Amen.

[51] And it came to pass, while he blessed them, he parted from them, and was carried up into heaven. [52] And they worshipped him,

and returned to Yerushalayim with great joy: [53] and were continually in the temple, blessing God.

[9] And when he had said these things, as they were looking, he was taken up; and a cloud received him out of their sight.

[10] And while they were looking steadfastly into heaven as he went, behold, two men stood by them in white apparel; [11] who also said, Ye men of Galil, why stand ye looking into heaven? This Yeshua, who was received up from you into heaven shall so come in like manner as ye beheld him going into heaven. [12] Then returned they unto Yerushalayim from the mount called Olivet, which is near unto Yerushalayim, a Sabbath day's journey off.

Appendices

Appendix 1:

The Laws of the Sanhedrin Regarding Trials

1. There was to be no arrest by religious authorities that was effected by a bribe (Ex. 23:8).
2. There were to be no steps of criminal proceedings after sunset.
3. Judges or members of the Sanhedrin were not allowed to participate in the arrest.
4. There were to be no trials before the morning sacrifice.
5. There were to be no secret trials, only public.
6. Sanhedrin trials could only be conducted in the hall of judgment of the Temple compound.
7. The procedure was to be first the defense and then the accusation.
8. All may argue in favor of acquittal, but all may not argue in favor of conviction.
9. There were to be two or three witnesses, and their testimonies had to agree in every detail (Deut. 19:15).
10. There was to be no allowance for the accused to testify against himself.
11. The high priest was forbidden to rent his garments (Lev. 21:10).
12. Charges could not originate with the judges; they could only investigate charges brought to them.

13. The accusation of blasphemy was only valid if the name of God itself was pronounced.

14. A person could not be condemned on the basis of his own words alone.

15. The verdict could not be announced at night, only in the day-time.

16. In cases of capital punishment, the trial and a guilty verdict could not occur at the same time but must be separated by at least 24 hours.

17. Voting for the death penalty had to be done by individual count beginning with the youngest so the young would not be influenced by the elders.

18. A unanimous decision for guilt shows innocence since it is impossible for 23-71 men to agree without plotting.

19. The sentence could only be pronounced three days after the guilty verdict.

20. Judges were to be humane and kind.

21. A person condemned to death was not to be scourged or beaten beforehand.

22. No trials are allowed on the eve of the Sabbath or on a feast day.

Appendix 2:

Maps and Illustrations

The maps on the following pages were designed by Debra Riley and first published in the author's work, *The Historical and Geographical Maps of Israel and Surrounding Territories*, (San Antonio, TX: Ariel Ministries, 2015). Slightly modified to better serve the purpose of this harmony, they show Yisrael (Israel) and Yerushalayim (Jerusalem) during several important events in Yeshua's life.

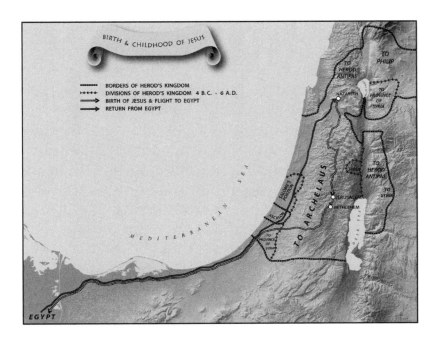

Yeshua's Early Ministry: The map below shows several important locations, such as where Yeshua was baptized, where He was tempted by Satan, and where He performed His first miracle.

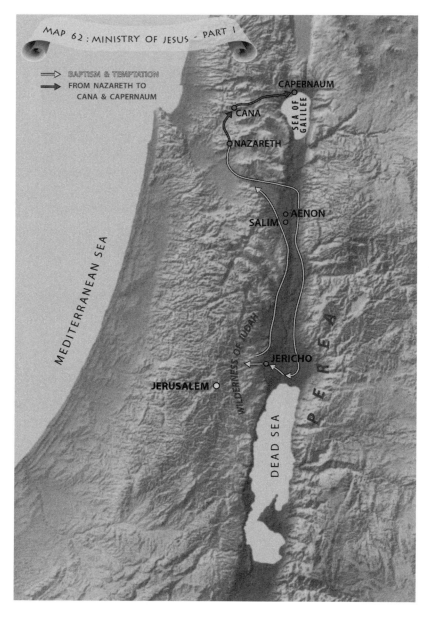

Synagogue in Kfar Nachum: Yeshua set up His headquarters in Kfar Nachum, located on the north shore of the Sea of Ginosar and strategically positioned on a busy trade route called *Via Maris*, which ran from Egypt through the land of Yisrael to Mesopotamia. The art work below was painted by Denise Hayden. It depicts the ruins of the synagogue at Kfar Nachum which is considered to have been built not long after Yeshua's time on the foundation of the synagogue that He taught in (Jn. 6:59).

Yeshua's Galilean Ministry: The map below shows Yeshua's Galilean ministry. He visited Magdala on more than one occasion. It was here that He cast out seven demons from Miriam Magdalit. Between Ginosar (Gennesaret) and Kfar Nachum (Capernaum), He preached the Sermon on the Mount. Most of His miracles occurred in Kfar Nachum, Korazin (Chorazin), and Beit Tzaida (Bethsaida). In Gergesa, He confronted a legion of demons and cast them into a herd of swine. His walking on the water occurred between Kfar Nachum and Beit Tzaida, and the storm at sea occurred between Kfar Nachum and Gergesa. The map also shows the cities Yeshua cursed.

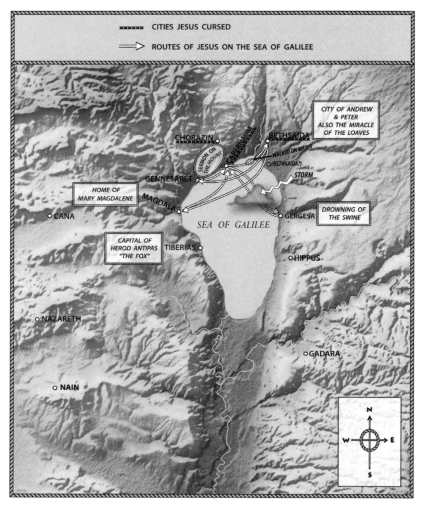

Ministry in Gentile Territory: Yeshua traveled at least four times to Gentile territory. One of these trips led from Kfar Nachum to Tzor (Tyre), where He encountered the Phoenician woman. Another trip brought Him to Caesarea Philippi, where Peter made his confession: "You are the Messiah, the Son of the Living God." After leaving Caesarea Philippi, Yeshua climbed Mount Hermon, the highest mountain in Yisrael, where the transfiguration occurred. We also find Him traveling back to Gedara (Gadara) and returning to Beit Tzaida (Bethsaida). The map below also shows His final journey to Yerushalayim by way of the Beth Shean Valley. From there, He probably crossed the Yarden (Jordan) River and walked to Perea before crossing back over near Jericho. From Beit Anyah (Bethany), He made daily trips to Yerushalayim for the last week of His ministry.

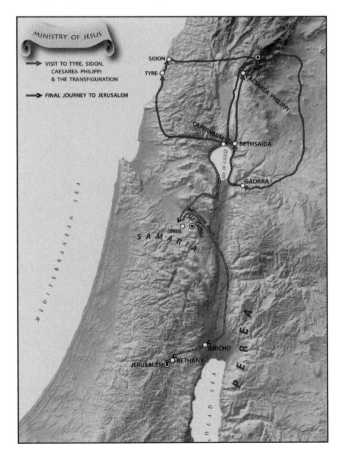

Herod's Temple: The illustration below, designed by Jesse and Josh Gonzales, depicts Herod's Temple during the time of Yeshua. The buildings were completely destroyed in A.D. 70.

Yeshua's Final Week in and around Yerushalayim: The map on the next page shows Yeshua's final week.

(1) On the first day of this week, He rode into Yerushalayim on a donkey. This became known as His triumphal entry. The people waved palm branches and cried, "Hosanna!" In the days to follow, Yeshua made daily trips from Beit Anyah to the Temple area where He taught, allowing everyone to examine His teachings.[1] At night, He returned to Beit Anyah.

(2) On the night of the Passover, He entered the city and made His way to the Upper City, which included modern-day Mount Zion (the biblical Mount Zion was the Temple Mount). It was there that He held His last Passover in the Upper Room with His family of disciples. The map shows an approximation of where that Upper Room may have been, but it could have been anywhere in the Mount Zion area.

(3) After the Passover meal, Yeshua went to the base of the Mount of Olives at Gat Shemen (Gethsemane).

(4) There, He was arrested and forced to walk to the Upper City where the homes of the high priests were located. He underwent the trial before Chanan (Annas) and then Kayapha (Caiaphas) who condemned Him to death on the basis of blasphemy.

(5) From there, He was taken to the Antonia Fortress where He underwent the first stage of His Roman trial before Pontius Pilate. However, Pilate, learning that He was from Galil, sent Him to Herod Antipas, who stayed at the Hasmonean Palace. There, Yeshua underwent the second stage of the civil trial. Herod sent Him back to Pilate at the Antonia Fortress, where He was flogged and eventually condemned to death.

(6) Then, He began His slow walk along what is known today as the Via Dolorosa from the Antonia Fortress to just outside the second wall, a place called Golgota.

---

[1] Despite what is depicted on the map, Yeshua never entered the Temple building itself. The law prohibited anyone except Levitical priests of the line of Aharon from entering the Temple proper, and Yeshua was of the tribe of Yehudah. Therefore, His activities were limited to the inner and the outer courts.

Based upon Messianic Jewish history, as well as early church history, the Church of the Holy Sepulchre marks the actual spot of Yeshua's death and burial.

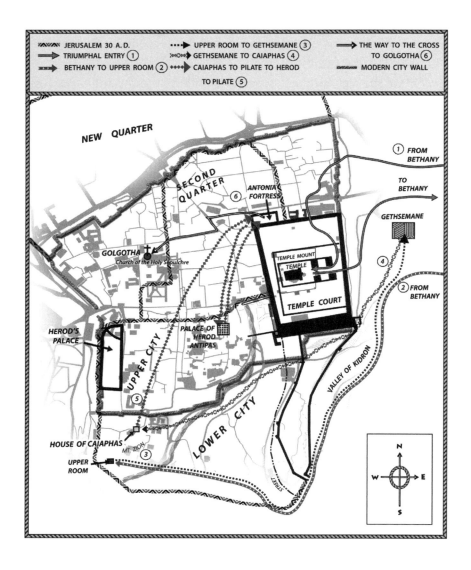

Scripture Index

Mark

Luke

John

Acts

I Corinthians